A Time to Love . . .
A Time to Die

A Time to Love . . .
A Time to Die

PRINCE LEOPOLD OF LOEWENSTEIN

Foreword by Canon Edward Carpenter,
Archdeacon of Westminster

DOUBLEDAY & COMPANY, INC., GARDEN CITY, NEW YORK

1971

LEE COUNTY LIBRARY
SANFORD, N. C.

Grateful acknowledgment is made for the use of the following copyrighted material:

Excerpts reprinted from THE PROPHET, by Kahlil Gibran, by permission of the publisher, Alfred A. Knopf, Inc. Copyright 1923 by Kahlil Gibran and renewed 1951 by Administrators C.T.A. of Kahlil Gibran Estate and Mary G. Gibran.

Excerpt reprinted from MEMORIES, DREAMS, REFLECTIONS by C. G. Jung, translated by Richard and Clara Winston. Copyright © 1962, 1963 by Random House, Inc. Reprinted by permission of Pantheon Books and Routledge & Kegan Paul, Ltd.

Dedicated to
Rosamond, Rosemary, Rosica, Stella,
Helga, Hubert
and to
Elizabeth

Nec mea mutata est aetas, sine crimine tota est:
 Viximus insignes inter utramque facem.

Never did I change with the years, but lived beyond
blame from the torch of the bridal chamber to that
of the grave.

> (Propertius 'Elegy to Cornelia': Book IV. xi
> 45–46)

Foreword by Edward Carpenter

It must always remain difficult to distil into words 'the precious life-blood' of a truly distinguished person. Human nature is too subtle an existence to allow itself to be so imprisoned, or to be held fast in rigid categories of thought. At the centre there is mystery, and even resort to imagery, to the language of suggestion and evocation, will not lay the self bare.

To conjure up a person we must catch him when he takes the wings of the morning and is in flight, or we must quietly be with him, when he is alone but without solitariness. Perhaps this is to say that people are only known, indeed only become themselves, in and through a marriage of true minds. Profundity in such encounter moves in so final a world that it is difficult for us to know precisely what happens when 'deep calls unto deep'. Certainly the imagination is kindled, insight is quickened, barriers are broken down, and the divide which results from what Sartre might call 'alienation' is bridged—not by human effort or agony of will but through the grace which self-giving in mutual awareness attracts. This is a kingdom which we do not take by violence, but it is within experiences of this kind that we begin to discover what love is, or rather, not what it is but what it does or effects. The aura in which we come to see the object of our veneration enfolds others, and we see them in this light. A new world is born around us.

It is within the context of such reflections that Prince Leopold of Loewenstein's sensitive study *A Time to Love . . . A Time to*

Die has meaning and comes alive. It is difficult, I repeat, ever to catch the fragrance of a human person; it becomes the more difficult when the person delineated is so rare a spirit as Diana Loewenstein. That the author has succeeded in so challenging a task is due, I suspect, first of all to the fact that what he writes is not so much 'emotion recollected in tranquillity' as a present and continuing exploration into the being of another. To use a very hackneyed word, but shedding it of philosophical implications, this book is existential in character. It recalls the past, but it does so in such a way as to suggest that that past has a present—and a future.

This book bears witness to the coming together of two persons who exposed themselves to each other and found in this exposure the basic and structural experience which leads to greater understanding and wider vistas.

My wife and myself had the privilege of knowing Diana Loewenstein intimately. The currency of language is so debased in daily speech that one hesitates to use certain words, since their pristine and austere character have lost vitality. She had the beauty which comes not simply from loveliness of form, grace of movement, and modulation of voice, but from a wholeness, sacramental in its manifestation and outreach. In her the paradox was true. She stood out clearly in a unique distinction; yet at the same time she melted into her background and became a part of it. I cannot remember anyone in whom there seemed to me greater coherence and clarity, yet always with a suggestion of that something more which shades off into mystery. Her communion with nature was a living expression of Schweitzer's 'reverence for life'. From it I learned to appreciate more keenly the psychological mood (if not the philosophical propriety) which constrained Shelley to write of John Keats:

> He is a portion of the loveliness
> Which once he made more lovely: he doth bear
> His part, while the one Spirit's plastic stress
> Sweeps through the dull dense world, compelling there,

All new successions to the forms they wear;
Torturing th'unwilling dross that checks its flight
To its own likeness, as each mass may bear;
And bursting in its beauty and its might
From trees and beasts and men into the Heaven's light.

There is no need for me to comment upon the story which Prince Loewenstein unfolds in the following pages—the agony and the ecstasy which like Blake's 'joy and woe' are woven finely into one texture. I am grateful for the integrity with which he has written, and so, I am sure, will be the many readers of *A Time to Love . . . A Time to Die*.

Part One

Then Almira spoke again and said,
And what of marriage, Master?
And he answered, saying:
You were born together, and together you shall
be for evermore.
You shall be together when the white wings of
death scatter your days.
Aye, you shall be together even in the silent
memory of God.

(KAHLIL GIBRAN *The Prophet*)

One

In 1963 we had known each other for nineteen years, and we had been married for sixteen years.

As with a piece of tapestry fashioned by loving hands from thousands of coloured threads there comes the moment of completion when, but for a few details, the artist's vision is fully revealed, so our marriage reached its accomplishment about that time.

If only time had stood still then. But time did not stand still. Like distant lightning on a perfect summer evening, fleeting intimations of changes and sorrows to come began to flicker on the fringes of my consciousness. At first it was nothing more than this; nothing tangible. Our life ran smoothly, also outwardly expanding, because for the first time we were relatively free from the financial worries which had clung to us like our own shadows over so many years.

We were able to do things which hitherto we had been unable to do, or only with the feeling that we ought not to do them. For example, we were able to spend some money on the improvement of our flat; to buy new curtains, replace broken wastepaper baskets, complete our sets of plates, cups, glasses, silver, all of which we had bought incomplete at sales when we had first moved into the flat.

We were able to give a few dinner parties, go to the opera, and to travel more frequently and in greater comfort than before. We could buy a car. This happened in 1964; it was a decision which I have never regretted. In her pocket diary for that year I found an entry on 4th June, written in large block letters, CAR, with an exclamation mark after it.

It was to mean so much to her; away from the noise, congestion and frustrations of the big city (which she had come to dislike more and more as the years went by), week-ends in the country, the prospects of trips in England and of journeys on the Continent. But it came to mean much more than all this. Whatever she did, whatever we did together, whatever experience came to her or jointly to us, she transposed them from the ordinary level of event and action onto a level of imagination and magic where they assumed a life of their own, a wider and more real life, from which the experience in actuality gained new dimensions of significance. She transformed all life from the ordinary to the extraordinary. *For this was the kind of woman she was.*

And so, also this car, this very commonplace possession, assumed a life and meaning of its own, far beyond that of its automotive function. It became part of our private world of enchantment. Now, years later, as in the same car I drive about alone on the main roads or across country in Surrey, Sussex and Kent where we had driven so often together, she feeding me with coloured fruit drops or lighting cigarettes for me, pointing out items of interest which I could never see, trying to make me pull up at antique shops when we had just passed them or had a car close on our tail; now that I drive alone, with only the sound of my radio as my companion, the enchantment of those days still enfolds me. I hear her voice—'Look out, Mister P.' (this was her favourite name for me in recent years), 'keep your eyes on the road . . .' and I pull myself out of my reverie.

I had first met Diana early in June 1944, at her parents' country house between Reading and Newbury. This is how it came about. Coinciding with the landing of the Allied Armies in Normandy, the bombardment of southern England by flying bombs

4

had begun. Life in London had become very unpleasant. At all hours, day and night, the sinister missiles could be seen and heard as they made their way towards the centre of the capital. One knew with each one as it approached, there would come a moment when its engine would stop, and then in a matter of perhaps thirty seconds, it would plunge from the sky to cause death and destruction as it exploded amidst the houses and streets that lay in its path. No place was safe, no time was safe. It was a nerve-wrecking business, and one began to long for fields with yellow buttercups and the woods in the fresh green of Spring, beyond the reach of the infernal machines.

Diana's father* lunched almost every day at a certain well-known restaurant near his office in the West End of London. I had known him for a number of years, but not on terms of intimate friendship. From time to time, during that period of the war, I also lunched at the same restaurant. On these occasions we would exchange a few friendly words in passing. But one day, as he was leaving, he stopped by my table and said, 'Would you like to have a few days of peace in the country? If so, why don't you come and stay with us for a week?' Without a moment's hesitation I accepted.

On my second or third day in the country, I was told quite casually over lunch: 'Our daughter, Diana, is coming from Oxford this afternoon and will stay until Sunday.' Her mother would go by car to meet her at the station which was a few miles away. I asked if I might accompany her. We were late in starting. Half-way to the station we saw the train arrive and leave, and a little later we saw the figure of a girl walking across the fields in our direction. We stopped and waited. I saw Diana first through the window of the car. I got out and she stood before me.

She was dressed in a flared skirt of blue linen with embroidered braiding at the hem, a white blouse and a loose, sleeveless jacket of the same colour as the skirt. She wore white ankle socks and

* The late Sir Victor Gollancz.

5

flat shoes, and she wore functional, unattractive spectacles. She was conscious of it: when we shook hands, she lowered her eyes. My first thought was: 'These we shall have to do away with as soon as possible'.

Two

We had little opportunity of speaking to each other in those few days of our first meeting in June 1944. Her father's massive, overweening personality filled the house. In his presence Diana and her sisters hardly ever spoke, for fear, as I soon discovered, of being chided by him or held up to ridicule. These distressing performances usually happened at meal times. Frequently, also, he made indelicate jokes at their expense.

As I have said, I had known him for a number of years. I knew him, as many other people did, as a successful publisher, writer and public speaker; as a promoter of humanitarian causes and ardent socialist, who exercised a certain amount of influence behind the political scene. Before the war, I had admired him for his courageous denunciation of the Nazi regime at a time when many prominent British politicians, newspaper proprietors and other public men were turning two blind eyes on the events in Germany. And there existed certain intellectual affinities between us. But not until that first visit to his country house had I seen him within the intimate setting of his home and family.

And so at first I could not understand how a man of his intellectual stature could derive satisfaction from deriding his own daughters, who at that time were not children any more, but young girls. In particular, I could not understand why he should single out for special obloquy so beautiful a girl as Diana. She had dark, luminous eyes, sensitive, aristocratic features, a delicately sensuous and perfectly shaped mouth. Her hair was the

6

colour of dark burnished amber, with coppery lights in it. Her expression was thoughtful, perhaps even a little grave but this 'grave little face', as someone was to call it many years later, shone in the light of heaven when she smiled. Her voice was strong, but low-pitched; her laugh was like a silver bell. I thought her then, and was to think her until her dying day, the most beautiful woman I had ever known.

Diana was the only one of the daughters who did not meekly submit to her father's uncharitable bantering. More than once in my presence she clashed with him.

Diana's mother, whom I had only met once or twice before and with whom I had never exchanged more than a few formal words, seemed to me an eminently practical and capable woman who filled her day with unceasing useful minor activities. She was still beautiful, with regular features and an almost Greek profile. She was calm, matter-of-fact in everything she said and did, and strangely impersonal. In particular I noticed that she seldom committed herself to a direct exchange of views and avoided face-to-face conversations which would have demanded the use of the personal pronouns, 'I', 'we', 'you'. Instead she spoke remotely, indirectly, and in general terms.

This, for me, inhibited human relations on all but the most superficial levels. She found emotional fulfilment if somewhat vicariously in causes: in Judaism, socialism; in the idea of women's rights; in her husband's activities, success and fame. And she found it in the impersonal concept of righteousness with which she became identified. Not once during that first visit did she ask me a personal question; not once in the 23 years that followed.

In vivid contrast, Diana's father spent hours talking to me. Even in the presence of his family, at meals and after dinner, he addressed himself almost exclusively to me. He was an indefatigable talker, voluble, assertive and idiosyncratic. And unlike his wife he was always fully and personally committed.

One afternoon, when I found myself alone with her father, he hinted darkly that Diana had great psychological problems, but

7

would not confide in her parents. I said that I thought this quite natural; girls of her age—she was then twenty-three—usually do not tell their parents about personal problems; more especially, they do not tell their father. When I probed further into the nature of these problems, he said that her very secretiveness was part of the over-all problem. Even when she was a small girl she had been secretive. She painted and would not show her pictures; she seemed to 'know things', but would not tell. And this tendency had become much stronger with the years. She would never reveal her ideas or only by hints and allusions. She showed no interest in the burning social problems of the day. She seemed to live in a world of her own.

This was true. The secretiveness to which her father took such strong exception was her way, the only way, in which she could maintain her inner independence and personal integrity in the face of the collective pressure of her family to make her conform to a pattern of thought and a *Weltanschauung* which were not her own.

Her father's reproaches, on the surface, merely boiled down to this: Diana would not conform. In this his attitude was no different from that of Victorian fathers, even though he took great pride in his own nonconformism and enlightened progressive outlook. The real, deep causes of his strange antagonism, which I had suspected from the very beginning, I was to learn only some years later.

My visit ended on the day Diana had to return to Oxford. There was an interval of half an hour between the departure of her train to Oxford and of mine, going in the opposite direction, to London. Her mother took us to Reading Station by car. The train for Oxford left from No. 1 Platform. To reach my train, I had to go through an underpass to the other side of the station. Diana's train was already in the station when we arrived, and owing to some wartime disruption, did not leave on time. I was hoping that her mother would go as soon as Diana was in

8

the train, but to my surprise, she stayed on. After about a quarter of an hour, she turned to me and said: 'You will miss your train if you wait any longer.' I said goodbye to Diana and went off towards the underpass, looking back once or twice to see if her mother was still on the platform. Just as I reached the underpass, Diana's train pulled out.

I waited another five minutes and then returned to Platform 1. There was another train due to leave for Oxford in twenty minutes. I took this train. It was a slow one, stopping at every station between Reading and Oxford, and I had to stand all the way. I think it was about five in the afternoon when I arrived in Oxford. I went straight to Diana's 'digs' off St. John Street. They were in a small house at the end of a quiet cul-de-sac. A lamp-post stood in front of the house; in those days— the 'black-out' was still in force—it was never lit. A little later, however, in the autumn of 1944, the so-called starlight lighting was introduced which crowned the lamp-post outside the house with a tiny glow, almost invisible on a moonlit night and not much stronger than that of a couple of glow-worms on a dark night.

I revisited the street in 1968. It had not changed in the quarter of a century which has passed since my first visit. There was a flower-box in the window of Diana's room on the ground floor, and the house seemed a little shabbier than I had remembered it.

When I arrived that afternoon, the landlady opened the door and said: 'There is a note for you.' The note read: 'I shall be back at about 5.15, wait for me.' A minute later Diana arrived. We had not exchanged a single word about meeting again before she had left, but we had both known that this was to happen. It was in the pattern of our destiny. Her mother's stubborn waiting on the platform at Reading had merely delayed our meeting by two hours. I returned to London on the last train that evening to arrive around midnight in the middle of a flying-bomb raid, which continued until the morning.

Three

There are in our life a few climacteric moments when we must make a choice. We do not always recognize these moments for what they are, and only when looking back do we realize the full significance of a choice we made at a particular time. But it does happen that we are synchronized with our destiny and recognize the moment of decision, and also know what is the right decision. These are the moments of Grace; if we then choose—whatever the reasons—wrongly, that is, contrary to our true pattern, we sin against truth, we reject Grace. That moment of Grace had come to me when I met Diana; the choice was clear. Whatever the difficulties and obstacles, she would be my wife. Everything, therefore, followed logically upon that basic realization.

Some time in June 1944, I moved to Oxford, where I remained until the end of the war in April 1945. Looking back, almost as a historian recording an epoch with all the relevant documents before him, how completely consistent were the beginnings with the subsequent unfolding of events.

I have before me many of her early letters to me and the few letters I wrote to her before we were married. Like most people, I have written and received a good many love letters in my life. How very few, when read years later, have stood the test of time. Passionate letters, foolish and shallow ones, some full of vows and promises never fulfilled; some that make one blush on re-reading them. How could I (or she) write such nonsense? Because seemingly true at the time when they were written, one knows now that they were not true, not true in the sense that they did not express one's own inner truth and the truth of the relationship which, at the time, seemed so all-important. Those letters, however, which Diana wrote to me and I wrote to her, were true, and

10

are still true today. Not that they were necessarily very profound letters, nor were they literary masterpieces. (Yet even then I was struck by the beauty of her phrasing, the originality of her thought and imagination, and her Lewis Carroll type of irrational humour by which she turned the absurd into the sublime. This was to be a source of never-ending delight to me, almost to the moment of her death.) What made her letters, and mine, true and as fresh today as when they were written, is the absolute certainty which informs them, the certainty of two people who, when they first encountered each other, knew they had encountered their common destiny. The vision and design of that magic tapestry was there in June 1944; it shines through those early letters. Then, over the years, it moves towards its completion.

We married in the summer of 1947, when Diana was in her twenty-sixth and I in my forty-fourth year. There was thus a difference in age of some eighteen years between us. But it did not matter; in her eyes I possessed the secret of eternal youth. This kept me young, and strange as this may sound, the fact also that we lived in a state of complete economic insecurity, also kept me young. Life still seemed to lie before us, full of promise and wonder. This is as it appears to me, looking back; this is how it appeared to her in those years of completion, when we gained a measure of relative security.

But in the early years of our married life, when difficulties and adversities were more numerous than strokes of good fortune, when, in the language of the later years, our little ship first encountered those rough seas of an insecure life which was to be our lot, Diana was often frightened and anxious. How were we going to manage? We had no furniture, no goods and chattels of any kind. We lived in two, not properly self-contained, rooms— the upper floor of a minute house in Chelsea—with no prospects of ever having a home of our own.

There was not much money. All my attempts to find a suitable position seemed to lead to nothing. It was always the same story. UNESCO, the COUNCIL OF EUROPE, other international organizations, industrial concerns. It always looked hopeful at first. Some-

11

times I was within a hair's-breadth of securing a good job, but it all invariably fizzled out. Diana had no professional qualifications or training that would have enabled her to earn money. She had been at the Slade and Ruskin Schools of Art before the war, but her studies had been cut short by the war. Her training had not been in commercial art, and even had it been, in the immediate postwar years there existed very few openings in this field, or if they existed we did not know of them. We could not look to her parents for assistance of any kind, not even for advice, nor would have wished to do so. But whereas I was not frightened by the whole concept of money, Diana was.

In the formative years of my childhood and youth, I had lived in a world separated by tradition and privilege as effectively from the world 'outside'—the world of professions, commerce, ambitions and struggle—as a medieval castle by its ramparts and moats. I had lived in complete security. It turned out to be a sham security, for, as I was to learn even before I reached adulthood, this world of castles, coaches, horses, liveried servants, gamekeepers, French governesses, tutors, in which I spent my childhood, was based on very weak financial foundations. The whole elaborate, yet so deceptive, edifice crumbled into dust after the First World War.

But so powerful are early childhood experiences that, real or sham, justified or not, the material security of those early years gave me a carefree and detached outlook on life and the material concerns of life, with consequences, both beneficial and bad. On the one hand, it kept me free from the worry of 'What shall we eat' or 'What shall we drink' or 'Wherewithal shall we be clothed' and enabled me to face adversity of every kind with a high degree of equanimity. On the other hand, the harsh economic realities of life show themselves quite indifferent to a man's philosophical outlook. Unless one wishes to spend one's life meditating in a cave, one has to play the game of earning a living according to established rules.

Looking back, I wish I had had advice more practical than my father gave me when I asked him at the age of eighteen:

'What do you think I should take up as a career; what do you want me to become?'

'What do you mean, "become"? You don't have to *become* anything, you *are;* is not that enough?' This, it cannot be denied, is a profound truth, but it does not cover all the contingencies of life.

Yet again, one must look at a man's life as a whole, and I find it difficult to visualize how my life could have been other than it is. Speculations such as, 'What would have happened if . . .' are not profitable. If anything had been different, the whole would have been difficult; in other words, not my life.

Diana's background and the circumstances under which she grew up, were very different from mine. Her father had to make his own way, for there was no wealth, real or imagined, in his family. The circumstances of his own childhood, to which I shall refer again later, acted as a powerful spur. Contrary to my father and the aristocratic caste to which he belonged, who regarded their privileged position as their birth-right and could not conceive of any other way of life, he was haunted by the spectre of poverty and was early on acutely aware of those harsh realities, social and economic, which for us did not exist. By the time he had a family of his own, he had already begun to make a mark as a publisher, and to lay the foundation of what was to become a not inconsiderable fortune.

His growing prosperity was soon reflected in his possessions and his style of life. And so Diana and her sisters also grew up in conditions of material security, which, though it depended on a more modest concept of life, and could only be maintained by unrelenting endeavour, was solid and real in contrast to the illusory security of my own childhood. Yet the dread of poverty never quite left her father, and this dread he had passed on to his daughters.

And so, whereas with me, illusion created confidence and optimism, with Diana the relatively modest yet real and ever-expanding prosperity of her parental home had produced the very opposite effect. To her, anything to do with money was laden

13

with awe-inspiring overtones. The dire consequences of being without money, of which her parents had never ceased to remind her, haunted her like a constant *memento mori* in those early years of our marriage.

This fear became coupled with—perhaps even caused—a lack of confidence in her own abilities. The latter never quite left her. As to her fear of poverty, it became transmuted in this process of spiritual alchemy, which she applied to life as a whole, into a true abnegation of worldly advantages and possessions.

In those early days of our marriage, when at times she showed faintheartedness and lack of confidence, I reproached her for failing in *tenue*. This was a concept which my father had instilled into us when we were children. *Il faut toujours avoir de la tenue!* Meaning that whatever befalls, one must remain unflinching, undismayed, serene; never show weakness, never admit defeat. It was the code of the ancient Samurai. I very much doubt that the Loewensteins strictly adhered to it, for I vividly remember the lamentations that arose in my parents' home when dividends failed to come up to expectations. But if Diana had not always shown the degree of serenity I expected of her in the face of everyday difficulties, the day came, when those difficulties had become part of a cherished past, when she taught me the true meaning of the Samurai code—the fortitude which does not carry the reward of a happy ending—*tenue* in the face of death.

Four

To mark the passage of time, films use the device of showing in a rapid succession of shots blending into one another and rushing away from the viewer, dates superimposed on a suitable background such as calendars, newspapers or diaries. When the sequence begins to slow down, we know we are near the point where the narrative opens or is resumed. What happened in the intervening years?

I have Diana's pocket diaries covering most of the years between 1947 and 1967. Every Christmas I gave her one of those elegant feather-weight pocket diaries, which came bound in many different kinds of leather and a variety of colours—dark blue, green, bright red, ox-blood, maroon, pigskin. And every year she gave me one. As in the film sequence, these neat, small pocket diaries in many colours pass before my eyes. What do they contain? Lunch and dinner dates, appointments with dressmakers, doctors, dentists; week-ends in the country, brief illnesses at home, visiting someone in hospital, the occasional theatre, the yearly holiday; telephone numbers, addresses, old friends, passing acquaintances; hopeful business contracts that fade away after a few entries; notes on laundry, titles of books, and every now and again brief comments. Like the bank statements, the spent cheques, the receipted bills which clutter up our drawers, these pocket diaries tell the story of the routine of life.

One day perhaps, someone will come upon my own pocket diaries and will open some at random, glance at the pages and think, 'How uninteresting!' Is this all there is to life? A handful of empty shells found on the seashore? It is not all. The essence of life; all that which happened in the intervening years fills the empty spaces between those routine entries in the diaries. These are the memories of the heart which rarely see the light of day.

In the metaphor of the film sequence of the rushing years, it is on the dates 1963 and 1964 that the camera would begin to slow down, the time when I had the first intimations of 'changes and sorrows to come'. They were foreshadowed also in her diaries and sketchbooks of those years. Short notes begin to appear on premonitions and prophetic dreams. Several times she refers to dreams in which she is subjected to sacrificial immolation, in a setting of distant antiquity, dreams which always follow the same pattern. There is another recurring theme; the dream in which she finds herself climbing a staircase inside a vast, apparently gutted house. The staircase is narrow and is precariously attached to the

15

wall, but has no protective railing. As she mounts higher and higher the chasm beneath her becomes more and more threatening, but there is no turning back. Finally the staircase ends by a small door let into the wall at the very top of the building. She opens the door and beholds a panorama of mountains and valleys stretching into infinity, but below her there is a sheer drop of hundreds of feet. She realizes this is 'journey's end'. There is another dream, converse to this one, yet similar in 'tone'. Here she wanders along corridors that end in doors which lead to further corridors, again ending in doors, and yet further corridors, and so *ad infinitum*—journey without end.

There is another dream on the theme of immolation, the *Albatross* dream she called it, that came a year or so later. In this dream she finds herself among a group of young people on a bridge. She takes a bow and arrow from one of her companions, aims and loosens the arrow at a huge bird flying above. The snow-white bird is hit in one wing. As it falls into the water below the bridge, the injured wing extended and flopping helplessly, she recognizes it as an albatross. With deep distress, she sees the bird's blood spill over its white plumage and colour the waters. She goes and confesses what she has done to a priest, saying, 'It was entirely my fault.'

This dream is particularly significant as a symbolic portent of disaster, for according to age-old legend, the killing or wounding of an albatross brings ill luck and worse upon the offender. Also, from time immemorial, birds have been symbolic of the human soul; thus her wounding the bird again stands for self-immolation. There is a further powerful symbolism in the crossing of the bridge. The bridge stands for transition; transition from one state of existence to another. (The Roman term, *Pontifex Maximus,* which became the designation of the Pope, literally means the 'Supreme Bridge Builder', the one who builds the bridge between God and man.) In her dream, Diana stood half-way across the bridge, and underneath flowed the river of irreversible time.

Diana may not have fully understood the symbolism of all these dreams; she barely mentioned them to me at the time and I had long forgotten them, but there is a note of anxiety in her comments which shows that she was aware that they had some special significance; she was aware that something was happening over which she had no control.

Coinciding with these descriptions of dreams are short notes on her health which began to trouble her; coinciding also, reflections on the transitoriness of life and on the spiritual path. There is one entry in a self-deprecatory, humorous vein. Only I could understand its significance, because only I knew to what it referred. She had slim, elegant legs and ankles and narrow feet, but a very slight malformation of the big toe on one foot. It was due to an enlarged joint, the result of ballet dancing (she had wanted to train for the ballet) at an early age. Like so many beautiful, gentle women, she never thought of herself as beautiful, and was deeply conscious of what she considered her own imperfections. The entry reads: 'Ugly feet are as good a reminder of the spiritual path as a skull on the table.' Another entry, a quotation whose origin I do not know, reads: 'It is only in what is loveliest, most fugitive, that eternity reveals, as in a sudden flash, as in the vanishing facet of a second, the beauty of all beauty; that it whispers in the purple hollow of the dancing flame the incommunicable *word.*'

At that time (1964) she first began to assemble material for an anthology of passages from her favourite books, which she planned to write and illustrate. A few such passages begin to appear in her sketchbooks; here are two of them: 'In the shadow of pain one may hear the footsteps of joy.' And shortly after this: 'If you would indeed behold the spirit of death, open your heart wide unto the body of life. For life and death are one, even as the river and the sea are one.' This is taken from *The Prophet* by Kahlil Gibran.

I did not at the time know of those entries in her pocket diaries and notebooks. However, much of what she felt and thought must have directly communicated itself to me. And quite independently also I was becoming aware of a process of change in her. It began around her fortieth year and expressed itself in her

17

painting, in the maturity of her thought and judgement, and in her increasing detachment over worldly affairs.

Often she spoke as if life in the physical body, life with all its needs, appetites, vanities and imperfections, was a burden to her which she would gladly shed. There were times when I had felt discouraged by what seemed to me her pessimism. Yet I knew that she did not reject life. She strove for perfection. Consciously since her Oxford days, but intuitively, probably since early childhood, she followed that inner vision. In whatever she did, in her painting, her stone carving, embroidery, flower arrangements, dressmaking, whatever the task she applied herself to, down to the most humble chores, such as polishing silver, brass or furniture, or merely dusting the room, she was guided by this ideal. And in whatever she did, she had what has been called *le geste essentiel*. The term can best be rendered as the *appropriate action*, the action which, with a minimum of exertion and time, achieves most effectively the desired end.

To make it possible, certain basic conditions must be fulfilled. Above all, one must acquire a complete understanding of the properties of the substances or materials on which one works and the laws that govern them. This in turn demands careful observation and study, but beyond it, empathy, a capacity of 'tuning in'. In its highest forms this becomes a complete 'at-oneness' with every single aspect of the action on which one is engaged, with its means (material or otherwise) and its ends.

For example, in painting we must become one with the subject we paint; in carving, with the stone we carve; in metal work, with the metal we shape; in archery, with the arrow we shoot, the bow from which we release it, and with the target we hit. I mention this particular example because in *Zen and the Art of Archery,* which was one of Diana's favourite books, the acquiring of this supreme mastery and the philosophy behind it, are beautifully described. It is shown there that to attain to the point of mastery, in whatever task one has set oneself, the point where art becomes 'artless', where everything happens as though of its own volition, one must persevere in the face of all obstacles, difficulties and

18

setbacks. No time, therefore, that has gone into careful preparation, study and practice, is ever wasted.

The *geste essentiel* is the secret behind Japanese unarmed combat, painting, flower arrangement, swordsmanship and archery. It was the secret behind the work of the men who built our great cathedrals, behind the work of the great painters, sculptors and craftsmen of the past. The main theme which ran through all Diana's creative work, especially her painting and stone carving, was that of the emergence and manifestation of the spirit in the living structure of the phenomenal world. As a little girl at the bleak, wind-blown resorts on the Kentish coast, where she and her sisters, watched over by an authoritarian nanny, spent their summer holidays, she discovered and was fascinated by the beautiful pebbles, crystals and shells on the beaches, and by fossilized plants and ammonites embedded in the chalky cliffs. She also became interested in rock formation and their structural composition. Collecting pebbles that had been shaped and polished by the sea over millions of years, and later of crystals and semi-precious stones, knowing their names and mineral features, became one of her great passions and an inexhaustible source of inspiration for her work.

A few years after we were married, she found a shop in Chelsea which specialized in stones of every kind and kept a vast selection of unusual specimens from all over the world. She spent hours at that shop, asking questions, making copious notes on the composition and origin of the stones and the metals associated with them; about their system of crystallization and their scientific names. Sometimes she bought semi-precious stones to be mounted later on a ring; sometimes she bought a particularly beautiful crystal formation in which she saw the very structure of the universe. She gave crystals as presents to friends, making her choice with the utmost care, so that they would fit the surroundings for which they were destined, and the personality of the recipient. She was fascinated not only by stones and rock formations, but also by rocky and desert landscapes and primeval oceans. They held visions for her of the world in its beginning.

19

When she began carving in stone, she first made the most exhaustive enquiries into the properties of the various stones and conducted a long correspondence with firms all over England which imported stone from Austria, Switzerland, Africa, India and China. Her studio began to look like a quarry with samples of all shapes and sizes littering the floor. She was not satisfied until she had found the stone which, in composition, hardness and texture, came nearest to what she required. She taught herself the necessary techniques, not only of the actual process of carving, but also of polishing with special grinding powders and oils. Here again she consulted books and spoke to experts until she completely mastered every aspect of the work. Then she applied the *geste essentiel.*

At one period she took up embroidery in the style and tradition of ecclesiastic embroidery. She set to work systematically, buying real gold thread, glass pearls and coloured beads. She had a special wooden frame made to her own specifications. The result was a series of velvet belts, embroidered with the most exquisite golden and jewelled designs which she composed as she went along. She vaguely hoped that she might sell them to couturiers or boutiques, but soon realized that to make the venture pay (she would work weeks on one belt) the price would have to be very high. But this had not been the main purpose of the venture. She followed her vision of perfection, and these embroidered belts were merely one aspect of it.

The theme of creation, of 'In the beginning . . .', can best be traced in the development of her painting over the years. It was there in her early pictures, in the boiling rocks, the steaming waters, the dark red glowing clouds through which break the first shafts of the divine Light. It appears in many variations in her later paintings which depict organic structures of nature as they emerge well ordered from the primeval chaos. Later she expressed it in series of rocky landscapes in a mystical Blakeian style, and finally she returned to it, in the miniature paintings destined for her anthology. These miniatures, all of them abstracts in strong and vibrant colours, are visionary interpretations of the inner

20

core of nature, where matter, energy and spirit interpenetrate to form the basic pattern that underlies the visible world.

But they are more than that. Looking at them (some of them were enlarged by her to full-size pictures) is to look into the world of microphysics, and into the vastness of the universe at the same time. They convey in a manner quite unique Dante's vision of the universe which he expressed in the words:

. . . e cominciò: le cose tutte e quante hann' ordine tra loro; e questo è forma che l'universo a Dio fa simigliante . . .

(Paradiso, Canto I: 103/105)

(. . . and began: All things whatsoever observe a mutual order; and this is the law that maketh the universe like unto God.)

Diana was convinced that underlying all appearance and beyond all imperfections of the world there was this scheme of harmony in which everything—*le cose tutte e quante*—from the humblest pebble on the beach to the most exalted orders in the celestial hierarchy had its appointed place. This conviction informed her life, this was the vision she followed. Her detachment over most of the things that matter so much to the great majority of people—money, position, success, health—should not therefore have surprised, let alone, alarmed me. It was part of her spiritual unfoldment, the opening of the 'Thousand-petalled lotus blossom', in the symbolic imagery of the East. But from 1964 on I had the inescapable feeling (which reasoning would not dispel) that there was a meaningful connection, other than the obvious one, between her extraordinary spiritual flowering and the complete 'at-oneness' and harmony which we had achieved on every level of our relationship. It was like listening to the last movement of a great symphony, when all the themes had been gathered up and were now rapidly moving towards their climax and final resolution.

Five

In 1965 Diana's health began to cause me real anxiety. She was often pale and listless. She tired easily. Her monthly periods were accompanied by unusual physical and mental distress. 'I am not much good to you as a wife,' she often said. 'Poor old Diana, there is always something wrong with her somewhere.'

I urged her to see a gynaecologist, but for a long time she would not hear of it. She had little faith in doctors. Then there came a time when she began to suffer from a strange allergic condition of throat and nose, characterized by prolonged sneezing fits, as in acute hay fever. An eminent specialist found a name for the complaint, but the vigorous local treatment which he applied gave no relief, nor did treatment with antibiotics. The trouble would suddenly disappear of its own accord, only to return in regular intervals, usually coinciding with the monthly periods.

I was reading Dr. Jones's *Life of Freud* at the time. One evening, when Diana's complaint was particularly troublesome, I came across a passage in the biography describing the friendship and collaboration, in the nineties of the last century, between Freud and Dr. Wilhelm Fliess, a nose and throat specialist who achieved a certain fame with his theory on periodicity.

According to this, all vital processes and events of life have the tendency of occurring or recurring in definite phases or cycles, and this tendency to which he gave the name *periodicity,* is determined by menstrual periods in women and its corresponding phase in men. Fliess elaborated his theory, in which numerology played an important part, into an all-embracing cosmic doctrine. He claimed that, given the relevant date, it was possible to predict all major events in a person's life, including exact dates and duration of illnesses, and the date of death.

22

Freud was for almost fifteen years under the spell of this brilliant but eccentric man. This was all very interesting, because it showed aspects of Freud's character which are not generally known. However, to me the main point of interest in the passage on Fliess was a reference to his other theory on the inter-relationship between the mucous membrane of the nose, genital activities and menstruation. In 1897, Fliess announced a new syndrome which he called the 'Nasal Reflex Neurosis' which comprised most of the symptoms from which Diana suffered, including widely distributed neuralgic pains, disturbances of digestion and catarrhal swelling of the mucous membrane of the nose with all the accompanying, distressing manifestations. According to Fliess and Freud, *all* these symptoms could be relieved, almost magically, by applying cocaine to the nose.

I had always suspected that Diana's allergic nose and throat trouble was not a localized affair, but was part of a more general condition. Here then was a confirmation of my views and an important clue as to the nature of her condition. It was now clear to me that Diana suffered from some deficiency or glandular malfunction due to a hormone imbalance. This made sense also in the light of her previous medical history.

'One has to go back seventy-five years to some of the more speculative theories of two Viennese doctors to make a correct diagnosis,' I said to Diana. 'Why have none of the doctors we consulted thought of it?'

One could not really expect it. The days of the family doctor whom one could consult at leisure and who *knew* his patients, have gone for good. With the ever-increasing specialization in medicine, it is now virtually impossible to find a doctor who can or will make a comprehensive assessment of an abnormal condition against the full background of the patient's health record, constitution and personality. Once a condition has been clearly diagnosed, one may expect excellent specialized treatment, but one can no longer look to a doctor for general guidance or expect him to take the initiative.

Diana's allergic affliction continued for some time, until, everything else having failed to give relief, she was given a powerful hormone injection. This stopped it at once and it never returned. Another proof, so it seemed to me, that my own diagnosis had been correct. Her general health, however, did not greatly improve.

Six

One day, towards the end of April 1966, she said to me: 'I have an appointment with Mr. M. Tuesday next at 3.30 in the afternoon.'

Mr. M. was a well-known gynaecologist and surgeon. Diana had made the appointment without having told me of her intention to consult a specialist. I was not too alarmed over the news; I thought she had acted wisely, yet I asked myself why she had been quite so secretive over it. It was not the last time I was to ask myself the same question.

When Tuesday came, I wanted to take her to her appointment, but she refused. 'Will you ring me at the office when you have seen Mr. M.?' I suggested.

'No,' she replied, 'there is no need for it; I will tell you when you come home for tea.' However, she did ring me at the office shortly after four o'clock. 'I have seen Mr. M.'

'What did he say?'

'Everything is fine,' she replied. And before I could put another question, she added, 'You try to be home by five. I shall have a nice tea ready for you.'

I was back at the flat at a quarter-past five. She had prepared tea on the trolley. She had made little sandwiches—tomato and cucumber—and on the way back from the doctor she had stopped at a continental patisserie and bought some special gateaux—chocolate-coated sponge spheres filled with whipped cream. I was very fond of these, mainly because they evoked pleasant childhood memories.

Often in the past, when one of us had some good news for the other and had intimated by the vaguest of hints that there was good news (it might be something quite unimportant, or something of real importance, but it would be *good* news), we would not tell immediately on meeting, but hold back for a while in order to prolong the pleasure of anticipation. Then when the right moment had arrived, either the bringer of the good news or the recipient would broach the subject. 'Shall I tell you now?' or 'Now tell me.'

This time it was I, having finished my sandwiches and about to start on my gateau, who gave the signal: 'Now tell me, what did Mr. M. say?'

There was a brief silence. She looked at me across the trolley and quietly said: 'I have to have an operation.'

It was so unexpected that I automatically fell in with her quiet, undramatic tone. 'When?' I asked.

'As soon as possible,' she answered. 'M. is making the necessary arrangements. He will ring me in the morning.'

I felt my composure go. As someone who has quite unexpectedly sustained a serious injury may, because of its very unexpectedness, not immediately become aware of the pain, it took me a few minutes to register what had happened. But then it was like a piercing pain. 'But you told me on the phone that all was well, darling, why did you say that?'

'I did not want to upset you at the office,' she answered. 'At the same time, I needed to hear your voice, it gave me reassurance.'

I remained silent, took her hand and held it firmly. This was not distant summer lightning any more. This was the first rumbling of the storm which, within less than a year, was to shatter our life.

'Tell me exactly what happened.'

'There is nothing to worry about, not really. I must have a hysterectomy. Many women at my age or younger get this kind

25

of thing.' And then she told me that it had taken Mr. M. less than five minutes to establish that she had swellings in the wall of the womb which he diagnosed as 'fibroids'. The surgeon had reassured her at once. Ninety-nine per cent of these types of tumours were non-malignant. Hysterectomy was no longer considered a major operation. Not only, therefore, was the prognosis excellent, but as one knew from hundreds of identical cases, once the shock of the operation had been overcome, women's general health usually improved quite dramatically as the result of it.

'Latest, six months after the operation,' Mr. M. had told her, 'you will feel a different person.'

'Let's not worry, Mr. P., all will be well. I will be as good as new, in fact, much better than I have been all these years.'

Her main concern was to arrange things so that I should not suffer any inconvenience. 'I have already spoken to Rosemary,* you can stay at her house, and over the week-end with Eileen,† while I am in hospital.'

But I did worry. I worried because of all my premonitions, because I felt that a pattern of inexorable events was beginning to emerge. I also worried on very rational grounds. Experience had shown that whenever there had been anything wrong with Diana's health, her condition had *invariably* been worse than first suspected. With most people, sudden indispositions, pains and symptoms of illness which cause alarm and distress both to the sufferer and the onlooker, in the majority of cases happily resolve themselves quickly and prove less serious than at first feared.

It was different with Diana. Whenever she had a cold, a gastric upset, 'flu or even a headache, she became much more ill than seemed warranted by the nature of the condition. She never wanted to admit illness. 'Don't fuss, leave me alone, I am all right,' were her standard reactions. She had been seriously ill only twice in twenty years, and each time the illness had been short; each time also it had been frightening in the violence of its

* Rosemary Lowry-Corry.
† Eileen and Milorad Petrovitch.

26

manifestations. Each time she had symptoms, such as excruciating pains in the back of the head, temples and neck, vomiting, photophobia, which seemed to point to an inflammation of the brain tissues.

In her first illness which happened in the second year of our marriage (the illness was the result of a mild sunstroke), Lord Horder, one of the most brilliant diagnosticians of that time, had warned me that she had a hypersensitivity of the tissues of the brain. 'You must watch any symptoms of that kind very carefully,' he said. 'They must never be taken lightly.' His words were to prove prophetic.

Diana had her operation in the first week of May 1966. All went according to plan, and, as the doctors had confidently predicted, there was no trace of malignancy. When, in the afternoon of the day of the operation, I arrived at the private patients' wing of the hospital, there was no one about. I waited for a while and then went into her room. It gave me a shock. Diana had not yet woken up from the anaesthetic, but she was not sleeping peacefully as one might have expected. Her face was flushed, her breathing came heavily through her open mouth. There was an air of helplessness and suffering about her, such as I had never seen before.

Mr. M., who came in shortly afterwards, reassured me. There was nothing abnormal about the way she looked and her breathing.

'The room is just a little too hot,' he said. 'Come back in an hour's time; she will be awake by then.'

I returned later and was able to exchange a few words with her. The next morning, when I entered the room, she was sitting up writing notes of thanks to friends who had sent flowers.

She was most particular about such things—thanking friends for invitations, dinners, week-ends or presents, or herself sending flowers and messages to friends when the occasion demanded. Her writing was small and exquisitely beautiful, and she hardly ever wrote a letter or even a short note without some small picture to embellish it. These illustrations would vary from a simple vignette, a flower or painted initial (as in illuminated

27

medieval manuscripts), to paintings which covered the whole page and into which she incorporated the message. Even the envelopes carried some picture or elaborate floral motif.

There must be many such letters in the hands of friends all over the world. Everything that had to be written, except business letters (which she was never able, and refused, to write) was written by her. She mastered the art of letter writing which is fast disappearing in our age of mass and instant long-distance communication.

For the two weeks following her operation, I found myself shuttling between my office, the hospital in Marylebone and the houses of my friends in Chelsea and Campden Hill. How quickly an abnormal situation can become normal routine!

Diana was making good progress; there were no complications. Soon she would be back home to convalesce and then, in a few months she would, as the doctors had said, be in much better health than before. Often, when driving to or away from the hospital, I pondered over these things; I told myself that now that we had dealt with the causes of her ill-health, there was no reason to be anxious any longer; on the contrary, there was every reason to be happy. Yet my heart remained heavy under the load of an ordeal, not yet revealed. *Le coeur a ses raisons que la raison ne connaît point.*

In almost twenty years this was the second time only that we had been separated for any length of time. The first time had been a few years ago when I had an operation for appendicitis. But then she was with me every day from morning to night, almost taking over from the nurses. It was not, except for the nights, a real separation, merely a transferring of headquarters from the flat to the hospital room. This time it was separation. I went to see her twice a day, but could never stay more than a short time, for I had my psychological consulting job to attend to.

But what made it a real separation was her absence from the flat. Every piece of furniture, every object in it—the pictures, the cushions, the flower vases (now empty), the many little knick-knacks on the mantelshelves and on the tables—all lovingly assembled and put in their respective places by her—they all needed her presence to come to life. She was the animating principle to which they responded. Without her the flat was not merely deserted, but in a state of suspended animation. This communicated itself to me every morning as I came to collect the mail. Never, I felt, could I live here without her.

It was not before the eighth year of our marriage, in 1955, that we had been able to move into a flat of our own. It was situated in an old-fashioned 'mansion' type of block on the western fringes of South Kensington on the very borders of 'bed-sitter' land. The block, a vast three-fronted complex, has no architectural distinction but its great attraction, which no one passing by would suspect, is a large, beautiful garden. It is enclosed on three sides by the block; the fourth side gives on to the backs of the houses of the adjoining square. It is thus a little secluded patch of country into which the noise and the fumes of the streets do not penetrate. Only the tenants of the flats have access to it. The garden has many trees: acacia, lime, cherry, sycamore, chestnut, crab-apple; an ancient mulberry and a row of tall plane trees. It has flowering shrubs of every kind, well-tended flower-beds and gravelled pathways. The lawns slope and rise, suggesting a miniature landscape with valleys and hillocks.

In summer the leafy branches of the nearest trees touch our windows. Every autumn on Guy Fawkes Night we watched mysterious clusters of coloured lights below as children let off their fireworks. From time to time a rocket would detach itself with a swishing noise, rise bravely for a few seconds and fall back again, its incandescence prematurely swallowed by the night, or spluttering fitfully away in the rain-soaked grass. In winter on the rare occasions when the garden was covered by a thin layer of snow the children would bring out their toboggans and slide down those minute hills.

The flat and its garden: they were the setting of our daily life for twelve years, eleven of which were those 'intervening' years when nothing happened worth noting down, except life itself in

29

all its richness. Looking back, there was perhaps an element of *hybris* in our self-contained happiness which the gods would not allow to go unpunished. If this is so, I can only plead that at no time in my life have I been actively and consciously engaged in the 'pursuit of happiness'. It came to me by Grace. There can be no regrets for Grace received; nor can there be reproaches against fate when it is withdrawn. For this is the very nature of Grace: it is always undeserved.

What I had always desired, even when I was quite young, was the gift of experiencing everything with the greatest possible intensity. It is still my quest now: intensity of experience which gives significance to every fleeting moment. In this lies the secret of happiness which must, of needs, include both sorrow and joy, the little sorrows and the little joys as well as the great sorrows and the great joys. Rejection of experience may shield one from many adversities and disappointments, but at a very heavy price. Grace does not come to those who would shut out life itself; happiness not to those who take no risks.

I had had the desire for intensity of experience and I had the latent gift. But, had I not met Diana I might never have achieved it. She, as I have said, possessed that inner vision of perfection which enabled her to endow with significance the most ordinary object and event. (This is what distinguishes the intellectual and spiritual élite of mankind from the common herd: the former will raise everything to a higher level of significance; the latter will bring down the level of significance.)

Even the worst stupidities and vulgarities of our modern world as epitomised by the popular Press, advertising and certain aspects of television became transmuted by Diana's sense of humour and detached, kindly tolerance. For example, out of crudest, most arrant nonsense in television commercials that offended the intelligence, she distilled her own supra-rational sense, so that even these commercials became a source of delight when we watched them together.

These may be trifling things, but everyday life consists of trifling things. She animated them as she animated the surroundings in which we lived. Her private world to which her parents took such exception because it did not conform to their own pattern of thought, was really an advanced state of consciousness, a more highly differentiated form of awareness which took in dimensions of life not readily accessible to others.

I lived in the magic of this private world of hers; it surrounded her like an aura which penetrated every corner of the flat and reached me wherever I happened to be, carrying its life-giving message as on an ultra-ultra short wavelength to which I alone was tuned in.

Her imagination was inexhaustible. She had created for herself a vast circle of 'friends', imaginary personages, benevolent 'little' people and strange animals who were as real to her as any of the people we knew. She conversed with them, she gave them form in innumerable comical drawings with which she adorned letters to children and notes to me; she brought them into our conversations and quoted their opinions. Children do this kind of thing, but she had brought it to a fine art, for she had, as someone said after her death, 'the innocence of a child and the wisdom of the ages'.

These imaginary personages were vehicles for her thoughts and at the same time symbols that stood for meanings and shades of meaning which discursive thought could not adequately convey.

The same held good for the names she invented for me. Never, from the moment when we first met, never in the twenty years of our marriage did she call me by my Christian name, never did she use it in her diaries or notes when referring to me or when talking to friends about me. Never did she use it when she was angry as so many married couples do when they wish to bring it home to themselves and to one another that a temporary breach has occurred in their relations. Even when she wrote out a cheque to me or bought something for me, it was not my Christian name that appeared on the counterfoil but one of those special names.

There were the main names which would remain substantially unchanged over a number of years or undergo slow and subtle transformations or co-exist in two or three versions of equal validity. These main names reflected in their symbolic way the

31

main themes of our life. Then there were the less stable names which would come and go at much shorter intervals; some would eventually graduate to the status of permanency; others would vanish, to re-emerge at some later date, changed or unchanged; others would vanish for good. I once made a list of the names I could remember: like geological strata they date the various periods of our married life. None of these names were contrived or deliberately 'thought up'. They were spontaneous outpourings from her imagination. Like her paintings, flower sketches, comic drawings and her handwriting, they were uniquely and unmistakably her own.

From the great variety of names three or four remained unchanged through the years. I will not give examples, for such names belong to the most intimate sphere of human relationship and do not convey much to others. There is, however, one which I have already mentioned and which will be mentioned throughout because it was this one which she used to the very end of her life. If I had omitted it or rejected it by a more conventional name, I would be doing an injustice to her memory, for the very fact that even in the final weeks of suffering and in the chaos of dissolution she still called me by this name, is itself a testimony to the extraordinary strength and originality of her character. This name is 'Mr. P.' As to its etymology, it is merely an abbreviation, to the first letter of 'Prince'. When it first began, I think even before we were married, this 'Mr. P.' introduced a note of comic ceremoniousness into our relationship. It never quite lost this implication which contrasted so vividly with the complete intimacy of our relationship.

All married couples, in the course of years, create their own special language, a kind of code which grows out of the joint experience and the imponderables of their relationship. To the psychologist these private languages would give important clues on the nature of married relations. Our private language fully reflected Diana's animistic world picture. To any outsider it would have been totally incomprehensible.

She never fully mastered German though she had made several

32

gallant attempts to learn it including a course at the German Institute in London. Yet she liked the language. She thought it quaint and amusing with its complicated declensions, conjugations; the articles of *'der'*, *'die'*, *'das'*; its plurals, pronouns, prepositions governing genitives, datives and accusatives; its divisible verbs and composite nouns. It seemed to give infinite scope for imaginative constructions by its rich blend of woolliness and precision. She also loved the earthiness of some of the terms with which she became familiar under my own private tuition. German became part of our secret language. Having a perfect musical ear, her pronunciation was faultless.

There were certain things I could express to her only in German. For example when talking about the German 'high nobility' —the initiates of the Almanach de Gotha. There are no adequate English terms to describe the social anthropology of that strange world which was also the world of my own childhood. I explained to her the designations, titles, styles by which the various subspecies of the German species knew of their respective identities, beginning with the lowest common denominator of 'doctor', gradually climbing the ladder of evolution to *'Herr von . . .'*, *'Freiherr'*, *'Graf'* (count). Here one reached the great divide between the lower and higher orders of life. There were two types of count; the ordinary count and the one who bore the style of 'Illustrious Highness'. Above the latter type of count came the Prince (of the Holy Roman Empire) who bore the style of 'Serene Highness' which made him 'co-equal' with Royalty. If Providence had placed you there, you had no further need or desire to aspire to higher things. In my father's words, *'you were'*, i.e. you existed in your own right—almost a non-contingent being.

It was all pretty absurd and unreal. Yet it was Diana, coming from a world so very different from my own who understood and could interpret my world to me with extraordinary psychological insight, objectivity and compassion. She saw the absurdities of life without condemning them. She made me re-assess my childhood in a new light, made me appreciate what had been valuable about

33

it and made me come to terms with its unhappy and traumatic memories.

Diana had her secrets; they were on two levels. One was the level of activities. She did not always want me to know what she was doing, but long experience had taught me that those secret activities were of childlike innocence, invariably connected with some happy surprise she wanted to prepare for me or with preventing or dealing with some difficulty or unpleasantness she wanted to keep from me.

She was incapable of deceit. 'I could never be unfaithful to you,' she told me once, 'because, apart from the fact that I simply couldn't, I would not be able to conceal anything from you. I would be forced to come to you and ask you for advice and how to go about it; how, for example, to arrange it if I wanted to meet a prospective lover. That would finish it before it had even begun.'

The second level was that of her innermost thoughts. Whereas on the level of her secret activities I was often curious, wanted to know what she was doing or why she would not tell me, on that deeper level I never wanted to probe. However intimately we know another person there is in everyone an ultimate realm of mystery in which resides his uniqueness as an individual. This realm must remain inviolate. Nor must the manner in which this uniqueness expresses itself in the personality as a whole be subjected to criticism, however well intentioned. Criticism may bring about changes which the one who criticises may think desirable, but there is always a heavy price to pay. In marriage both partners pay: outward behaviour ceases to reflect the inner truth of each one and the inner truth of the relationship between them. This is how marriages founder; even those which, judging by outward appearances are happy and are experienced as such by husband or wife or both.

We cannot change others. We can, if we work hard enough, destroy them, but we cannot make them into what they are not, however desirable this might be in some cases.

What love can do, and therein may lie its fulfilment, is to bridge the gap of 'ego-consciousness' which separates us from one

34

another and establish a direct link between the mystery of the one and that of the other; between, in Martin Buber's terms, the 'I' and the 'Thou'. A common pool of mystery is then established which contains the images and treasures of each, and in which new images and treasures derived from joint experience are stored. They become joint property and each may freely draw on them.

Love of this kind, marriage built on these foundations, can withstand any difficulties, trials, quarrels, misfortunes; almost anything. But here again there is a price to pay. The closer, the the more absolute the mysterious link between two people, the greater the psychic catastrophe for the one, at the death of the other.

There was no need for me to explore the innermost secrets of her thoughts; they flowered all around me in the thousand facets of her love. Never had I been more conscious of this than in that last year of our life together.

I was never happy when she was out alone for any length of time. And when she did not return at the time expected I became worried. Had anything happened to her, and if it had, how would I know? She never carried her pocket diary on her or any other means of identification. After all, accidents did happen in a big city and she was short-sighted and never wore her glasses in the street. (If she had gone by bus, I always hoped that her point of destination would be on the same side as the bus-stop, so that she need not cross the street.) The longer she stayed away the more intense became my anxiety. I would pace up and down in the flat from one room to the other all the while trying to listen to the sound of the lift outside. Was it coming up to our floor or would it stop on the floor below? My ears were so finely attuned to every sound that might indicate that she was back that I would sometimes know from the very rhythm of the steps in the entrance hall three floors below, whether it was she or someone else walking towards the lift.

The truth was that she was well able to look after herself; also that she was never very late. The explanation would always be a simple one. The traffic had been bad or she had been kept waiting in a shop. And so, underneath all my anxiety there was the blissful certainty that she would return and that all was well—for the time being.

I have often since asked myself if the constant anxiety I had when she was out by herself did not also contain an element of premonition that a time would come when, however long I might wait, whatever the sounds I might hear from the lift, whatever the kind of steps in the corridors, there would in the end not be the sound of her key in the lock to announce her safe return.

Seven

In May 1966 she did return, and after three weeks at home we went for one week to the Isle of Wight. We intended to take a proper holiday in the South of France in August. 'You must do a lot of swimming this summer,' the surgeon had told Diana. 'That is the best tonic for your abdominal muscles.'

We were back in London about the middle of June. Soon afterwards I learned that my consultancy contract had been terminated. I received three months' severance pay but was not required to attend the office after the 30th of June.

Were we once again entering upon a cycle of financial difficulties? Something deep in me, an optimistic faith carried over from childhood, that things get always better as one proceeds on the road of life (is not modern man's belief in the inevitability of progress of the same order of fantasy?) made me reject the idea. After all, things had become so much better in recent years; why then should they return to what they had been before?

Yet, I could see no immediate prospects of a new job. Men much younger than myself were losing their positions because of the prevailing economic crisis. And, if I could not find a suitable job, where was the money to come from? I had given up my literary free-lance work. Also, long experience had shown that the worst time to start anything new was the summer. Most of the people one wanted to see would be away, and even those who had not left town were not particularly anxious to enter into business discussions or take an interest in new ideas. Summer is not the season for sowing but for reaping. In like manner people also like to enjoy the fruits of their labour in the summer.

The metaphor may not be very exact, but I see all life closely linked to the rhythm of nature, and human activities, even the most contrived, artificial and sophisticated, as expressing—however remotely—something of that basic rhythm or law of nature. Everything that goes counter to this I have always regarded as profoundly unsatisfactory; for example ice-skating in summer or eating fresh strawberries in winter; or getting bad news on a sunny day.

The summer had always been to me the season of fulfilment and to be enjoyed as such.

When, therefore, as it unfortunately had happened so often, we had found ourselves short of money in the summer and hence had not been able to make any plans for going away on a holiday like most of our friends, I would announce to her that, as from the 15th July to the 31st of August we would be on holiday. We would during that time not worry about money but pretend that all was well and relax.

It was not always easy to carry out this resolve, but somehow we succeeded. We would get up leisurely; we would, as far as possible, dispense with shopping, cooking, washing-up; instead we would have picnic meals in our garden or in the country. Kew Gardens was one of our favourite spots; we sometimes would spend most of the day there, I reading or writing, Diana sketching. If the weather was bad we would visit museums as though we were tourists in a foreign country. But perhaps, most important of all, we would not dress formally but wear holiday clothes and deliberately dissociate ourselves from any activity or thought which we felt did not fit into this season of rest and recreation.

It was an elaborate piece of self-deception; an act of illusionism which we staged for ourselves. But the happiness it gave us was real. Would I have to do it again? I doubted it. I felt this summer would be different.

I did not discuss the matter with Diana. I wanted to save her from worrying over money. But she was aware of my preoccupations, and her thoughts seemed also to have gone back to those summers of imaginary holidays.

I found recently among her notes one entitled *The Value of Self-deception*. It is dated July 1966, and reads:

> Self-deception can engender a mood of optimism. The *'facing facts'* propounded and recommended mostly by those who on the whole have to face only pleasant facts, as opposed to those who have to face unpleasant facts, is not very helpful because those facts can be so grim that no amount of facing them can change them. Whereas a certain degree of self-deception which engenders a different mood, might suddenly reveal that the facts are not what one thought them to be, but that there are additional or different facts. Also self-deception may allow time to intervene and new solutions of which one had not thought to come up spontaneously. At certain moments in life non-action is better than action. . . .

It is, of course, quite possible that this reflection did not refer to money matters. I shall never know.

We had decided that whatever the financial problems facing us, we would go on our holiday to the South of France in August.

Diana was to see her surgeon at the end of July for a final check-up. She had made a good recovery from the operation but was still delicate and needed much rest. She spent most of her time at home. She had finished an illustrated book for the little daughter of friends of ours and was now starting to work on the illustrations for her anthology. I bided my time and made no determined efforts to obtain another consultancy. I felt that this was one of those moments in life when 'non-action was better than action'. We could not influence events; we had to wait upon them.

One night towards the middle of July I had a very vivid dream. In it I stood at the edge of an open-air swimming-pool, an unusually wide pool when I suddenly saw Diana being pulled out of the water on the opposite side. She appeared to be unconscious. I tried to run along the edge of the pool over to the other side, but I could not run. I remained transfixed on the spot. I could not run, nor could I jump into the water and swim across. When finally I reached her—I don't know in what manner—she was dead.

I woke up; it was about seven o'clock in the morning and the sun was shining into the room. Diana was sleeping by my side. Usually when one wakes from a bad dream and sees that all is normal around one feels reassured. It was not so this time. I lay with pounding heart for several minutes. I never told her about the dream. I knew I could not, and should not, tell her.

Prophetic dreams are often heavily disguised by symbolisms. This one hardly was. I could not get across: I could do nothing to save her.

The surgeon told Diana, after a cursory examination, that all was well and that she could go away whenever she wanted. 'There will be no need for me to see you again,' he added. Another successful operation, a normal recovery, all bills rendered and paid; the case was closed. 'Enjoy yourself on the Continent, and don't forget—plenty of swimming.'

Meanwhile we had had to revise our holiday plans. Our friend Julia* in whose villa above Cannes we were going to stay had let the house for August. Diana was not particularly disappointed. She felt she was not ready yet to go abroad. September would be the best month for the South of France. Also, for the first time in years, she was beginning to worry again about money. The pattern of those years of insecurity which we had thought were well behind us, seemed to repeat itself. Once again, as she put it

* Julia Ward.

39

in her quaint fairy-tale language, we were 'two little people in their little boat in a stormy sea' with no port in sight. I tried to reassure her; but could offer no positive grounds for my confidence beyond the empirically established truth that our 'little ship' had weathered many storms and was not likely to founder now.

However, all these preoccupations with money affairs seemed to me quite unreal. It was not lack of money which menacingly darkened my horizon. What was it?

We were now at the beginning of August. The weather was bad. One still spoke hopefully of 'summer'; yet we were half way through summer, and it once again looked as if it were to end before it had properly begun. Yet the countryside was beautiful; we had our car and no special reasons for remaining in London all the time. We went for drives, we spent the week-ends with friends. We still had our own enchanted world.

One afternoon—it had stopped raining, and the dripping leaves sparkled in the sun—I was walking in our garden as I often did when I wanted to collect my thoughts and form an inner vision of our future. As I stood by one of the flower-beds looking at a rose tree covered with particularly beautiful large flame-coloured blooms, I saw something glinting in the ground close by the tree. Half buried in the loose soil I found a small crucifix of polished wood, the figure of Christ in silver. I picked it up and saw that let into the reverse side of the cross there was a tiny glass phial filled with water. Engraved under it was the word *Lourdes*.

I took the crucifix and went back to our flat immediately. Diana was in the sitting-room where she had laid the tea. 'Look what I have just found,' I said, handing her the crucifix.

She looked at me with a deep, searching expression such as I had rarely seen on her face and said: 'What do you think this means?' She took it and put it on the table beside her bed. It was to be with her to the end—and beyond.

Towards the middle of August Diana surprised me by saying:

40

'Soon I shall take you on a lovely holiday; I think we might even take the car.'

As the holiday was a foregone conclusion I was a little puzzled by the way she put it. 'You take me, my pet, and I take you,' I answered; 'we take each other, but I am not sure about taking the car. That will make it more expensive.'

'Don't worry about that, Mr. P., I have certain plans.' She would say no more. I was mystified. Had she perhaps sold a picture or been commissioned to do some well-paid commercial art work? I did not want to probe.

Eight

17th August 1966. From now on the camera must slow down even more to concentrate on smaller units of time: on single days and soon on single hours, for time is beginning to run out.

In the last few days she had been uncommonly busy, uncommonly tense, uncommonly animated, and alternating with these moods, uncommonly quiet and withdrawn. Once or twice she came back to the question of the special holiday hinting that soon she would be able to tell me more. Several times also she had urged me to go out in the afternoon to see friends or go for a walk. 'A man should not always stick around the house; it is bad for his morale,' she had said.

In the morning of 17th August a letter came for her. I recognized her mother's handwriting. She did not open it in my presence, and later when I asked her what was in the letter—for letters from her parents were very rare—she said: 'I will tell you later today; it could have something to do with our holiday.'

For the afternoon she had arranged for us to go and see our friend Eileen in whose house I had stayed for a few days earlier in the year. As often before, we had tea on the small vine-covered

41

terrace that led from the drawing-room to the garden at the back of the house. After tea Eileen took Diana upstairs to show her some new curtain materials. They were away some considerable time, and when they came back to the terrace, Diana seemed very anxious that we should leave immediately.

Back at the flat she said: 'Now, Mr. P., I have something to tell you.' She spoke in a matter-of-fact way.

'Has it something to do with what you said this morning? I mean, something about our holiday?' I asked, not because I thought I might really hear good news about the holiday, but as a last desperate attempt to delay the impact of something which at that moment presented itself to my mind like a huge tidal wave inexorably moving towards me. When it broke over my head a minute later I was prepared.

She said: 'Come, sit by me and hold my hand.' Then, in the same quiet and gentle tone in which she had told me about her forthcoming operation three months before, she continued: 'I have to have another operation.'

'What is it, darling?' I asked, clasping her hand tightly.

'I have a lump—a very small lump—in my right breast.'

'How long have you known?'

'I discovered it about ten days ago, the week-end when we stayed with Mrs. A.'

'That must have been only a few days after the doctor told you that all was well and you should forget all about ever having had an operation.'

'It was five days after I saw him,' she answered, 'but never mind that now; it has nothing to do with it.'

Up to now I had remained as calm as she herself appeared to be. But now my pent-up emotions sought an outlet and the most obvious one was to put the blame on the doctors. Somewhere, somehow, I felt they had bungled things. 'Why did he not examine you properly, instead of just talking smoothly?' I burst out in anger and anguish.

'It obviously did not occur to him at the time,' she replied, 'but he has examined me since.'

42

'When was that?'

'Now, Mr. P., darling,' Diana said—it was she who was now trying to comfort me—'don't work yourself up so much. There may be no reason for it. Try to be calm and let me tell you everything from the beginning.'

Everything was now falling into pattern: my dream, my constant anxiety, her strange reaction when I gave her the Lourdes crucifix, her moods, her activities during the last week; it all now was beginning to make sense, terrible sense. 'Before you start,' I said, 'there is just one thing I want you to tell me: why did you not mention anything to me sooner? After all, it is now ten days . . .'

'I simply couldn't,' she replied, 'but wait, this is all part of the story . . .'

One night on that week-end at Mrs. A.'s she had woken up about three o'clock in the morning. On waking up she had become conscious of a very slight tugging sensation—it was not a pain, merely a suggestion of a twinge—in her right breast. At first she had disregarded it, but when it persisted she put her hand to her breast feeling with her fingers around the nipple. She thought she had felt a small knot about one inch above the nipple. It must be a mistake. She again put her finger on the spot. No, it was no mistake, there was a distinct point of resistance, a small lump the size of a pea.

A week before we had both seen a television documentary on cancer of the breast in which a number of patients had described their own experience, from their first discovery of that tiny lump, to operation (removal of the breast) and complete recovery. The message of the documentary was: if dealt with in time, there is every chance for cure; so never delay when you notice anything which strikes you as suspicious.

At that moment, in the still of the night, she remembered the documentary. Was it *that,* the lump, cancer of the breast, operation, removal of the breast, the end of her life as a woman, perhaps the end of her life? Should she wake me? She decided not to. 'There would have been no point in waking you, and so I made

43

up my mind not to tell you until I knew for sure.' She lay awake for a long time; eventually she went to sleep again. When she woke up at about eight in the morning, the whole thing did not seem true to her any more. Surely, it could not be; everything seemed completely normal. There was her husband still asleep. Soon he would wake up. It was a lovely day. There would be breakfast, reading the morning papers, leisurely dressing after breakfast. . . .

Her hand went to her breast. No, there was no lump . . . yes, there was . . . there, about one inch above the nipple. She could feel it clearly now, like a small somewhat elongated pea. Nothing, nothing could think it away. Just then I had woken up and asked her how she had slept. And I remembered now, as she was telling me about it all, that she had said: 'I did not sleep very well; I was restless.' That was all she said. The routine of that morning had been exactly as she had visualized: breakfast, morning paper, dressing leisurely after. But there was the *lump*.

I interrupted her: 'But why, why did you not tell me in the morning? Why, why did you not tell me in the days that followed? How could you bear it all alone?'

'I thought it all out carefully,' she replied. 'I realized that I might have to have another operation; I realized that it might be cancer, but I was not certain; it could be a harmless cyst. And, wanted to make sure, and then . . .' She hesitated.

'And then, what then?' I pressed her.

'Well, you know, Mr. P., I began to think about money. You say all is well and we need not worry. But I know you do worry. You have no job. I did not want to spring this all on you at this moment. I thought that if really I had to have another major operation, where was the money to come from?'

'But we are covered by our insurance.'

'I know, but there are always extras, and there is our holiday. I wanted to make certain financial arrangements so that, after my operation, we could go away for a good long holiday knowing that we would not be coming back to money worries as so often in the past. I simply could not burden you with all these things.'

44

On her return from the fateful week-end she had immediately made an apointment with Mr. M. and gone to see him two days later. He confirmed the presence of what he declared to be a harmless cyst. However, he said, it should be removed; this was a minor matter which would necessitate her staying at his hospital for not more than forty-eight hours. On further examination he found deep down in the right armpit a hard, enlarged gland. 'We shall remove this at the same time,' he said. Diana asked him whether there was a connection between the swollen gland and the little cyst. 'It could be, but it need not be so; but it would be just as well to remove it.'

When would he wish to do the little operation, Diana asked him. He said it could be done within the next two or three days. Only then did she tell him that I knew nothing about it and asked if the operation could wait for a while because this was a very inconvenient moment.

'For how long did you think you would wish to postpone it?' Mr. M. asked.

'Until October, if possible . . .'

At this, Mr. M.'s manner which up to this moment had been very lighthearted, changed. If she wanted to postpone the operation, he would not want to take the responsibility for the decision. A second opinion by a specialist would be required. He remained quite firm on this and promised he would contact either Mr. X. and Mr. Y., both great experts in this particular field. For the moment it was left at that.

'Then came the most difficult part of the whole business,' Diana continued, 'namely to see my father and discuss financial matters with him. You know how I dread having to talk to him. I get tongue-tied and muddled and am almost incapable of formulating my thoughts and presenting my arguments in an intelligent coherent manner.'

She was determined to face the ordeal. She took a couple of tranquillizer pills, rang him at his office, succeeded in making him listen to her and to agree to meet her later in the day at his flat. It had never been her intention to ask him for financial help, but merely to obtain his authorization to raise a certain sum from her trust fund. 'I was prepared to put up with anything, provided I got what I wanted.' The ordeal proved quite as bad as she had anticipated.

However, in the end he gave his consent. 'When I left I felt greatly relieved,' Diana said, 'I was quite cheerful, and I sang a little song to myself. "At least," I thought, "I have relieved Mr. P. of this extra worry."'

After a brief pause she continued: 'You understand now why I could not tell you before.'

'I understand, my love, but I wish you had told me all the same.' I remembered the message of the documentary film on breast cancer. I also felt that if Mr. M. had been certain that the small lump was merely a harmless cyst, he would not have proposed an immediate operation, and failing this, have insisted on a second opinion.

'We must not lose any more time now,' I said, 'so what do we do next?'

'Tomorrow, I am afraid, won't be a very jolly day,' she replied. 'We have to see three doctors, one after the other, in the afternoon. First Dr. G. (the senior partner of our own doctor who was away on holiday), then Mr. M. and finally Mr. P. G., the surgeon whom Mr. M. has recommended.'

She had organized all that quite unbeknown to me. I was amazed. As a woman intending to deceive her husband might lay elaborate plans to enable her to meet her lover without arousing suspicion might, for example, enquire quite casually what her husband's movements would be on a certain day or throw out hints of lengthy appointments with her dressmaker or hairdresser, so Diana had worked out and followed a plan which required very precise timing and co-ordination in order to see her doctors and to make those other calls: on women friends, on her parents, calls whose sole purpose it was to relieve me as far as was in her power from financial and other worries. Only when she was satisfied that all this had been done did she break the news to me. For almost two weeks she had carried alone the terrible burden

46

of that agonizing knowledge that had come to her in the still of the night on a week-end in the country. To prepare me for news which she knew would come as a shocking blow to me, she had spoken of a special holiday which, indeed, she had been preparing at the same time. I doubt if any man could show such selflessness and heroism. I know I would not have been capable of such *tenue!*

'It must not have been easy for you, my pet, to make all these arrangements without betraying yourself in some way or other,' I said. 'You know how carefully I watch you.'

'It was not easy, Mr. P., especially as you were at home most of the time. That is why I suggested once or twice that you should go out.'

'But why did you not tell me last night after you had seen your father; why did you wait until now?' 'Well, you see,' she replied, 'Rosemary is away; I had to find out from Eileen whether she could put you up again—unfortunately she can't—and also I wanted to be quite sure that the financial arrangements had been made which I discussed with my father yesterday. I only knew when I got the letter this morning . . .'

'What did the letter say?'

She smiled. 'When it comes to it, Papa is generous. He sent me a cheque for £500 with a curt note saying, it would be better not to bother the trustees at this moment.'

We went out that evening to dine with Rosamond.* 'Let's not mention anything to her today,' Diana said, 'it would spoil her evening.' Some time later Rosamond told me that we both appeared to be under some strain during dinner.

The next day at three in the afternoon we went to our first appointment. Dr. G. was among the two or three most fashionable physicians of London. 'Everybody' went to him. On certain days, at certain hours in the afternoon, his waiting-room presented the picture more of a social gathering than of an assembly of the sick in desperate need of healing. He addressed most of his women patients by their Christian names or called them 'my

* Rosamond Lehmann.

47

dear girl'—whatever their age. He was an excellent diagnostician and an experienced doctor. And underneath his sometimes disconcerting off-hand manner he was a kindly man who took the welfare of his patients very much to heart. That afternoon he brought us face to face with the stark reality of the situation.

Having examined Diana (I was present during the examination) he offered us cigarettes and took his chair behind his desk. 'There is, without any doubt, a small lump in the breast and an enlarged gland deep down under the right arm. No one can tell at present whether the two are connected, but as to the lump . . .', he looked at me . . . 'I think you know enough about these things to know that any lump in the breast, however small, must be removed as soon as possible. There is no other way.'

Diana sat quietly, listening to him. He then looked at her and continued: 'As you probably also know, the nature of the growth cannot be determined beforehand; it must be examined during the operation, and if it is malignant'—he paused—'the whole breast must be removed.'

I looked at Diana. She seemed quite calm; there was but the slightest terror of her eyelids at these fateful words which must strike terror into a woman's heart. Dr. G. went on: 'Perhaps the worst about it all, my dear girl, is that you will have to go into the operation, not knowing whether or not the breast will be removed. You must have the courage to face this agonizing uncertainty. . . .'

Before we left, Dr. G. mentioned that there was now a school of thought followed mainly by the French, which favoured treatment of breast cancer entirely by radiation in preference to surgery. 'Your own surgeon will have to decide; I am not competent to pronounce on this.' As he saw us to the door he said once more, almost tenderly: 'Courage, my girl . . .'

We stood outside his house under a cloudless sky of a hot summer afternoon. This was indeed bad news on a sunny day. We spoke little; there was not much one could say. I took her by the hand and we walked around the block to our next appointment with Mr. M.

48

In contrast to Dr. G. he had the perfect consultant's consulting-room manners. He received us, all smiles and radiating confidence. He spoke in diminutives about the impending operation, its consequences and length of stay at hospital. He discouraged all speculations as to the nature of the condition and made little reassuring jokes.

As it had already been decided that he would not do the operation, the object of our visit was merely to hear his views on the two surgeons he had originally suggested and on the third, Mr. P. G., who had finally been chosen. All three were top men in their field; Mr. P. G., being the youngest, was probably the most up-to-date.

In as much as it gave us confidence in the surgeon into whose hands we were going to entrust Diana's life; in as much also as it did restore in us for a short while the precious mood of self-deception, our visit to Mr. M. served a good purpose. It also gave him the opportunity of retiring gracefully from a case which it may have been unwise of him to offer to take on in the first place, for on his own admission, it was really 'not his cup of tea.' I doubt whether, to this day, he knows that Diana died. I never heard from him again.

Our final appointment, the most decisive of all, was with Mr. P. G. He received his private patients in his large and airy flat overlooking Regent's Park. One of the sitting-rooms served as waiting-room. Instinctively I tried to assess the owner's personality from the decor, the furniture, the colour scheme and the general atmosphere of the room. It was all very pleasant but impersonal: a couple of modern settees (in pastel colours like everything else), the latest TV set, a few reproduction antique tables, magazines strewn around, among them one on fly-fishing.

This gave me a clue. 'There is a man,' I thought, 'so immersed in his arduous profession that he has little time for other interests and activities. What he needs and seeks above everything else is air and light. Fishing in Scotland or Ireland is probably his only hobby.' All this proved correct. It made him a sympathetic figure in my eyes; I felt we had come to the right man.

Diana was with him for a very long time while I waited alone with my thoughts. I did not want to speculate too much on the outcome of the consultation; I would know soon enough. But what seemed certain was that she would have to have an operation, and, putting self-deception aside for a moment, what seemed almost equally certain to me as I reflected, was that the growth would prove to be malignant.

It is a strange sensation when suddenly one realizes that, from a certain moment on, one's life will not be the same ever again; that some radical change has already taken place which as yet is not outwardly reflected but soon and inevitably must be. I had this kind of feeling on that beautiful Sunday morning in September 1939, when war had just been declared. People were coming out of church. Suddenly the air raid sirens sounded in what proved to be a false alarm. Then all was normal and peaceful again. Every flower in the garden looked as it had looked before; the meadows were green and lush, the crickets and grasshoppers chirped and I sat under a tree in the dappled sunlight as before.

But one knew that something quite irremediable had happened which would, as it began to unfold in accordance with its own logic, give the lie to everything that now still looked so utterly right, so completely justified and well established. All this would not be true any more, was in fact no longer true even then.

It is a strange sensation also to realize that the 'future', that vague and nebulous abode in which we conveniently lodge our hopes and our fears, is suddenly with us *now,* the precise, clearly defined, inescapable present. And that when death comes it is always *now.*

At last the secretary came to take me into the consulting room. Mr. P. G. was a man in his early fifties, of slight build, diffident in his manner but precise and methodical in approach. I could see that Diana had established an immediate and good rapport with him.

'I have discussed everything fully with your wife, and we have agreed that it would be best not to delay things. I shall probably

50

do the operation at the West London Hospital early next week, probably on Wednesday the 24th.'

I looked at him questioningly: 'How long . . .' I began.

He followed my trend of thought and said: 'She will only have to be two, at most three days in hospital, for I have decided that even if the lump is malignant, and this we shall not know until we have examined it, not to remove the breast, but to treat her by radiation only . . .'

I felt tremendous relief at his words. No major operation, no disfigurement. I remembered Dr. G.'s remark about the French school of thought; obviously Mr. P. G. was a follower of that modern school.

Yet, at the back of my mind there was a nagging doubt. Could it mean that he suspected a cancer that was already too advanced or of such malignancy that a radical operation would only make things worse? I had heard of such cases. I dismissed the thought and smiled at Diana who also seemed happy. Mr. P. G. then told us that he would arrange for Diana to see Dr. L., the chief radiologist at a well-known hospital in our immediate neighbourhood, tomorrow. 'In case radiation treatment should prove necessary, it would be best to prepare everything in advance; certain measurements have to be taken and other details have to be worked out. . . .'

'Quite a day,' Diana said when we were outside; 'at least we can be happy that I don't have to have another major operation. I can tell you now it gave me quite a shock when I heard Dr. G.'s gloomy pronouncement.'

'I know, my sweet, I was equally upset.'

There is a certain street through which we had passed so many times, never pausing, but sometimes with a fleeting pang of discomfort immediately relieved by the thought 'not for us'. It is the street of the Cancer Hospital, now no longer so called. This street was to become 'our' street for the next three months, the street of our secret life.

On Friday, the 19th of August, we went for the first time through the swing doors of the side entrance which led to the radiology department. Dr. L. had been briefed by Mr. P. G., but we had the impression that he had been briefed very vaguely or had already forgotten what he had been told. He asked all kinds of questions that irritated Diana. Although he looked a kind man and spoke kindly she did not take to him.

When Diana joined me again in the small waiting-room she told me that her chest and back had been subjected to minute measurements 'with calipers and slide rules' and that figures had been entered into a chart. 'They seem to be taking it for granted that I shall come for treatment; not very reassuring.'

On Tuesday the 23rd of August, I took her to the West London Hospital, a forbidding, gloomy place, built in mid-Victorian days. The private patients' wing had a number of single rooms, cell-like, with thin partitioning walls between them. She suddenly noticed that there was no private telephone, and for the first time her courage failed her. She saw herself cut off from me and she refused to stay unless a telephone was installed that very day. Fortunately the Floor Sister who had quickly sized up the situation managed to engage her in a conversation, having arranged meanwhile for a call to be put through to Mr. P. G. Just as we were about to walk out of the hospital, the surgeon came through on the telephone and persuaded Diana to stay, saying that the operation might otherwise have to be postponed for two weeks.

This, then, was her second entry into hospital.

The next day, August 24th, shortly after breakfast Mr. P. G. rang me: 'I thought you would like to know that we have just finished the operation; we have removed the lumps (plural!) and a certain amount of tissue. Now she will have to have a little radiation treatment.'

'What you are telling me,' I answered, 'is that there is cancer.'

'Yes, *but it is not nearly as bad as I had suspected.*'

Here, then, was the true reason why he had decided, after examination, not to risk a radical operation. As I had suspected, the cancer was of special malignancy. Who can now tell whether it was the right decision?

52

'When and how are we going to tell Diana?' I asked the surgeon.

'I shall go and see her early in the afternoon when she has fully come round,' he replied, 'and break it to her gently, but I think she is very intuitive and will be prepared for it.' Mr. P. G. further told me that the radiation treatment must start almost at once; if possible, the next day. 'We must at all cost, prevent a spreading, and we must knock out that gland under the arm.'

I knew that nothing would ever be the same again.

I went to see Diana in the afternoon. She received me smilingly. 'Hullo, Mr. P., I am a dreadful nuisance; am-n't I.' (That was part of her special language.) 'Now, I believe I have to have radiation treatment.'

'Who told you?'

'The anaesthetist; a very nice young man. He came to see me a couple of hours ago. I am afraid I was sick when I came round. Poor young man, he was so embarrassed. He couldn't even find a bowl. But now let's have a chat; I'll ring for another cup of tea.'

I told Diana that she could come out before the end of the week but that they wanted her to have the first radiation treatment if possible tomorrow. I would hire a car and take her to the other hospital and bring her back to Hammersmith again.

As I was leaving I met Dr. G., the physician, in the corridor. He had been told of the outcome of the operation, and had come to pay a brief visit to Diana. I told him that I wanted to have a word with him and would wait.

In less than five minutes he was out of the room again and we walked down the corridor together.

He seemed in one of his gloomy moods. 'What are the chances of a complete recovery?' I asked him.

'Fairly good; eighty per cent,' he answered.

'What exactly does this mean?'

'It means that, if there is no recurrence within five years, she will be all right.'

I wanted to continue the conversation, hoping he might say

53

something from which I might derive real comfort. 'How do you think did this happen?' I asked. 'Is there any connection with the condition which necessitated the hysterectomy three months ago?'

'There is a school of thought ("this must be one of his favourite concepts," I reflected) which holds that unless you also remove the ovaries when performing a hysterectomy, over-production of hormones may provoke cancer of the breast.'

'Surely Mr. M. must have been aware of that,' I replied, and at once the suspicion came back to me that something had been 'bungled'.

'No doubt he was aware of it, but . . .' and Dr. G. made one of those inimitable Central European gestures which are so much more eloquent than words, '. . . the point is that no one really knows.'

No one really knows. The truth of this statement was to be borne in on me relentlessly over the next six months.

On Friday Diana was sufficiently strong to go by car to the other hospital for her first radiation treatment. She was immediately taken into Dr. L.'s surgery and there under his supervision, she was 'mapped out' for treatment. A number of small blue crosses in indelible ink were painted around the area to which radiation was to be applied. Later on as the area was extended, more crosses in different colours were to appear on her skin and as the treatment continued, coloured lotions of many hues were applied (to protect the skin from burns) until her right side from the neck to below the chest and around the right shoulder looked like a painter's palette.

Soon the little crosses, blue, magenta and red, became a familiar sight to me as I watched patients going in and out of the radiology department. I saw them on necks, throats, cheeks, bare chests; on shaven heads of men and on the yet hairless heads of tiny babies who lay like waxen dolls in their hospital cots.

The department in which the treatment was given, into which we now descended for the first time, consisted of a central wide

54

corridor which housed the control panels or consoles which governed the radiation units. Those control panels looked exactly as I had imagined them. A series of levers, switches, dials, flashing lights, all neatly arrayed, sending unseen impulses to the working end of the system.

Our lives are increasingly governed by these innocuous looking, impersonal panels, attended by white-coated operators, male or female. Buttons, switches, dials, flashing lights. Nothing much to distinguish those here in the radiology department of a hospital from those installed in guided missile submarines where they are used for remote-control destruction or from those in automated steel mills, or in space rocket launching sites. Nothing much to distinguish them, except perhaps size and complexity and our knowledge of their intention.

On either side of the central corridor were the radiation chambers. Two of the largest ones lay behind heavy metal sliding doors; the smaller ones seemed to need no such protection. By the side of each chamber there were small panels of thick glass let into the wall, through which the therapists could watch their patients during treatment. Over the entrance of each radiation chamber warning lights were placed: green when the chamber was unoccupied; red to indicate that treatment was in progress.

I never obtained more than a fleeting glimpse of the chambers themselves and of the treatment units, ungainly monsters that looked like a combination of dentists' chairs, operating tables, X-ray apparatus equipped with pullies, wheels, levers and swivelling platforms to allow for every possible angle of radiation onto every afflicted part of the patient's body.

Skill, conscientiousness, and attention to the minutest detail were required on the part of the therapist in setting the machine to the required angle, the 'head' containing the radioactive element exactly at the right distance and within the confines of the treatment area mapped out by the coloured crosses. Surrounding areas of the skin had to be protected by means of leaden plates covered in leather. Getting the patient into position was time consuming and a nervous strain on the patient

55

who had to co-operate in this procedure of being lashed to and immobilized in the arms of the contraption from whose sinister-looking 'warhead' powerful rays were about to be released into his body; Beelzebub driving out the Devil, as it were.

Once the therapist had left the chamber and switched on the ray, there was nothing for it but to endure, while taking comfort at the thought that inevitably the moment would come when the mechanism would click to a standstill and one would be released. But to remain seven to eight minutes in a not too comfortable body-posture, which one is not able to alter, is itself a severe test of endurance. Added to this is the patient's awareness of the implications of the process, his alone-ness and inability to communicate; it may become something of a torture, especially for anyone with a tendency to claustrophobia.

Fortunately Diana was free of this. To her the worst of the actual treatment, apart from the ever-present fear that she might receive too large a dose of radiation, was the strange smell she associated with the radiation chamber: a mixture of oil and ozone which gave her a kind of nausea. The ozone, it was explained, was produced by the splitting of the oxygen in the air through radiation. (At least this is how she understood it.) And since the treatment rooms seemed to have no proper system of ventilation, the atmosphere became stuffy. It made her feel faint. On that first day she was given a short treatment lasting some seven minutes, and mainly concentrated on the gland under the arm. It was obvious that the doctors were very anxious to 'knock out' this particular trouble spot as quickly as possible.

After the treatment I took her back to the West London Hospital, again by hired car which I felt was less bumpy than our own car.

She returned home on Saturday, the 27th. The following Monday the radiation treatment began in earnest. According to the doctors it was to last for 'three to four weeks', five days a week, with the week-ends free. In fact, it continued until the middle of November, more weeks being added each time we thought we had reached the end.

The reason given for this very long treatment was that she 'stood up to it so well'. I think she must have received the maximum dose of radiation which, it is thought, the human system can stand.

Every day, Mondays to Fridays, for the next two and a half months I took her to the hospital, and after treatment back home again. I was glad I had no office to go to. For the first two months the sessions varied in length from seven and a half minutes (when radiation was applied to one area only) to twenty-four minutes divided into three phases of seven to eight minutes each, when all areas under suspicion, namely chest, neck and right shoulder, were treated. These were the most exhausting sessions, that drained her vitality and left her so weak that on several occasions especially as the treatment entered its later stages, she was, on leaving the hospital, hardly able to walk.

I waited for her, sometimes in the central corridor where I watched the girls at the control panels, or, when the sessions were very long, at the pub at the corner of the street.

This was our 'secret life', which began on August the 29th.

After a cold and rainy summer there came a warm and sunny autumn that was to stay on beyond its season, and, pushing past a feeble, self-effacing winter, would stretch out its hand to catch the hand of an eager, early spring.

Many an afternoon, mostly between three and four, I sat in the brilliant sunshine on one of the wooden benches outside the pub under a sky that was often as blue as in Italy or the South of France where we should have been at this very time. I sat there, thinking of our life together: almost twenty years of constant struggle and difficulties, but twenty years also of unbroken happiness.

I did not dare to contemplate the future, for underneath my hopes and my fervent desire that she should recover I felt there was no future to contemplate. I think it was during those waiting hours outside the pub in the early autumn of 1966 that the idea first came to me that one day I would write a book about her.

57

I always kept an eye on my wristwatch, and if at the expected time—I knew how long the treatment would last—she had not joined me, I walked back around the corner to the hospital. Often I would meet her half way; sometimes I would find that she was still in the radiation chamber, the beginning of the treatment having been delayed for one reason or another.

A good many years ago, I had seen a film on the life of St. Vincent de Paul, missionary to the poor and founder of orders of charity (d. 1660). The film showed harrowing scenes of men, women and children afflicted in body or mind, huddled together outside and besieging the entrance of his hospital—a cross-section of suffering humanity in a 17th-century setting, yet timeless and symbolic of man's frailty and of his helplessness in the face of suffering, illness and death.

In our age we are spared the sight of the maimed, the crippled, the blind; we are spared the sight of open sores, gashing wounds and repulsive disfigurements. Most of it is concealed. It is concealed by the gleaming white ambulances that take the sick and the dying swiftly away; by the casualty wards, the white-coated doctors and nurses; it is concealed by modern methods of treatment and public welfare.

No one can doubt that suffering has been greatly alleviated, and much of the terror of illness been banished by modern medical care. And yet when one penetrates inside the walls that separate the sick from the healthy, one becomes aware that the helplessness of man in the face of illness and suffering has essentially remained the same as in the days of St. Vincent de Paul. Anyone moving in the corridors and wards of a big hospital is soon caught up in it.

Pitiful figures, prostrate on stretchers and trolleys or wrapped in red blankets, in wheelchairs, pass constantly before one. Grey-faced and listless, or unnaturally animated, patients sit on benches, waiting for treatment or consultation. Anxious relatives converse with their charges in forced cheerfulness. The air is thick with anxious anticipations, frustrated hopes, concealed knowledge, open sorrow and unspoken words.

58

It is a world totally different from the world outside, yet the dividing lines are very thin. A tiny lump in the breast, an unaccountable pain, a small error of judgement in driving a car, and it becomes *your* world.

I became familiar with it in the course of those many weeks, more so than Diana, because I had time to wander around and to observe much of the routine of the hospital, especially the radiology department.

And as I became more familiar with the place it lost its dread for me, but with the dread went much of its magic as an Aesculapian sanctuary of healing.

I overheard conversations between doctors; between nurses; and between doctors and nurses. There was none of the confidence here which they displayed when talking to patients or their relatives. It was all much more tentative, uncertain, casual, haphazard; even slightly muddled. It all seemed based on trial and error and hoping for the best.

I also began to know some of the patients who regularly came for radiation treatment; to know also the location of their particular cancer (the little coloured crosses!) and to draw certain conclusions as to their condition and prospects. I thought I could detect those who would be cured and those who would not. Like one of the principal characters in Thomas Mann's *The Magic Mountain* I began to develop the faculty of spotting the *morituri*—the 'candidates for death'; it was an uncanny feeling.

Twice a week Diana had to undergo medical examinations by Dr. L., blood and other tests to check up on the effects of the radiation on her general health and on areas under treatment. It was of the utmost importance to avoid severe burns of the skin, which might lead to open wounds and other complications. All this was done with thoroughness and professional skill. After three weeks of treatment the ominous gland under the arm had gone back to normal, the breast had healed completely, and there were no signs of any spread of the disease. 'We are ex-

59

tremely pleased with the effect of the treatment,' the doctors told us.

Diana herself was full of confidence. I suspended all judgement but watched her carefully all the time. Every afternoon, on coming back from the hospital, I made her rest for several hours, and we rarely went out in the evening. We did, however, see some of our most intimate friends, and as far as possible we tried to keep up the appearance of a normal life. No one knew the routine of our *secret* life.

The worst day was always Friday, after five consecutive treatments during the week. I think it was in the sixth week towards the middle of October that Diana was put on to the cobalt-ray machine every other day. The cobalt ray, the most powerful yet devised for radiation treatment, could be applied only for a maximum of one to one and a half minutes at a time. The implications made one shudder, for one inevitably thought of the ultimate threat to humanity, the cobalt bomb, one of which would suffice to poison half the population of the world.

Sitting under that ray frightened Diana—the machine itself had something particularly sinister to it—and even the shortest exposure made her feel ill.

There were, however, the week-ends when she could recover and regain her strength which she always did to an astonishing degree. I took many snapshots of her during those sunny autumn days in October 1966. They show her in the perfection of her beauty.

Towards the end of October we again began to speak of our holiday in the South of France. As everything seemed to have gone according to plan and there were no signs of any complications, I was optimistic. We knew of two or three women who had gone through the same ordeal of illness and treatment and had made a complete recovery. They were now, years after, in normal health. So, why should she not also recover?

But then, one afternoon in the first week of November, when I sat waiting in the corridor of the hospital, I spoke to the staff nurse who usually attended the weekly check-ups and was familiar with all the details of Diana's case. I had noticed more than once in her eyes an expression of tenderness and sadness whenever she looked at Diana. That afternoon, as she was passing, I stopped her and said: 'Would you say that my wife is making good progress in her treatment?'

She hesitated for one brief moment and answered: 'The treatment is going very satisfactorily, and she has an excellent chance of recovery.'

There could be no doubt as to the implications of her words. I said: 'You mean, it is by no means a foregone conclusion that she will be fully cured?'

She knew she had to speak the truth, and she said: 'I am sure you realize that our present methods of treatment—excising cancerous tumours by surgery or knocking them out by radiation, incidentally knocking out a good many other things besides—is crude in the extreme. One day these methods will appear to people as primitive as those of medieval medicine appear to us today. The truth is, we don't know any better. And our methods are often very effective; many patients are being cured by them. What else do you want me to say?'

'So there is a good chance that she too may be cured completely?' I insisted. 'Especially as we seemed to have caught the disease in its very early stages?'

'Yes, there is a very good chance,' she answered, 'let us hope —and pray.'

Part Two

In the depth of your home and desires lies your
  silent knowledge of the beyond;
And like seeds dreaming beneath the snow your
  heart dreams of spring.
Trust the dreams, for in them is hidden the gate
  to eternity.

(quoted in the Anthology from
KHALIL GIBRAN *The Prophet*)

One

At last the treatment came to an end. It was on the 17th of November that I sat for the last time in the basement room where the neat, wholesome-looking girls manipulated the controls. It was a 'short' treatment, only one minute and forty seconds under the cobalt ray.

How often had I anxiously watched the red light come on over the radiation chamber indicating the beginning of the treatment, and followed the hand on the face of my watch going round, hoping that at the very instant when the exact number of seconds prescribed for the day's treatment had ticked away, I would hear the mechanical whirr of the time switch which preceded the cutting off of the ray, and looking up, I would see the green light come on showing that all was now clear. How often had I thought: 'Perhaps they might make a mistake and not set the time switch correctly; perhaps I ought to tell them.'

Of course, this never happened. These highly trained girls made no such mistakes. And yet, we had found that there were great differences between the girls and the way they carried out their task. With some girls we felt safe; with others we did not. When one of the latter was on the controls I was always nervous and tense during the whole duration of the treatment. On those occasions a thirty minutes' wait in the radiation department or at the pub on the other side of the street could be agony.

The awesome power of the rays, gathered into these machines from the very heart of the universe, and like the god Shiva impartial destroyers and givers of life, cried out for the redeeming Grace of human compassion and love. Not all the girls had that gift. The silent cry for compassion was written in the faces of the patients whom, day after day, I had seen in that department of the hospital. There were the patients in an advanced stage of the disease who were wheeled in from the wards—some mere shadows of what had once been human forms. There were the less ill who came accompanied (sometimes supported) by relatives, often talking urgently and intensely in Mediterranean or Middle East tongues. There were those who came alone, like the little man in work-a-day clothes with the tell-tale blue cross clearly visible on his chest through his open-neck shirt. And the other red-faced bull-necked character whom I had often seen purposefully striding along the streets of Chelsea. It could be seen from his markings that he had cancer of the throat. And the young Arab boy who had several of these crosses on his shaven head and who sat silently staring into space by the side of his tutor or personal guard. And even the beautiful, elegant young woman who when she had come for her first treatment some days before had walked in briskly in front of her husband, throwing back her head and dark locks as though in defiance of the purpose which had brought her to this place (of whose existence she had probably never heard before), even she after a few days—still proud and erect and perfectly groomed, but walking less briskly —even she bore this silent plea for love and tenderness in her face.

It was customary, I had observed, for patients who had completed their treatment to give small presents to the girls who had looked after them. Mostly people gave boxes of chocolates which the girls handed round to each other; others gave stockings or pieces of costume jewellery.

The day before the final treatment we had been to the shop that belonged to Caldey Abbey, the Cistercian monastery off the coast of Pembrokeshire, where the monks made many kinds of perfumes, lotions and scented preparations from the flowers they cultivated to this end. Caldey Island was one of those places which we had wanted to visit and never did. The year before we had been invited by the Abbot to come and stay for two weeks as his personal guests, and he had added a message to his invitation assuring us that we need have no misgivings as to the quality of the food, since brother kitchen-chef was a Frenchman.

Diana very much wanted to go. The whole idea of monastic life and of the ancient arts and crafts practised in the monasteries had always had a special appeal for her. But twice we had to cancel our intended visit; I blamed myself for this; I had felt—wrongly as I now know—that I could not afford to take the time off. 'Next spring, I hope that we shall be able to come,' I had informed the Abbot. *Next spring.* She did not live to see it.

We had bought all our perfumes at the Caldey Abbey shop in London for years; especially at Christmas and on other special occasions. The perfumes, essences and lotions were exquisite—fragrant, fresh, natural; the bottles and containers and boxes of elegant design. We visualized the monks tending and harvesting the flowers, distilling the essences in old-fashioned retorts in vaulted chambers. (In fact, they employed the most up-to-date methods.) But Diana preferred to think of it that way. 'Most probably there is always one monk who reads aloud from the works of St. Thomas Aquinas or other holy books while the others silently apply themselves to their presses, cauldrons and retorts. . . . That is why the perfumes are so much better than ordinary commercial ones. . . .'

And so the day before, Diana had selected presents for the girls who had given her treatment over the past nine weeks. Rose-essence for the bath for one of them. 'I think we give this to the pretty, fair-haired girl.' Lavender water for one of the older therapists. 'Island gorse'; 'Caldey No. 2.'; 'Caldey Cologne'; 'Fern'; each one carefully thought out with the prospective recipient in mind. Each one separately wrapped and adorned with coloured ribbon.

When Diana had emerged from the radiation chamber we distributed the gifts among the girls and told them that the perfumes had been made by the monks of Caldey Abbey. 'Goodbye and good luck,' said the senior therapist. And so we took leave from the place of our secret life.

Half way through the treatment Dr. L. had gone abroad to attend various medical gatherings. His assistant, Dr. J., a shy, taciturn man, had taken over. This non-communicative assistant was now waiting for us at the end of the corridor.

He took a red ball-point pencil from a row of six or seven in various colours which adorned the breast pocket of his white coat like so many badges of distinction and entered some notes into the treatment chart handed to him by the Sister in charge. 'Dr. L. will want to see you on his return from Japan in about a fortnight.'

We asked him when he thought we might be able to go abroad on our long delayed holiday. 'Not for a little while yet,' he answered. 'Dr. L. will tell you. In any case you must wait until all the skin has peeled off over the area of treatment.' This was one of those things which had been revealed to us only gradually as the treatment proceeded: that the skin would come off as it does after severe sunburn.

We shook hands with Dr. J. who looked down at the tips of his boots. 'Thank you very much.' He was too shy to answer.

We passed the doorman with whom, every day, I had exchanged a few words about the weather. He looked at us with eyes that had seen much heartbreak and tragedy and had forgotten how to smile. Then we stood in the damp air of a November afternoon. Diana took a deep breath. 'Thank God, I won't have to smell this horrid mixture of ozone and oil any more,' she said. 'Let's hope this is really the end of the treatment.'

'I am sure it is, darling. Let's go home and have tea.'

Our secret life had come to an end. About one month and a half of near-normal life was left to us.

Two

Only a few intimate friends knew of the nature of Diana's illness; knew about her operation and the radiation treatment. Outwardly she showed no signs of the ordeal. She had not lost weight; she looked normal; some people even thought she looked uncommonly well.

But she tired easily and had little appetite; the rays seemed to have affected her digestion; she always craved for acid and highly spiced foods—tomatoes, cucumber, sweet-sour gherkins, curry, yogurt.

I would not allow her to go about on buses or do any but the lightest local shopping. Nor was she allowed to do housework which put strain on her right arm and shoulder. No exertions, but rest, peace and quiet . . . and then, if all was well, the long delayed holiday in the South of France. She was now my charge —she had been for the past few months; but now that the doctors had done everything that *could* be done (no further radiation would have been possible), now I stood alone in her defence with hope and faith my only allies. She was my wife, the tender, passionate, all-loving, all-caring companion of my life; but she was also my child, my *Sorgenkind* (as I told her in German), my child of sorrows.

Never had I been more conscious of the significance of the words 'To have and to hold . . for better, for worse, for richer, for poorer, in sickness and in health . . .': We had experienced it all in the twenty years of our marriage. But now more than ever I had to look after her, surround her with care, to *love* and *cherish* her, come what may. Nothing else mattered.

Our daily routine, which with slight variations had been the same over the years, now changed. For example, it had always been Diana who got up first and made our breakfast. She would bring it into the bedroom on the trolley and sit on the edge of the bed while I remained in bed. But from May 1966 onwards the roles had become reversed. I made the breakfast and brought it in on the trolley. She stayed in bed—she always felt guilty about it —and I sat cross-legged in Yoga posture on the bed, spreading around us napkins, plates, cups and saucers as though we were having a picnic on the lawn. These were moments of happiness; moments of happiness on borrowed time.

We rarely went out in the evening, and only to dine with our closest friends. She was obliged to wear dresses with a high neckline because the various colours with which she had been painted during the treatment, as well as some of the tell-tale crosses, were still visible on her shoulder and on the right side of her neck. 'At last I am well equipped for the evening,' she said to me one day, 'I have all these pretty evening dresses; and now I shall not be able to wear them.'

'In a month's time,' I answered, 'you will be able to wear them and then we shall go to the opera.'

We spent most evenings at home watching television—I noticed that her eyes had become oversensitive, even after an hour's watching she would develop severe eyestrain and headache —or we would read.

Before her illness our reading interests coincided only on certain subjects, mainly Eastern wisdom and religion. Usually it was I who discovered new books on these subjects: 'You must read this, my pet, this is a most interesting book': *Hara* (*The Vital Centre of Man*)—*Foundations of Tibetan Mysticism—The Sufis —The Embossed Tea Kettle*—a new edition of *The Secret of the Golden Flower* and many others in the course of the years. She read them most thoroughly, making marginal notes and under-lining passages as she went along. 'You never read the books you recommend to me,' she often said. 'Why don't you? I would like you to read them so that we can discuss them.'

'I read them, know them, through you, my love,' I would answer. And this was true, and not only for books: I knew through her. How true it was, I was to learn not many months later.

It was not that I never read the type of books I gave her; I read some of them, and I read books on the same subjects, with a different approach. But we came to the same conclusions and could discuss what we had read, and compare. Often, though, we were in direct competition. We might be reading different books on the same subject at the same time. Suddenly a passage would strike me as being of special significance, and I would say to her: 'Listen to this, this is very important.' She would look up from her book, and I would begin reading the passage. After a while I would say: 'You are not really paying attention.'

'Yes, I am, but I was just reading something very important myself; let me read it to you . . .' Then she would read and I, steeped in my own thoughts, would listen while still glancing at my own book. 'You never listen properly,' she observed.

There were other categories of books in which I took little or no interest: books on Celtic lore, on Druidism and on early Christianity in Ireland and the Western Isles, in particular Iona, 'the lamp of Christ whose flame lighted Pagan Europe'. She knew every book by Fiona McLeod (William Sharp) on the subject and also the tales and strange novels by Charles Williams, author of Arthurian legends, inspired interpreter of Dante, poet and Anglo-Catholic mystic, whom she had first met in Oxford during the war where at that time he exercised a powerful influence on a whole generation of undergraduates.

These and other books of the same kind were her own special and private concern, part of her secret world to which I have already referred. I knew of their existence, of the care with which she treated them; I knew she annotated them, but it was not until after her death that I looked at them.

Towards the end of May 1966, when she was at home recovering from her first operation, I began to read to her every evening. Soon this became a regular habit which continued through the summer and autumn almost without a day's interruption. The books I read out to her were mainly history and historical biographies, subjects very different from those which constituted

71

her normal reading. In her formal education—if this term can be applied at all to the few years she spent at a co-educational school in Devonshire, followed by one year at a girls' school near London—history seemed to have been missed out altogether. In her parents' home, in the years leading up to the outbreak of World War II the atmosphere was so highly charged with the passions engendered by contemporary history that there was little incentive for a sensitive young girl to aquaint herself more fully with so distasteful a subject.

But no woman married to a Loewenstein can for long live outside history. In contrast to my brother Hubert, who is a sound historian with a grand and universal conception of history, I am a mere amateur with a certain insight into the motives of men. Accordingly, the *dramatis personae* on the stage of history, with their personal vanities, ambitions, virtues and failings, and how their complex motivations and conflicting aims shaped history, is of greater interest to me than the grand design which, according to some historians, shapes history independent of men.

What had always fascinated me about my own family, was not its role in history—important up to the end of the 15th century, but negligible since—but the occasional flashes of eccentricity and genius which down the centuries light up and mellow those stern unvarying features of the family face. Genius with us was in fact always linked to romance, for whenever it occurred it was as a result of an unusual marriage. Indeed, our branch of the family* owes its existence to a romantic streak in the character of the Elector Palatine, Frederick I, the 'Victorious' (1425–76), who fell in love and secretly married a beautiful girl of non-royal birth of whom it is said that she could read and write, do fine needlework, sing and play the lute. Two sons were born of the marriage; one died at the age of sixteen, the other, Ludwig of Bavaria, was created Sovereign Count of Loewenstein by the Emperor Maximilian in 1494.

The pattern of romantic marriages repeated itself; always detri-

* The House of Wittelsbach, Bavaria.

mental if judged by the criterion of power, prestige and property, always beneficial if judged in terms of human values.

Diana loved to listen to my historical tales, and with her extraordinary power of empathy and her sense of 'having been here before', brought it all to life as though it had happened only yesterday. Often she would refer to Frederick (dubbed by his enemies 'Wicked Fritz'): 'I am sure you look exactly like him when you are angry'; and to his rough Bavarians, for she was convinced that they were a rough lot. Whenever I came into the bedroom without having wiped my shoes on the doormat or when I spilled water over a polished surface or munched cheese-sandwiches dropping the crumbs on the floor, she would attribute such uncivilized habits to my Bavarian forebears, 'those peasants with their battle-axes', as she called them. I would protest and say that we had never been peasants but always superior beings, clad in shining armour and wielding gigantic swords, but gentle and loving out of armour; when sitting by the fire in our great halls, surrounded by our womenfolk, we would listen to music, play chess or hold discourse with learned men.

She conceded that there must be some truth in what I said because, as she remarked: 'You and your brothers, and also other members of your family, you are all to a certain extent like that; none of you have extravagant tastes and strange habits; none of you are great eaters or drinkers; all of you have scholarly minds.'

But one cannot entirely disown one's heritage and upbringing: thirty-two generations of ancestors, all to a greater or lesser extent concerned with the business of war, must leave a mark. There is a secret hankering after martial glory in the heart of every Loewenstein, however scholarly his mind, however remote from war his profession.

I had always wanted Diana to know something about the history of France from the reign of Louis XIV to the Napoleonic Empire, and it so happend that during 1965/66 a number of books on that period, written for the general public, made their appearance. It was those I read out to her. The last complete book I read out to her was on the battle of *Austerlitz*. It demanded a good deal of concentration on the part of the listener because of the detailed description of the battle plans on both sides and the names of the many marshals and generals, French, Russian and Austrian, and the disposition of their troops. The book also contains many sketch-maps which have to be referred to constantly.

'Are you in a mood for strategy today, darling?' I would ask her when I wanted to continue the story where we had left off the evening before.

Yes, she was, whereupon we would recapitulate the main developments in the preparation for the battle or the battle itself. We became experts with a strategic grasp of the situation equalled perhaps only by Napoleon himself. We knew exactly how many men, how many pieces of cannon, how much infantry and cavalry were involved on both sides; we knew that on the right flank of the allied, Austro-Russian army was Prince Bagration with his corps facing Marshal Lanne's infantry and Murat's cavalry; that to the left of Bagration was Prince Lichtenstein's cavalry, and a little further back the Russian Imperial Guard. We knew the exact position and the subsequent moves of all the other units under their various high-born commanders; above all we knew Napoleon's battle plan which neither the Russian Czar nor the Austrian Emperor, nor any of their general understood until it was too late and the day irretrievably lost.

We both looked forward to our evenings' history readings; she lay beside me, very close while I read. Often she kept her eyes closed because the strong light of my bedside lamp hurt them, but she always listened with complete attention, asking questions and making comments.

'I think we will stop now; let's switch off the light and cuddle down.' So ended every evening, every evening's precious, unrepeatable, final experience. This is what I felt when, in the darkness, I put one arm gently around her (for I dared not put my arms firmly around her; she was still too bruised) and had kissed her goodnight. 'One more evening gone; how many more?'

74

As I lay in the stillness of the darkened room, in those closing weeks of the year I could not help thinking back on how since April the 'changes and sorrows', of which I had had the first intimations at a time when our happiness seemed complete, had step by step revealed themselves and had always been graver, more sinister than one had feared. I could not, hard as I tried, free myself from the oppressing feeling that, as in a Greek tragedy, some inexorable process had been set in motion which would run its full and predetermined course.

When would the next 'change and sorrow' be with us, what form would it take; how would it first announce itself? Would she tell me in her calm and gentle way: 'Mr. P., I think there is something not quite in order with me,' and then tell me the symptoms? Or how would I myself first notice that there was something amiss?

But the stillness of the night also held its comforts. She was with me, real, reassuring in her physical presence: her head close to mine on the pillow, her open hair all around my face. From top to toe she was beside me. I could kiss the nape of her neck; I could signal to my toes to touch her toes, or I could pass my hands lightly over her hips. She was still with me. And when I drifted into sleep, all seemed well and as it should be.

But with the morning the gnawing worries returned. How did she feel, what would she say? I watched her anxiously. Remembering that twice before she had dissimulated the true situation, I looked out for any clues in her appearance and general condition. Did she look well? Was she paler than usual? Was she losing weight? Was her appetite normal? Why did she not smoke? (I knew that when a person who smokes develops a sudden intolerance to smoking, this could be a symptom of cancer. She never smoked much, and so perhaps this was of no significance, but all the same, it worried me.) I watched her moods. Did she seem preoccupied? Was she more silent than usual, more withdrawn? *Would* she tell me if she discovered some new symptoms? And if the illness had not been cured, would she be suddenly dramatically ill or would the new onset be insidious?

Economic problems were again beginning to press upon us. For the past few months, while she was under treatment, I had made no serious attempts to find another consultancy. But this could not continue for ever. Our 'unearned' income (an absurd term which seems to carry the pejorative meaning of 'undeserved') provided no more than a fraction of what we needed. Reserves were dwindling fast, and, even if by some freak of fortune an appointment had been offered to me at that time, could I have put my heart into it? I could not see the way ahead; I could not see ahead, except in flashes of forebodings which touched realms of experience in which jobs and money were of no real significance.

And yet, there they were, the hard realities of pounds, shillings and pence. I could not ignore them. 'How are we off for money?' Diana would ask me from time to time.

'All right,' I said, 'don't worry.' Strangely enough, I did not really worry. I do not think out things logically. I think pictorially and decide on a course of action in accordance with the clarity of the picture before my inner eye. It is like bringing a photographic slide projected onto a screen into focus, except that the bringing into focus happens by a largely unconscious process.

At that particular moment there existed an inner picture of a possible development. About a year before I had, in connection with some business, met a group of people, partners in a small but successful company. I had met them again more recently. Imperceptibly these few encounters had begun to generate a momentum of their own which pointed to a more lasting and significant relationship. This was the picture which, at first vague and blurred, but gradually clearer in outline and depth, presented itself before my mind.

'I think,' I said to Diana one day, 'that I might try to link up with these new friends of mine. I like them all and I can see quite a number of things we might do together; besides, I am fed up with the whole idea of being employed by anybody.'

Diana was delighted at the thought, and from then on my association with the little group whom she affectionately called

76

'the boys' (and who have since become close friends) became a source of constant interest and joy to her; the last source of world-directed happiness. She knew that I had made the right decision and she backed it with all the power of her love and the conviction of her incredibly strong personality. It was she who, on what proved to be one of her last public appearances—tea at the Oxford and Cambridge Club on the 30th of December 1966 when she met all the 'boys' together—obtained from my not unwilling partners important concessions which consolidated my position within the new company.

Having made my decision, I put aside worries over finance. I knew we would not make money immediately and perhaps not for quite some time, but at least we would no longer depend for our living on other people's decisions and whims. Cautiously, tentatively, we began to make plans for the future.

The making of the decision (which in retrospect proved to have been a very important one) also helped our morale. It released us, if only for a short while, from our state of passivity, restored to us some measure of initiative. Diana now devoted most of her time to her anthology, with renewed zest and complete dedication. She had selected all the passages during the summer and autumn, and now set them out in her beautiful small script in a sketchbook, and to each quotation she painted a miniature picture, expressing the spirit of the text as she understood it.

I could not help feeling, even at the time, that the anthology was her testament which at all cost she wanted to complete. It remained incomplete, but this unfinished anthology is a work of great beauty and spiritual insight; the work of someone who had indeed (as expressed in the quotation from Kahlil Gibran), 'beheld the spirit of death' unflinchingly and had made her peace with the world.

77

Three

We had made our bedroom into her studio and living-room. I had put a small table by the window for her to work on, and there, surrounded by ink bottles, paint tubes, brushes, papers and books, she would sit all afternoon writing, sketching and painting. I went to my 'new office', strictly speaking, not my office yet, in the West-end. I drove along the most convenient and pleasant route through Eaton Square, past Buckingham Palace, down the Mall to St. James's Square, where I parked my car, to walk another five minutes to the office. This route which I still drive almost daily now was soon to become associated with the most poignant emotions—anxiety, compassion, love, hope, sorrow, despair and spiritual exaltation—of which I am capable.

Even now this route, twice a day in every kind of weather— in bright sunlight, in rain, in gathering darkness according to the season—brings back the story of those last months of her life.

In those weeks, from the end of November 1966 to the end of January 1967, I would usually come back home in time for tea. Late in November, on days when I returned home in the early afternoon, I would, driving west along the Mall, see Buckingham Palace and the Royal standard on its tall mast against the last glow, pink, yellow or purple, of the setting sun. It would hold hope or sad forebodings; it would reflect or highlight my own feelings of the moment. In December, when the days were at their shortest, it was always dark when I returned. And often I found Diana anxiously waiting for me.

'I am glad you are back; I have been listening to the sound of the lift, and every time it came up I hoped I would hear the sound of your key at the front door immediately after.' She had never in the past worried even when I had been home later

78

than expected, whereas I had always worried when she was late.

I reassured her: 'My darling, it is not really late, but it gets dark so soon; if it were summer you would now be sitting in the garden and would not think that it was late at all.'

Soon the days would lengthen once again; each phase of that cycle of light and dark would remain indelibly imprinted upon my mind.

One Sunday morning early in December, Diana said to me: 'The back of my neck aches, especially when I turn my head.' She said it in a casual way and added: 'It must be some kind of fibrositis.'

'Yes,' I answered, trying to sound equally casual, 'it is not surprising after all this treatment,' but a shiver went down my spine. I asked her: 'Is it the first time you noticed it?'

'No, not really, I have had it for a few days, but I paid no attention to it. It is not bad at all, just a bit of a nuisance.'

We arranged to have lunch with Stella and Leon* at their house at Ascot. Knowing her way of understating her condition whenever she felt unwell, fearing that there was worse news to come, I said: 'Are you perhaps not well enough to go to Ascot; shall I ring up Stella?'

'Nonsense, nonsense,' she replied, 'I am quite well enough; besides, we have arranged to see Mr. P. G. next Wednesday for a check-up. We'll discuss the matter with him then.'

This gave me another shock, for I could see that she was worried and must have been thinking of seeing the surgeon, perhaps for the last few days. 'I am going to ring Mr. P. G. right now,' I said, 'I am sure there is no need to worry, but let's have a word with him . . . he said we could ring him any time.'

Diana protested for a moment, saying we should not disturb the surgeon on a Sunday morning, but then she agreed. Mr. P. G. seemed not at all surprised: 'This always happens after the treatment; there is absolutely nothing to worry about, I can assure you,' he said.

Superficially I felt reassured and we drove out to the country.

* Sir Leon and Lady Bagrit.

Was this the first intimation of more changes and sorrows to come? I tried hard to dismiss the thought. After all, the surgeon ought to know—but did he?

Later in the afternoon when I was alone with Leon—Diana was resting—I voiced my misgivings. We were standing by the window in the small library from where one could see the lake, now reflecting the pale pink that lit up the sky in the setting wintry sun. After I had spoken we stood silently watching a flock of giant geese take off in formation from the surface of the water. 'We don't know where they go for the night,' Leon said, 'but every evening just before dusk they assemble at the call of the leader and fly off, to return in the morning.'

We went to see Mr. P. G., as had been arranged, the following Wednesday. I waited in his large drawing-room while Diana was with him. I remembered our first visit to him in the middle of August last, when I had also waited in the same room for the results of his examination. Then I had been prepared for the worst. This time, as I paced up and down casting an occasional glance at some illustrated magazines lying on a small table, I kept on telling myself 'I am sure it will be all right.'

After about twenty minutes I heard the door open on the other side of the hall. I heard his and Diana's voice. This reassured me. 'There would be silence,' I thought, 'if he found anything amiss, or he would have called me in as he did that first time.'

'Everything is in perfect order,' Mr. P. G. said as they came into the room. 'I have examined Diana most carefully and I am completely satisfied!' He then explained that the muscular aches were due entirely to the effects of the radiation treatment; they might continue for a while, might also affect other parts of the body, and, he added, they could even return for quite a number of years during winter or when the weather was damp. 'But there are no signs whatever of anything being wrong; I have examined all the glands and the spine . . .'

'Why the spine?' I asked.

'Well,' he said, 'this is very important, the treatment can sometimes affect the bones through de-calcification, but there is no indication of this.' We left in a happy mood.

The aches did not subside, but they did not get worse during the next few days. As Mr. P. G. had suggested they shifted, but—and this he had not anticipated—they also changed in character. From one day to the next the skin on her back, around the shoulders and along a clearly defined band around her chest became very sensitive. The right side which had been exposed to the radiation was more affected than the left. The sensitivity also began to radiate down the right arm. She began to experience a slight discomfort when raising that arm. Twice more we went to see Mr. P. G.; each time he reassured us. The last time we saw him in December he said there was no need to come back for the time being, and he fixed a date: the 20th of February, when both he and the radiologist would see her for a general check-up.

We decided we would take our holiday to the South of France, so often postponed, at the beginning of March when spring would be well advanced there.

Our semi-normal life continued. I went to my office; she worked on the anthology; in the evening we watched television, though this increasingly gave her eyestrain and headaches, and I read to her. Her own reading became confined to one of her best loved books: Arthur Osborne's Life of the great Yogi, Sri Bhagavan, whose teachings had made a profound impression on her.

Four

There is a last time for everything in everybody's life, but it is perhaps not very often that one human being can observe, be aware of and recall in detail another human being's 'last times'.

But since the beginning of her second illness in August 1966, I began to register in our everyday life one small event after another which for her was to be the last of its kind. At first the recognition that this was the 'last time' was below the level of consciousness; nevertheless, whenever it happened, something like a distant alarm-bell sounded in my mind; sometimes it was like a premonition; sometimes a fleeting thought quickly dismissed; sometimes like a missed heartbeat which makes you feel faint for an instant. Later, as the final illness began to declare itself, the awareness became more and more clear and conscious, until, towards the end, I saw and I knew: This is the last time.

There was the last time we went to a cinema together: one afternoon in September during her radiation treatment. I had been waiting as usual at the hospital, but when she came out, instead of taking her home, I said to her: 'Shall we go to a cinema; do you feel well enough?'

It had been a day of short treatment, and she did not feel too tired, and so we went to the Chelsea Classic at about 4 o'clock. The sun shone brightly, and the day was warm; the cinema was half empty. We saw a French film, *Les Amants,* which we had wanted to see for a long time, but had always missed.

'It is a "sexy" film,' I said to her as we settled down.

'That's just what we need,' she answered, 'it will cheer us up.'

It was indeed a film with stark erotic passages; but it also had some wonderful shots of French manor houses, small villages and tree-lined provincial roads which reminded us nostalgically of some of the car trips we had made in the past and intended to make again in the future.

We sat through the film, holding hands as we had always done. When we left we said: 'We ought to do this more often.' But it it was the last time.

Then there was the last time she came with me to the dentist. Whenever I had to have a tooth extracted or undergo some treatment which she thought might be painful or tedious, she accompanied me. She would sit in the waiting room, and when

82

I returned from the surgery, she would anxiously enquire: 'Was it not too bad; not too painful?' If it had been unpleasant, she would at once jump to the conclusion that the dentist had not done his job properly: 'I'll talk to him and tell him to be more careful next time.'

She came with me one day towards the end of November. I had told the dentist about her illness, and he had commented: 'She has an excellent chance . . .' He accompanied me back to the waiting room and greeted her: 'Your husband tells me that you are much better; I am delighted and I am sure you need not worry any more.'

'I don't worry,' she answered, 'I only worry about him.'

When I next visited the dentist she was no more with me.

From early December on, when she had developed those strange aches and pains, everything we did together began to assume an air of finality and unreality to me, and this despite my newly found and purposeful activities.

We discussed our 'coming' holiday in the South of France; we talked about the necessary re-decoration of the flat; she wore for the first time the first and only fur coat she had ever had; for the first time she seriously planned to have an exhibition: 'In about a year's time I shall have enough paintings for a one-man show, provided I work really hard.' We went to one or two small dinner parties; visited friends in the country, went shopping together . . . it all did not quite make sense to me; it seemed to lack continuity, to have no follow-up. A strange picture would sometimes appear before my mind's eye: a bridge over a river of which only the part on the near shore was still clearly visible, the rest seemed to end in mid-stream; a symbolic warning as in a dream.

Then came Christmas. We had decided to send only a few Christmas cards that year. As always she selected them, wrote them and posted them. It was the last time.

We had very little money, and so we agreed to give each other only token presents, also not to have a tree but only a few fir branches which I laid out on a table and enlivened by chains of tinsel and a few coloured glass balls. Our two small 'Swedish' Christmas angels, one in gold, the other in silver and with busy, determined-looking faces were 'on duty' as in previous years. Every year they would come out of their cotton-wool and tissue-paper wrapping to spend twelve days and nights suspended from a branch of the Christmas tree where they would gently turn and sway in the warm current of the candle flames. Then they would return to the obscurity of a drawer in my desk. This year they stood on the table, peeping out from between the green branches.

Another duty would await them three months later, but this was their last Christmas appearance.

Whenever Diana gave a present to me or anybody else, it would be accompanied by a small card with a special message illustrated (in the manner she illustrated her letters) by a pen-and-wash drawing or with a fragment cut out from an Old Master painting pasted on to it. This she would do especially at Christmas. These cut-outs—the face of a Saint, a detail from an Annunciation or of a Nativity, clusters of trees in a landscape, a skating scene—were never chosen at random, but always with due regard to the occasion, and, as with all her presents, in harmony with the personality of the recipient. I have a large collection of these little cards covering twenty years of birthday, Christmas and other presents.

Some years for Christmas she would give me as many as ten or twelve presents; each one had its own card, message and picture. Every picture expressed symbolically some past event or memory or some hope for the future.

That Christmas she gave me only two presents. The card to one shows a detail of a 17th-century Flemish painting: the angels bringing the glad tidings to the shepherds. This is what she wrote: 'My darling love, this very small present comes to you with my most special and tender love. Through all the tribulations you have been, every hour of every day, my happiness and joy and meaning. Little bird of my soul, Diana's solace, may this coming year bring you much happiness and no more trouble with your *Sorgenkind*. You are my only love and angel, like in the little picture. Big kisses, darling boy, your Diana.'

The other card shows a few figures; soldiers and peasants in a landscape. The message runs: 'My sweetheart, my dearest husband (and friend), may the coming year bring you great good fortune and satisfaction and good health too. A Happy Christmas (Home, Sweet Home), tea and little biscuits in bed, and kisses . . . D.'

The picture in my diary for 1967 is of a Dutch Winterscene with people skating on a large frozen pond. These were the last cards and written messages I had from her, and the last diary; though not yet the last present. My message to her, in her diary, reads: 'To my darling, sweet girl, with all my love and the most tender thoughts, always day and night; year in, year out and forever . . .'

On Boxing Day, for lunch, we went to the house of Eileen and Milorad who customarily invited a number of friends for drinks and a leisurely exchange of messages of good-will on this, the day of St. Stephen, the first Christmas martyr. I was not very happy because Diana was in discomfort, even pain, from what we now had begun to call 'neuritis', extending over her chest and right arm. She looked exquisitely beautiful in a dress in the new style, not quite 'mini', yet much shorter than most of her recent dresses. 'How very becoming,' I thought, 'this new style on a beautiful young woman; why have I not noticed it before.' She wore her hair open, falling down almost to her shoulders, and she wore some of her antique rings and bracelets.

She was standing with her back to the fireplace, her head turned slightly to one side. I looked at her reflection in the large mirror above the mantelpiece, and suddenly I realized with a profound shock that she looked very ill. She, too, had seen herself in the mirror, for she said to me later: 'I thought I did not look very well this morning at Eileen's.'

'Mirrors always make one look worse, especially in this dismal winter light,' I answered, 'I looked at myself and thought I looked quite awful.' But I knew that this time the mirror had told true.

The neuritis increased over the next few days, but the aches and pains around neck and shoulders ceased. 'The only thing that worries me,' she observed, 'is that my right arm seems a bit stiff; I notice it especially when I make up or do my hair; it is quite a strain.'

Then came December the 30th, when, at the Oxford and Cambridge Club, she met my colleagues and fought my battle for me. The 'boys' would never forget the touching beauty of her smile as she sat there in a vast armchair (surrounded by plates laden with buttered scones and crumpets) putting my case with faultless logic and quiet determination.

On New Year's Eve we did not sit up late. I lit the candles that stood on the table amidst the fir branches. I drank her health with a heavy heart. 'Happy New Year, my love, my sweetheart.' I held her close to me, kissing her lips, her eyes, her forehead.

So ended 1966.

Part Three

VIA DOLOROSA

One

Sunday, January the first 1967, was a springlike day in a winter that never became winter. Diana had been suffering from neuritis for several days. (Her pocket diary bore the entry: 'Neuritis 4th day'.) We had not gone away for the week-end, but as it was such a fine day we decided to have a very early lunch and go to Kew Gardens. She put on her old dark green Jaegar coat with the tartan-like overcheck. The coat had been altered and shortened more than once, but these attempts to keep it up to fashion showed diminishing returns. 'You cannot wear this ugly old coat any more,' I used to say whenever she proposed to put it on. Again that day I protested: 'It is Sunday, the first of January—*New Year;* you cannot wear it . . .'

'It will do for walking in Kew Gardens,' she answered.

I insisted that she should wear something new, something a bit festive on this first day of the year. As she put on an old headscarf I said: 'If you must wear a headscarf at all, why not the new Hermès scarf with the Napoleonic motifs; I have read you so much about Napoleon lately; you could wear the scarf. You know now so much more about his battles and all the rest . . .'

'It slips off my head,' she said, 'but if you like I will put it on.'

'Take your dark glasses, darling, the sun is very bright . . .'

She agreed at once: 'I will; the sun seems to be hurting my eyes.'

And so off we went to Kew Gardens as we had done often in years before; then by bus or underground—now by car. We walked along the paths and across the grass and we walked by the lake and up to the river from where we could see Sion House. It was a spring day; it was almost warm in the sun. The bulbs were beginning to push through the grass and the autumn leaves which had not been cleared away. The birds were singing. We had brought bread along to feed them but except for a couple of overfed blackbirds we found no customers. Diana walked gaily by my side; she did not appear to be tired or in pain. She had brought her camera, but there seemed nothing worthwhile to photograph, especially as we only had a black and white film.

'I'll take a picture of you,' she said.

'No, you have taken the same kind of picture so often; let me take one of you.'

'Not in this terrible coat,' she said. She never encouraged me to take photographs of her. 'I always look silly in photographs,' she said.

I am glad I did take a few pictures of her that last year of her life; one, in particular, which I took on a sunny morning in December. I said to her: 'Smile, my love.' She smiled but she shut her eyes because she was facing the sun.

When she saw the print, she commented: 'That really is a silly grin; we won't put this into the album.' I always have this picture with me.

But no photograph was taken that Sunday, January the first, at Kew. As we walked back in the slanting sun, with airliners overhead, 'homing' for London airport, I *knew* this would be the last time I would be walking with her in Kew Gardens. 'This is the first day of 1967,' I thought, 'this is the year of her death.'

She had three more months to live; exactly to the day.

I have her diary of 1967, the last in the series marking the passage of the years. In it she recorded the symptoms of her illness in terse remarks and brief sentences. Entries made before the end of December 1966, and in the first week of January 1967, show no trace of abnormality in her writing; after that the writing rapidly deteriorates until she could write no more towards the end of February. There the diary ends; the rest, most of the year that was still to come, is blank.

However, there is one entry beyond the last day when she was able to write. A solitary entry on the 13th of March: 'Mr. P.'s Birthday'. She must have written it at the very beginning of the year, for the writing shows but the faintest sign of a tremor.

Monday, the 2nd of January, the day after our walk in Kew Gardens, she spent mostly in bed. 'Bad headache and neuritis', reads the entry in the diary. The following day, on short notice, we once again went to see Mr. P. G., the surgeon. Again he assured us that there was nothing to worry. 'Come as arranged on the 20th of February for the general check-up.'

When we left, I said to Diana: 'Now we can be quite happy again, can't we? Let's go to Don Luigi's in the King's Road (a restaurant where we had been regular customers for some years).'

She smiled, not terribly convinced, and we drove to Chelsea. For the first time I noticed that her walk was not quite steady. 'There is this stiffness in my right arm, and now also in my legs, a sort of lumbago,' she observed. She had little appetite and we left soon.

The next few days she spent partly in bed; the headaches fluctuated. I see from the diary that we went out once or twice in the evening; also that we cancelled a number of appointments. I would not allow her to go out much, especially alone. I went to my office every afternoon but was always anxious to get back as soon as possible. She was keenly interested in my new venture, and every day I had to give her a detailed account of what I had been doing.

Every now and again she mentioned the slight stiffness in her right arm, but every time we found a rational explanation. I

91

think it was also at that time that she first told Doreen, our daily help, that it took her much longer to comb her hair and put on lipstick; there was this stiffness in her arm, and a certain unsteadiness in her hand.

Two

On the 14th of January, it was a Saturday, we dined with friends at a hotel in Knightsbridge. Diana had been told by Dr. R. not to drink alcohol—perhaps just a glass of wine or a small whisky—as long as her neuritis and lumbago continued. After dinner we sat for a while in the lounge. Diana looked tired, for we had been out most of the afternoon visiting a friend in hospital on the other end of the city. But she was gay and talked with great animation. I noticed—it was no more than a fleeting impression—that her speech was slightly slurred. This had often happened before, whenever she had a little too much whisky which with her meant no more than three or four small ones. I remember thinking, 'She has only had *one* small whisky.' I passed it over.

The next day, Sunday the 15th, she woke up with a slight headache. At ten o'clock the phone rang. It was my brother, Hubert, ringing from the airport where he had just landed from Germany, for a brief stop-over on his way to Dublin. He knew of Diana's illness and treatment and wanted to know how she was getting on. I told him that, except for certain aches and pains, she was quite well.

Half an hour later—I was still in bed—Diana came into the bedroom holding one of the illustrated Sunday magazines. She said: 'I must tell you, Mr. P., something very strange has just happened to me.'

So instantaneous was my reaction that before she had even

92

finished the sentence I felt all the blood draining from my face. I did not look up but answered as calmly as I could: 'What is it, darling, tell me.'

'It is not easy to describe what happened,' she said, 'but let me try to explain. I was reading this article'—she pointed to the open page of the magazine—'when suddenly I did not understand any more what I was reading . . .'

I had myself only just read the article and found it difficult to understand; it was confused and badly written. For a fraction of a second I felt relieved. I said: 'I am not surprised, I also could not make out what it meant; I gave up trying after the first three paragraphs.'

'I know it is badly written,' she replied, 'but it is not that at all; something quite different altogether, an experience which I have never had before.'

'Sit down, my pet, tell me.'

As always when she reported an event or experience, she was completely composed, lucid, measured, objective and precise in her description: 'I was sitting—you know where—reading this article; suddenly something seemed to go wrong with my perception; I don't know how best to describe it, it widened at the fringes at the expense of the centre. Now, keep still for a moment; this will help you to understand. You hear all kinds of noises; for example a bird singing in the garden, a car passing in the distance, steps on the floor above, perhaps even the radio in the flat next door—you can hear it now. These are all fringe perceptions; they are there, you take them for granted but they do not impinge on the main object or task on which you concentrate. This occupies the centre of your perception; for example my reading the paper or we now talking together . . .'

She was now sitting on the bed, and I had put my arms around her, holding her tight. 'Go on, darling, what exactly happened, tell me.'

'The fringe perceptions became very loud; I heard a Hoover in the flat above and every kind of noise including music; it all crowded in on me; and I don't even know whether they were

93

exterior noises or only in my head; whether the music was real or only imagined—and as they crowded in on me, these noises and disturbances as it were from both ends of the fringe, the main centre perception became smaller and smaller until I did not understand anymore what I was reading and what I was doing . . . it was quite frightening . . . what could it have been?'

'Are you all right now?' I asked.

'Perfectly, just a little upset,' she answered.

Here then it was, the dreaded moment that ushered in the new 'changes and sorrows'. Here then was the answer to the question I had been asking myself all these past weeks: 'How would a recurrence of the illness announce itself?'

I knew deep down in my heart that this was it; the beginning of the end. But, of course, my mind would not accept it, and all my feelings revolted against it. *No, it cannot be;* it is only one more of these after-effects.

It was Sunday and not much could be done. I did not want to frighten her by calling the doctor. 'I am sure there is nothing to worry about,' I said to her; 'when I get migraine I have similar troubles; sometimes I get quite muddled in the head . . . and you have had this migraine type of headache on and off for the past few days.'

'It wasn't really bad this morning,' she answered, 'but, as you say, let's not worry, I am quite well now, and I am looking forward to lunch with Eileen.'

We went to lunch with Eileen and her husband. Diana seemed quite normal, but she was very pale. When we returned home I asked if all had been well. 'There was a terrible moment before lunch,' she said. 'You were sitting at the other end of the room talking to someone. Milorad was talking, and suddenly the same thing happened; suddenly I could not follow what he was saying and, moreover, I was terrified that he might ask me a question, for I *knew* I would be unable to answer, that is unable to *speak.*'

'But during lunch you were chatting away quite gaily!'

'Yes, by then it had passed.'

94

The headache came back in the evening, and she was unable to watch television.

The next day, Monday, the 16th of January, she seemed to have recovered from the shock of the previous day. We had accepted an invitation for the evening, for drinks followed by a buffet supper at Gerard Irvine's, vicar of St. Cuthbert's, the Anglo-Catholic church which was five minutes' walk from our flat. Gerard had known Diana at Oxford, but only quite recently had their paths converged again. We had asked a friend to join us.

Diana spent the morning at home working on her anthology, and we had lunch together. After lunch she went back to the bedroom and I into my study. I had intended to go to my office at about three o'clock, and we had agreed that she would have a rest in bed until my return. But I had also decided to speak to one of the doctors during the afternoon, and this I did not want her to know. While I sat there thinking how best to do it and which doctor to see she came rushing into the room. This time she was in a state of distress: 'It has just happened again, the same thing has happened again, but much worse this time. I was painting my picture when noises and music and other things crowded in on me and . . .' she could not find the words, and when she found them she mispronounced them, jumbled them together, used them in a wrong context or used, instead of the word she wanted, the one with the opposite meaning. 'You see what is happening,' she cried, 'I cannot even find the words; I mix them up, I cannot speak at all . . .'

I tried to calm her. I took her back into the bedroom, laid her down on the bed and said: 'Don't upset yourself too much, my love, I am going to ring Mr. P. G. right now and we shall go and see him this very afternoon. Stay here while I ring from my study.'

I rang Mr. P. G., only to hear from his wife that he was ill in bed with a bad 'flu and could not be disturbed. I then rang Dr. L., the radiologist at the hospital. It happened to be the day when he saw private patients in the afternoon. Luckily I managed to speak to him and to hold his attention. I explained minutely what had happened and when I had finished, he said: 'If she is well enough to come, bring her to the hospital immediately, I will see her at once.'

By the time we had arrived at the hospital, in that familiar street so full of unhappy memories, so full of anxieties and hopes, she had, once again, completely recovered. Her mind was clear, her speech almost normal.

As we sat in the little waiting-room in the basement, the staff nurse who had been in charge of Diana's radiation treatment looked in. She shook hands with Diana and said: 'What brings you here; I thought you were not coming before the 20th of February?'

We explained that there was just a small matter to discuss with Dr. L. It was immediately clear to me from the way she answered, that she already knew the purpose of the visit. 'Dr. L. will see you in a few minutes.'

Dr. L., clad in his white coat, his concave mirror pushed back over his forehead, received us in his usual grave and kindly manner. He was not a man of many words. He put a few questions and then proceeded to examine Diana. The examination consisted mainly in testing the various reflexes in arms, legs, hands and feet, with a close scrutiny of the inside of the eyes. He checked the movement of her eyes, made her open and close her hand, hold things, press against objects. He also, and this was new to me, made her go through what appeared to me a series of grimacing movements with her mouth. Finally he examined her throat with the help of various lights and mirrors.

At the end he said: 'I cannot find anything abnormal anywhere.' Then turning to Diana he added: 'The symptoms which you have had and which your husband has fully described may be due to a number of causes, none of them serious. However, if they should come back, I advise you to see a neurologist, for this would be his province. If they don't come back, forget it. There is no reason why they should come back.' He then sent her to another department for a blood test. When she had left the room, he said: 'I wanted your wife out of the room so that I could have a word with you.'

He came very close to me, and speaking in a low voice he said: 'There are at present no definite objective neurological symptoms, except for a slight lack of co-ordination in her eyes when I made a specific test. But did you have the impression that the left side of her mouth was slightly drooping?'

I had not noticed it, but when he had said it I had to agree that there was perhaps a slight difference between the right and the left side of the mouth. The left was a little lower. I thought of her father who, after his first stroke, had developed the same symptom. It went together with his paralysis on the right side of his body. I said: 'Do you mean that she has had a very slight stroke?'

'No, but it might point to an irritation in the brain. This and the speech disturbances which you have so fully described do not allow us to dismiss the whole thing lightly. I don't want to upset you unduly; it is rare, very rare, that such cases metastasize. We have controlled the cancer in the breast; more we cannot do—there is the possibility, remote at present, of a secondary cancer—in the brain. This is not my province. I will arrange to speak to her doctor. She will have to see a neurologist.'

'Could it be due to the after effects of the radiation?' I asked. 'Like the headaches and neuritis from which she has been suffering for quite some time?' I knew this was a question which would not be to his liking, but I had to put it; I wanted to be shown one glimmer of hope.

"I doubt it,' he replied, 'but one can never tell.'

'But it could be,' I insisted, 'it *could* be?'

'It could be, but it is unlikely.' This ended the conversation, and I rejoined Diana, who was on the floor above still waiting for the blood test.

Primitive man believed in the magic powers of the witch-doctor and medicine man; but even now in our age of science something remains in us of that primitive faith in the magic powers of doctors. We rationalize this and not without justification, for medical science has enlarged frontiers of knowledge enormously and with it the means and methods of diagnosing and curing disease. Our faith in the healing power of the doctor has certain foundations in established facts. But it goes beyond this. We believe, we wish to believe, that the doctors' powers to heal do not stop at the frontiers of medical knowledge. Nor should one dismiss this faith as worthless; it is a source of hope and comfort and in many cases the ultimate results seem to vindicate it. Illnesses, even grave ones, get cured by a combination of medical skill, natural processes and the faith of the patient in the doctor which in turn stimulates the natural healing powers. Innumerable minor ailments vanish simply as the result of *seeing* the doctor.

But the frontiers are there. On that afternoon, when Dr. L. spoke to me, they rose before me like an impenetrable brick wall. Logic could not knock a passage through it. Faith had to detach itself from rational foundation if it wanted to carry hope across that forbidding wall. I realized also that it was not the faith any more in the doctors' superior knowledge and magic, but in the miraculous in which the doctors merely played the part of the beads in the rosary—tangible symbols to hold on to while the process of faith went its own mysterious ways.

But faith does not absolve from action. Everything had to be done, must be done, to combat the disease; every avenue must be explored, every method be used which skill, knowledge and ingenuity could devise, however heavy the odds against success. And, after all, I kept on telling myself, it was not *certain* yet that her condition was secondary cancer of the brain. It could be the result of the radiation treatment; even Dr. L. had reluctantly admitted this possibility.

Yet, whichever way I looked at it, the situation was menacing and frightening in the extreme. Would I have the strength to face whatever was coming? Would I have the strength to sustain her if her courage faltered? It was clear to me also that the burden of decision on whatever was to be done would from now on be mine alone. I could not help feeling that the great specialists in whose hands she had been up to this moment would vanish one after the other as actors vanish from the stage when they have said their part. Already I had detected an intimation of this in Dr. L.'s slight impatience and distant look when he spoke to me. There was an air of: 'Next case, please' about it. I was to prove right. Other specialists came and in turn faded away. But for their bills one would not have remembered that they had ever been there.

The stark truth, as it began to dawn on me that afternoon—its full implications were to be brought home to me in the course of the weeks that followed—was that the illness had got out of control and that I would not find a doctor who would take on the overall command.

I took Diana home. She seemed to have completely recovered from the shock of her earlier experience; her speech was quite normal, except for a slight faltering when pronouncing certain words. She did not wish to put off the arrangements made for the evening.

The first decision facing me was whether to tell her parents of the grave turn in her illness, and how to do it. Her father who had suffered a stroke a few months before was now back home, an invalid in a wheelchair. The parents knew of Diana's illness and treatment, but no more than the bare facts. Many extraordinary taboos had inhibited from very early on the natural flow of ideas, feelings and general communication between parents and children and had thus 'frozen' their relationship at a pre-adult level which once and for all prevented a further development when the 'children' had become adults. Among them was the one that ordained that all that concerned the parents was of supreme importance, relative to which importance anything that concerned the children—whatever their age or station in life—was only important in a random kind of way. Never should it be allowed to intrude upon the parents' consciousness sufficiently to deflect their attention from all those matters of *real* importance, e.g. political, social and humanitarian causes, intellectual, artistic and business pursuits on which they were engaged.

So powerful can such parental taboos be that unless they are specifically and explicitly lifted in time, their effects may far outreach the original intention or situation that brought them into being. This lifting of taboos never happened in Diana's family with the result that neither Diana nor her sisters (perhaps with one exception) ever wished to discuss their own personal affairs, worries and problems with their parents. Occasional, very half-hearted attempts to break through the barriers quickly ended in a barren wilderness of misunderstanding and frustration.

Non-communication between parents and children had become the established normal state of affairs. I do not doubt that there occurred moments when the parents (especially Diana's father) worried over this 'non-relationship', but on the whole they preferred to think that no news was better than bad news. This led to the tacit assumption on the part of the parents that all was well with the daughters (and their families) as long as there was no overwhelming proof to the contrary.

When Diana's fatal illness first declared itself, in August 1966, whatever may have been the true effect of the news on the parents, the taboos prevented any effective communication of concern or compassion on their part.

Between September and December—all during Diana's treatment—there was practically no contact between her and her parents. In October of that year a new element had entered with her father's grave illness. As a consequence of his stroke he also suffered from a complete amnesia which covered all recent events. As his memory gradually returned he began to make enquiries after Diana's health and was given to understand that she had recovered. In trying to decide now whether to tell her parents of what had happened I had to consider the effect such distressing news might have on her father's condition. I could not withhold it from them, for her condition might suddenly take a completely catastrophic turn.

I decided to convey the news to her mother alone, and the

100

only way of doing this was to go to the parents' flat in the hope that I could take her mother aside and speak to her without arousing his suspicions. Had I telephoned his suspicions would have been aroused at once, for the telephone was in the sitting-room where he spent most of his time.

I left Diana at home and, having told her that I would be back from my office within a very short time, went to call at her parents' flat. My carefully prepared plan went wrong from the start. Her mother brushed aside my attempts to speak to her alone, and at once took me into the sitting-room where her husband, who was much more intuitive than she, received me with an expression of anxious anticipation.

At the news of Diana's condition, and at once realizing the sinister implications of the symptoms, he gave vent to the most profound and heartrending expressions of distress—a distress which I felt rose from the depth of his being as though the sources of love and compassion for his daughter, so long closed, had suddenly burst open under the impact of this calamity. This was the moment of reconciliation. The barren years of lovelessness had been redeemed in this one moment of grace. My heart went out to him.

Before leaving we agreed that Diana must never know of my visit.

The same evening, at Gerard Irvine's party, Diana suffered another attack of mental confusion and aphasia. I had watched her anxiously across the crowded room. She was in conversation with Canon Carpenter when suddenly I saw her grow pale and distressed. I rushed over to her, and she whispered to me: 'Can you hear this motor horn honking all the time or is it only in my head . . . and all the other noises?' Then as she tried to explain, her sentences went wrong, her words went wrong; she held on to me: 'Take me away, I am ill . . .'

We arrived back at the flat. The woman friend who had been our guest came with us. Diana insisted on preparing a cold supper. I suspected she wanted to be left alone. This gave me the opportunity of telling our friend to be prepared in case Diana should again become ill.

Dinner passed without further incident, but towards the end Diana's head suddenly dropped forward. She remained in this position for a few seconds, murmuring: 'How very strange, how very odd, what can it be?' I wanted to take her back to the bedroom to make her lie down, but she became very agitated and told us to leave the room, she would do the washing-up and join us later. I knew she did not wish our friend to see what was happening.

We went into the sitting-room, but not many minutes later Diana came in in a distraught state. She broke down crying, 'What is happening to me?' 'What is happening to me,' she repeated, 'there is something terribly wrong here . . .' Then she turned quite angrily on us and said: 'I don't need any help in cooking, I can cook quite well by myself . . .'

I had put my arm around her and was holding her gently, her head against my chest. 'Darling, we did not want to help you to cook, but merely to help you wash up.'

'Did I say "cook"?' she asked. 'Of course I meant "wash up"; I get it all wrong, I mix up "dinner" with "lunch", "morning" with "evening", "before" with "after", and yet I know what I want to say.' And then, explaining her condition to our friend, she said: 'You must know, my dear, that something very unusual is happening to me; it started yesterday, and we don't know yet what it is. The doctors think it is the result of the radiation which has affected certain nerves in the brain . . . perhaps you will excuse me now, but I think I ought to go to bed.' She was as always exquisitely polite and considerate.

Later in the evening, as we sat on our bed, she talked with complete lucidity and almost scientific detachment about her strange 'attacks'. Every now and again she got a word wrong, usually words closely linked in meaning but not synonymous. For example: 'he' for 'she'; 'hot' for 'cold'; or 'bed' for 'chair'; 'door' for 'window'. But she invariably noticed it immediately and would say: 'Now why do I use this word instead of the correct one?' Or, catching herself mispronouncing a word, she would add: 'Why do I mispronounce this word?' Towards the end of our discussion she said: 'I think the worst is over. I don't think I shall have this kind of trouble again.'

She was right. After that evening there were only a few very minor incidents, moments of hesitation and searching for the right word, a few verbal slips and mental lacunae. She was to remain completely normal in thought and speech almost until the very end. It seems that the pressure on the centre of speech in the brain did not develop any further after the initial incidents.

From now on we lived in a world of the Unknown. It was like wandering warily in a thick haze in a no-man's-land with lurking dangers which at any moment, from any side, might be upon us. We held on to one another; I to protect her; she to support me in protecting her.

Her pocket diary for Tuesday the 17th of January bears the entry: 'headache at night.' This was new. There follow a few normal entries: 'tea with Mrs. F.': 'lunch with Rosemary'; 'lunch with Rupert'; 'dinner with Mr. and Mrs. L.'. I vividly recall these occasions. Each was a last one. Then, on Saturday the 21st: 'woke up with bad headache' and the next day: 'woke up with splitting headache at 4 a.m.'.

The nights now began to be disturbed. The days were still fairly normal. She worked on her anthology and painted a small picture. The stiffness in her arm prevented her from painting on larger canvasses. That small picture was her last one, and it remained unfinished. I continued to go to my office; once or twice she went out by herself, to the hairdresser and to do local shopping. There was silence from the doctors, but I understood that Dr. R. was engaged in making arrangements for her to see an eminent neurologist.

'What is the point of seeing a neurologist?' Diana asked. 'I am sure there is nothing he can do.' This was, of course, true. Neurologists cannot cure conditions. The best one can hope for is that they find nothing. A consultation with Dr. B., the neurologist finally chosen, was fixed for the 31st of January. The nightly headaches had now become an established fact; 'migraine' we began to call them. It gives comfort to name a thing; it makes it more manageable, less incalculable.

We developed theories on the cause of these 'migraines'. We found one which was not at all implausible. On the right side of her body all those parts which had been exposed to radiation— breast, right shoulder and neck—had become slightly swollen, 'puffy'. 'This is quite normal,' the doctors had said, 'it always happens after radiation' (and they explained why and how). There was absolutely no significance in this, and gradually, over the years it would subside.

I knew that all migraine, whatever its cause, produces a swelling of blood-vessels in the brain, and since the brain cannot expand there is pressure which causes the typical migraine headache and any other of those distressing symptoms associated with the condition. I had suffered from it for years. We therefore concluded that this swelling which visibly extended over her shoulder and neck, most probably also was present in some of the blood-vessels supplying the brain. The result was migraine. Thank God for this theory. Actually, it was not far out; there was swelling pressing on the brain; 'oedema', Dr. R. said when concurring with our theory.

In the night from Monday the 23rd to Tuesday the 24th of January, after a restless sleep, Diana woke up at five in the morning with a splitting headache. She switched on the light, and before I had time to say anything, she rushed out of the room and was violently sick.

I went after her and held her head as she was sitting, white and shivering, over the basin in the bathroom.

The quality of horror and distress of that night, and of those that followed is almost impossible to convey.

The implications of what was happening were only too clear, and I was helpless; helpless in the face of her immediate distress and suffering, helpless in the face of those terrible implications. And it was that hour before dawn when vitality dips down to

104

its nadir, when all is sinister, lonely and frightening, when only happy sleep can carry one to the renewed hope of the day.

The doctor came at about 8 o'clock in the morning. Not much was said; there was little that could be said. It was decided that she should have a nurse for the night as long as the present condition continued. Certain drugs were prescribed to alleviate the headaches, prevent sickness and enable her to sleep. From now on the drugs in ever-increasing profusion of colours, shapes and specific characteristics became the outward symbols of the doctors' unavailing fight against the mysterious disease. They served their purpose (less and less so as time went on) in alleviating pain and discomfort; moreover, though this was not their purpose, it enabled us to attribute certain particularly distressing symptoms to them rather than to the illness itself.

The night of the 23rd to the 24th of January was the last we spent together in the same bed. However difficult had been our days over these many years—and there had been long periods when the days were very difficult and disheartening—there had always been the nights, over seven thousand nights in twenty years of married life; the nights in which the difficulties of the day were resolved and forgotten in the intimacy of sleep: one sleep enveloping two people who had become one unit.

I had to think of Ronsard's poem:

> Vostre ame estoit dedans la mienne enclose,
> La mienne estoit en la vostre, et nos corps
> Par sympathie et semblables accords
> N'estoient plus qu'un: si bien que vous ma Dame,
> Et moy n'estions qu'un seul corps et qu'une ame.

> Thy soul was in mine own enclosed,
> My soul in thine and thereupon our flesh
> From sympathy and minds afresh
> Conjoined, were one; as if you, whom I adore
> And I were but one body, but one core.

This was not to be any more. On January the 24th I moved into my study. In the two weeks that followed we had four or five different night nurses who came on duty at nine in the evening and left at eight the following morning. With each new girl I had to go through the same distressing briefing procedure. 'We don't yet know,' I would begin, 'the exact nature of my wife's illness; it may be very grave, on the other hand it may only be the result of the radiation treatment she underwent last autumn. The critical moment is usually between two and four in the morning when she wakes up with intense headaches and may be sick . . .'

Diana had an old-fashioned brass handbell with which she summoned the nurse when she woke up during the night. The nurse was in the sitting-room adjoining the bedroom; my study was two doors further along the corridor. Every night, whenever I heard the sound of the bell, I would wake up with a start, my heart beating in fearful anticipation of what would happen next. I would not go to sleep again until all was quiet. Often I would hear hurried steps and whispered conversation. In the morning I would come into Diana's bedroom to hear the news of the night. It greatly varied; there were good nights and bad nights; nights when she had merely woken with a headache; nights when she had been sick. But she was invariably exhausted on waking up.

Her condition always improved during the morning, and there were days when she could dress and go about the flat, and even go out with me.

On January the 27th a new symptom appeared. The entry in the diary reads: 'slightly wobbly on legs'. This and other new sinister symptoms did not announce themselves in a spectacular manner; they came in, as it were, by stealth, unobserved, like burglars at night. But suddenly one would become aware that something had changed; something new had happened, some deterioration in her condition, some slight new incapacity or difficulty.

There was the increasing stiffness of the right arm, the new difficulty in writing and when putting on lipstick, a slight temporary numbness in the finger-tips of the left hand, increased photophobia; reluctance to read—she had difficulty concentrating on what she was reading. And now there was the wobbliness in her legs.

She said to me: 'You know, Mr. P., I am like a car with the steering gone slightly wrong; it is always pulling to the left, and I have to counteract it by pulling sharply to the right; you know what I mean, you must have experienced this with cars . . .' I knew exactly what she meant and, observing her as she walked down the corridor to the kitchen I noticed that she was in fact swaying to the left.

Then came the day when she quite casually remarked: 'Today, for the first time, I could not get out of my bath alone, nurse had to help me. My back and my legs are so weak.' And then came the day when she could not get *into* her bath unaided.

I think it was at that time that what I later came to recognize as my 'protective mechanism' first became operative. It worked like a shutter or a gate which allowed only a certain limited quantity of bad news to 'get through' to me at a time or to let the news through but cut out or alter the implications of the particular bit of bad news. One could also compare this protective mechanism to a transformer which reduces high voltage current into low voltage current, so as to remove the danger of injury and damage through sudden or sustained shock. The effectiveness of the protective mechanism grew in direct proportion to the pressures put upon it. But at no time did it inhibit action; on the contrary: by preventing panic and paralysing despair it freed the mind for action. At no time did it block the sources of compassion and diminish the capacity of suffering. It acted as a regulator that enabled one to adjust one's inner resources so that they could match the demands put on them at any given moment.

Twice more we went to the country by car; on January the 27th, the day when Diana had first become aware of difficulties in walking, but otherwise had felt quite well, and again on the 29th of January, which was a Sunday.

107

On that Sunday, Stella had rung from the country and asked whether Diana might be well enough to come out to lunch. It was a beautiful springlike day. Diana was not well, and for one moment I hesitated. But then suddenly I knew: it would be her last trip to the country; I did not want to deprive her of the joy of seeing Ascot Place, which she loved so much, once more. And I decided to take the risk.

All the time while I was driving, with her by my side, I kept on thinking 'this is the last time'. 'This is the last time she will see this cluster of trees, that group of houses, these other so familiar landmarks.' And when we had entered into the park through the wrought iron gates (which in the past she had always opened for me, but which this time I now had to open), I said to myself, 'She will never see this park again.' Visiting Stella and Leon at week-ends had become a regular feature in our life over the past two years. There were periods when we went to Ascot Place almost every week-end: we knew it in the winter, in spring, summer and autumn, and whatever the season, whatever the weather, it was a source of unending delight to her.

It was a place of magic natural and man-made beauty. There was the lake teeming with ducks, giant geese and every kind of minor water fowl through which majestic swans sailed like caravelles. Herons lived in the shrubs and trees at the edge of the water, and when disturbed would ponderously open their wings and take themselves off in ungainly hovering flight.

There were the bridges and the waterfalls on both ends of the lake; the 18th-century grotto with its interior of glittering felspar; there were the lawns, the huge rhododendron banks, the giant trees, the unexpected clearings in the wooded parts where a gracious temple-like pavilion stood. And there was the house itself, restored from its once ugly Victorian accretions to its original 18th-century purity of design.

Looking from the house towards the lake, the fields and trees beyond, one became conscious of a vast expanse of sky which seemed to enclose the estate—a little realm of its own—as in a

108

huge translucent cupola. It gave one the feeling both of freedom and security.

Diana used often to wander off on her own and take photographs, an art which she had only recently acquired, but with her unfailing eye for the essential—the heart of the matter—she soon produced with her cheap camera pictures of great beauty that radiated the enchantment of fleeting moments held still for a fraction of a second.

The lunch proved a great strain on her. We were fourteen or sixteen people around the huge extended dining-room table. Diana sat between Leon and a guest whom she had only just met, and I sat at the other end of the table next to Stella. All through lunch my eyes were on Diana watching her for the slightest sign of distress. However, she appeared to be enjoying the conversation with both her table neighbours.

After lunch we all re-assembled in one of the drawing-rooms. Diana now looked pale and tired, and she spoke little. I was sitting next to her on one of the settees when a woman guest asked if she could take a photo of us. At first I hesitated, but then, once again, the words 'this is the last time', flashed through my mind. I knew it would be the last pictures ever to be taken of her. I consented. The picture in colour and taken by flashlight is on my desk together with another of her alone, taken immediately after the first. Diana's expression is strained and other-worldly, almost transfigured. I am glad I had given my consent to the picture. She herself was never to see it. We took leave of our hosts at about five in the afternoon and returned to London; our last country trip together.

The same evening my brother Hubert returned to London from Ireland. I had left a message for him to await him on arrival at his hotel. The message told him of Diana's grave condition.

Diana was in bed when Hubert arrived at the flat. A moment before he rang the bell I thought: 'Perhaps he will bring me some water from Lourdes.' I took him into the drawing-room and, before saying anything, he handed me a small flask containing Lourdes water. He himself attributed a sudden dramatic recovery from a festering abscess on his lungs a few years before to Divine Grace mediated to him through the miraculous power of that water. That night, before the nurse arrived, I dipped a finger into the water and traced the sign of the cross on her forehead. I also moistened her lips with the water.

'Do you think this will help, Mr. P.?' she asked.

'It may speed your recovery, my angel,' I answered. Then the nurse came in, and I kissed Diana goodnight.

Every night from now on I went through this little ritual of the Lourdes water—with ever diminishing hope. 'It does not taste very nice,' Diana said on several occasions, but she never refused the water.

On the 31st I took her to Harley Street to see Dr. B., the neurologist. I waited downstairs while she was with him in his consulting-room on the first floor. I noticed that she had great difficulty in walking up the stairs; she held on to the banister and seemed to drag her feet.

The consultation took over an hour. Once again I sat waiting for a verdict which might be decisive. At last Dr. B. came into the room; he was alone. 'There is no evidence of any neurological lesion,' he said; 'everything seems normal.'

This was good news to which I immediately reacted: 'In that case,' I said, 'one can be pretty confident that all will be well, can one not?'

In view of what he had only just told me, his answer was quite unexpected and deeply disturbing. 'It is difficult to say, but there is always hope.'

'But you have said that there are no neurological lesions; this, after all, is the decisive factor?'

He avoided my gaze and answered: 'These cases of intracranial pressure are very obscure, one can never be certain; however, let us hope for the best.' (Later I heard that he was one of the foremost authorities in this field, and that from the beginning he had not had the slightest doubt on the true nature of her illness.)

Two days later the first series of X-ray pictures was taken; they showed no abnormality of any kind. 'Not the slightest indication

110

of any secondary deposits,' Dr. R. told me. My hopes rose again. However her general condition gave little ground for optimism.

The entries in her diary over the next few days read: 'Very bad night; terribly shaky'; 'Legs terribly weak'; 'Bad headache, terribly weak'; 'Very weak and exhausted'; 'Sick at breakfast, in bed all day'. In between there are entries about friends who came to see her, Rosamond, Rosemary and others. Several times when I was out, Rosemary stayed the whole afternoon and made tea for her because she was not well enough to look after herself, and I did not want her to be alone.

One day—there is no entry about it in the diary—I took her out to lunch at Don Luigi's. Even to walk as far as the car was an ordeal to her. She walked with tiny little steps, 'like a very old lady', she commented. My protective mechanism went into action: 'This is only temporary,' I thought. Arrived at the restaurant, we went to our usual table at the back. I noticed that the waiters looked at her; she barely managed to get to the table.

That helpless expression of a child looking at grown-ups for comfort and reassurance, that touching expression of a human being whose whole security rests in an absolute trust in others, in their love and kindness, which I had seen for the first time in her face one day after her first operation in May—I saw it again when she sat down at the table at Don Luigi's for what was to be our last meal together in a restaurant. I was to see that expression again and again in the weeks to follow.

Twice more after that day she came with me in the car: on February the 3rd when I took her to the frame-maker's shop; the second and last time, on Sunday the 5th, when we called on our friend Rosica* for a drink before lunch. On our way an incident occurred which proved to me that she was very ill indeed. As we were about to turn left into the square where our friend lived, a small car behind us tried to overtake on the wrong side. I could see in my mirror that there was no real danger. The impatient driver behind me could not go fast and realized in time that he could not overtake me. It was no more than one of those ordinary

* Rosica Colin.

111

incidents of the road to which one has become accustomed. Diana suddenly panicked; she flung her right arm around my shoulder and cried: 'Please, please stop at once; he is going to run into us!' Her sense of judgement which in all situations of life had always been perfect had suddenly left her. I reassured her, but she was shaking all over.

On February the 8th there is an entry in her diary: 'Worked on painting'. In that last week at home she also did a preparatory sketch of a gramophone 'sleeve' which had been commissioned by her agents for a gramophone club. (She had done a number of such sleeves, mainly for classical music, and each in the style of her miniature paintings.) It never went beyond the stage of that preliminary sketch.

'I don't think I shall be able to complete it,' she told me.

'I am sure you will,' I replied, 'leave it for a few days until your arm gets better.'

Ten days or so later when she was in the nursing home she telephoned her agents, saying that unfortunately she would not be able to complete the design. Later I found the sketch, an airy semi-abstract landscape in the style of the Japanese masters of the 18th century. And with the sketch were the instructions as to size and procedure which she had prepared for the firm of commercial photographers who had carried out this type of work for her over a number of years. She was precise and meticulous in everything and never wanted to let anybody down.

Two or three times a week an elderly woman now came to cook for us in the evening. I shall never forget the evening of Friday, the 10th of February. Diana had spent most of the day in bed, and we decided to have dinner in the bedroom. Everything had been carefully thought out by me as for an intimate *souper à deux* of two newly marrieds. I had put out our antique blue-and-gold china made at the Royal Prussian Porcelain factory at Potsdam, which we had been given as a wedding present. I chose table mats and napkins to match. Shortly before eight o'clock I had lit the candles in their tall silver candle-sticks.

112

Their colour matched the pink velvet of the curtains; their steady flame rose like a silent invocation.

At eight, Violet (that was the name of the cook) wheeled in the trolley. Diana, dressed in a pretty *négligée,* sat on the edge of the bed to which we pushed the trolley. I sat on a chair facing her.

If I could but forget just for this one evening the real circumstances and think that here in the stillness of this room with its pale green patterned wall paper, its Italian Master drawings, its pink curtains that shut out the world, in the soft light of the candles, we were once more enjoying *'la douceur de la vie'*. If only I could imagine that this was the reality and *'that other'* had been but a bad dream . . .

After the first course—a very light fish soufflé—Diana looked sad and pleading: 'I haven't much appetite, Mr. P., I don't think I can eat any more.' We were back in the real reality. Pink curtains, delicate pale green wallpaper, Italian drawings, soft candle-light, all this had suddenly become quite meaningless—nostalgic figments of the mind screening the grim picture of truth. The enemy was not without but within the walls of our home.

Clinging to the notion that appetite was a sign of good health and hoping (against my better knowledge) that by eating the delicious meal prepared with so much care and love she would prove that she was well, I said to her: 'But you said yourself, darling, that you were looking forward to the dinner, that you were hungry.'

'I know, Mr. P., I am terribly sorry, but I really have had enough; I just cannot swallow another mouthful.' That was our last meal together.

The night nurse, a new girl, came at nine o'clock. Once again I gave my instructions and said to her: 'The Princess will ring for you if she needs anything during the night. Should there be anything serious, you must wake me.'

At about 4 a.m. I was woken by the now familiar sound of the brass bell. I dozed off again after a few minutes, but was roused by an insistent knocking on my door. The night nurse came into

113

the room and said: 'I am afraid your wife is very ill; she has been sick several times and she has lost all feeling in both hands.'

'What will you do?' I asked. This time the protective mechanism did not work; once again it was that sinister hour before dawn when hope and life are at their lowest. I was prepared for the worst.

'I have already telephoned Dr. R., and he has given me permission to give her an injection of Pethidine. I shall give her the injection now, that will make her sleep.' The nurse continued: 'Dr. R. will come as early as possible in the morning.'

I tiptoed into the bedroom where Diana lay pale, her eyes closed in the light of the two candles which we had first lit a few hours before for our *souper intime*. She said: 'Hullo, Mr. P., I am not very well,' and then added with a little flicker of a smile: 'I am an awful nuisance.'

She woke up at about seven in the morning and was sick again. The doctor came shortly after eight and soon after him Rosemary came whom I had rung to tell her what was happening.

Dr. R. was still optimistic. Of the numbness in her hands, he said this occurred quite frequently as a result of violent sickness; besides it had passed already, except in two fingers of the left hand.

We now had to make a decision: 'could she remain at home or should she be taken to a nursing home?' I think both Dr. R. and I knew what the decision would be. It was impossible to look after her at home. There was no one to run the household; I had to attend to my office, and Diana could not be left alone during the day.

As usual it proved difficult to obtain accommodation in the private patients' wing of any of the more accessible hospitals or less expensive nursing homes. Finally we succeeded in getting a room in one of the best nursing homes in the West End. 'It is one of our best rooms,' the matron said over the telephone, 'and, I am afraid, also one of the more expensive ones, but it is the only one which is free today.'

We accepted. 'It will be for about a fortnight,' Dr. R. told the

114

matron, and in answer to her question as to the nature of the illness, he said: 'Severe headaches, sickness and muscular pains; we have to make certain investigations.'

Diana took the news calmly. 'It will make it easier for you, Mr. P.; at least you will be able to get some sleep.' But then she suddenly became anxious: 'But where will you go; you can't stay here by yourself with no one to look after *you*.'

'Don't worry, my pet, Rosemary will put me up for the time you are in the nursing home.' As always in a crisis, Rosemary had immediately offered to help. Seneca's words came to me: *Veros amicos reparare difficile est.*†

In the early afternoon we packed a small suitcase. We put in some of her prettiest pyjamas, nighties and bedjackets; handkerchiefs, slippers; her make-up case. She wanted to take only three books: *The Prophet* by Kahlil Gibran, her Prayer Book, and Arthur Osborne's book on Sri Bhagavan. 'You know I can't read much these days,' she said.

She also wanted to take her favourite photograph of me. She put on the ring I had given her on our tenth wedding anniversary and a bracelet of which she was particularly fond, and into her handbag went a few other of her most treasured possessions. I insisted that she also take the carriage clock which had stood by our bed all these years and a small transistor radio which had been given to us as a Christmas present.

'You might want to listen to music.'

'I might,' she answered doubtfully. She never did, but the set was put to another practical use.

She was not well enough to dress, but not ill enough to be taken by ambulance to the nursing home. Rosemary offered to take us in her large well-sprung car. Diana wore over her pyjamas a tartan skirt and a woolly cardigan; on her feet she had soft bedroom slippers. Her hair was open, framing her face and falling over her shoulders as she had mostly worn it during the past few weeks.

We left the flat at three o'clock in the afternoon, a sad little

† It is a difficult thing to replace true friends.

115

procession. The night nurse had stayed on to accompany Diana to the nursing home. (She remained with Diana for the next three weeks.) She supported her on one side and I on the other. The porter carried the suitcase and I the radio set.

We arrived at the nursing home, which was situated close to Wimpole Street and past which I had often driven or walked, little thinking that a time might come when it would be the centre of my life, a place of pilgrimage, a cup overflowing with sorrow and a shrine of worship.

The room, No. 116 on the first floor, was indeed one of the best rooms in the house. It was large and airy (though overheated) and pleasantly furnished. The moment I entered it, I *knew* that she would never leave it again, alive.

We put her to bed, unpacked the small suitcase and disposed the few personal belongings around her bed: my photograph on the table on the left, the portable radio on the adjustable bed table, the scent bottles and other small objects within easy reach. There were no flowers yet.

Then, for the third time in less than nine months, I had to fill in the hospital admission form: Age, religion, reason for admission, probable length of stay.

'Let's put ten days to a fortnight.' The Floor Sister, a Scotch woman, unemotional but with a dry sense of humour, took down the particulars, making a few routine jokes as she went along.

Diana took little interest in the proceedings. She lay pale and exhausted in her bed. Then I took leave of her, the third time in nine months. But this time it was quite different from the previous occasions. Though I felt a momentary relief to know her in proper care, I knew that this was but a momentary rest on a road whose course and destination had been traced by powers beyond anyone's control.

'I shall ring you later in the evening, my pet,' I said to her before leaving. 'And I shall be with you tomorrow morning.'

'You look after him, Rosemary, darling,' Diana said; 'you know **he** is quite helpless without me; and tell him not to drop the soap

116

into the bath and leave it there.' It was Saturday, the 11th of February 1967.

In the evening my brother Hubert left for Germany, and I moved into Rosemary's house in Smith Street, Chelsea.

Three

The next day, Sunday, began my new routine of life, of a life which in retrospect appears to me like one of those photomontages in which the central features within a narrow circle are magnified and sharpened under a powerful lens, whereas everything beyond the periphery is blurred and indistinct.

The focal point around which my psychic energy consumed itself in a white-hot flame, while ever renewing itself out of itself from depths unknown, was *she;* outside that ring of fire all was shadow and unreality; I myself as I moved in this world from which I had withdrawn all interest, was shadow and unreality.

The switchboard operator at the nursing home came on at nine o'clock in the morning. A few minutes after I would ring through to the Floor Sister to enquire how the night had been and what Diana's condition was in the morning. Her private night nurse had by that time made her report.

In the early days no one from the matron down suspected the true nature and desperate gravity of Diana's illness. She was at the nursing home 'for observation.' These were the assumptions on which the nursing staff had been briefed. The thought that this beautiful young woman might be what in medical parlance is known as a 'terminal case' occurred to no one. Consequently, the answers I received to my morning enquiries were of a routine kind: 'Quite a good night'; or 'a certain amount of headache';

117

'no, not much appetite'; 'yes, she was sick in the morning, but now she is resting comfortably'; 'she had to have a small injection of Pethidine . . .' (I soon came to dread that word, for these injections which at the beginning were only given in moments of acute emergency became a daily routine yielding ever-diminishing returns) '. . . yes, she is quite bright this morning . . .'

In the weeks to follow, though the substance of the morning conversation did not change much, the same questions and the same answers carried different meanings and implications; a tacit bond of common knowledge had created its own code.

I could never start my telephone call in the morning without having first lit a cigarette. Usually it was Rosemary who lit it for me and sat by me anxiously listening while I talked. The conversation would set the mood for the day, hopeful or sombre, but getting more and more sombre as the days and the weeks progressed.

After the telephone call I would finish dressing and then leave the house, a traveller into the unknown. I would first go to my flat to deal with correspondence, make a few telephone calls and try to put some sort of shape into the affairs of the day. I was like the lone sailor in mid-Atlantic who, in order to maintain a proper grip over himself, and with it command of his craft, must keep himself incessantly busy with the tasks at hand, and never allow himself to be idle, lest he be suddenly overcome by the realization of his own loneliness and intrinsic helplessness.

Mrs. F., our daily help, came every morning to keep the flat in order which was now deserted for the second time. The knowledge that she was there to receive me when I arrived at about ten in the morning gave me great comfort. The continuity of life had not been broken entirely.

From the flat I went to the nursing home where I spent the rest of the morning. After lunch, for the first two or three weeks, I went to my office on alternate days, and then back to the nursing home between three and four in the afternoon, where I remained most days until eight o'clock in the evening.

Diana's room was at the eastern end of the building where it formed the corner with a narrow mews that intersected the main

118

street at this point. Approaching the nursing home from the east, the first thing I would see was the windowless red brick wall, behind which, at the height of the first floor, was her room. I soon worked out the exact spot on the outside wall behind which, I knew, was the head of her bed.

To this day I cannot pass by the building without instinctively looking up to that patch of red brick wall behind which she lay and suffered for seven weeks; behind which she died.

Every year at the end of winter we had come to look at a particular almond tree that stands in the front garden of a house in St. Leonard's Terrace in Chelsea. It was this particular tree which announced to us the coming of spring.

St. Leonard's Terrace is a piece of early 18th-century London uniquely preserved. A row of Queen Anne houses built of red and terra-cotta-coloured brick mellowed by time; each house with its own front garden, stone-flagged and partly hidden from the street by trellis work, covered by creepers in summer; by flowering shrubs and small fruit trees. The whole terrace faces south over a green enclosed by hedges and bordered on the east side by old plane trees, towards the Royal Hospital built under Charles II as a home for old soldiers. Seen from the south St. Leonard's Terrace and its green could be in the very heart of the country. It is an ideal place to watch the changing pageant of the seasons, especially the coming of spring which to us became symbolized by the first pink blossoms of that particular almond tree.

The year before spring had come very late; it was not until the second week in March that the first blossoms had begun timidly to unfold their petals. This year it all happened a whole month earlier at the beginning of February. I saw our little tree first on Sunday morning, the 12th of February, as, coming from Smith Street, I drove past on my way to the nursing home. The tree stood in a halo of delicate pink.

From then on every morning, in what became my routine for seven terrible weeks, I passed the tree and watched its progress

119

and that of its companions in the adjoining front gardens. Not only almond, but also cherry, pear, apple, camellia, lilac, laburnum: I saw how one by one in ever-quickening pace they came to life, touched by the magic wand of spring.

She lay in a darkened room in the nursing home; she would not see the little tree; perhaps she would never see it again. Spring, this beautiful early spring was happening without her. I could not bear the thought of it. I could not bear to look closely at the gardens in St. Leonard's Terrace; I never stopped, and as the weeks passed I ceased to look altogether, but hurried past as quickly as I dared, my mind's eye fixed on that darkened room, north of Oxford Street.

For the first five weeks her room was always darkened; she could not bear light, it intensified her headache. In the hours of daylight the curtains were drawn. I never looked at these curtains very closely, but I remember they had a gay pattern of large flowers and leaves in yellows, pale browns and greens, against a lighter background. The light that filtered through was like very pale winter sunshine. In the hours of darkness, the only light in the room came from a lamp fixed to the wall at the head of the bed. It was one of those modern contraptions which could be extended, dipped, swivelled in all directions. For those first weeks it was always dipped below the level of her eyes and focussed on the polished surface of the built-in furniture unit which served as bedside table, chest of drawers and wardrobe. The reflected light gave the room a faint orange glow, barely bright enough for me to read out to her the messages that came with the flowers and the postcards and letters from friends wishing her a speedy recovery.

Even though the room was dark she hardly ever seemed to open her eyes. She opened them to look at me and to smile at me, and in the early days, to read some of the messages, to look at the flowers and to look at my photograph which stood very close to her on the bedside table.

Once in those early days she said to a visitor, apologetically and with the graciousness of a hostess showing her garden in

120

failing light: 'I wish you could see this room in good light; it is really very pretty with all those flowers.'

There was something so touching in what she said and in the way she said it; it brought tears to my eyes. It had a quality of heartrending generosity and beauty. This was the room which for her was associated only with pain and sickness; with darkness; with long hours of solitude; with perplexity and distress of every kind; a room in which she had to bear, to endure, to accept; a room over which she had less command every day; a room which soon she would not be able to see any more: the room in which she would die.

Yet, it was also a room filled with flowers; a room in which she was surrounded by care and love. In a strange way it was her home, and she felt responsible for it. She wanted the visitor to feel welcome—despite, as it were, certain shortcomings due to the hostess's indisposition. It was a pretty room indeed, but it was not a pretty room for her.

There was no dramatic change in Diana's condition during her first week at the nursing home. The headaches and the sickness (which she still recorded in her diary and on odd pieces of paper) were being kept under control by drugs, but she had no appetite and was visibly beginning to lose weight. She was still able to get out of bed and sit in a chair, wash herself and brush her teeth at the basin. The latter also involved the delicate operation of cleaning a very small plate with two lower front teeth. As a very young girl she had lost two front teeth as the result of a fall. Ever since she had to have two artificial teeth mounted on a very fragile plate.

She had always been conscious of this 'defect' as she thought of it; she hid it like a shameful secret. 'Very off-putting,' she said, 'a young girl with false teeth.' The secret of the plate was well kept. No one except her family, the dentist and I knew of it. Even at the nursing home they did not know for two or three weeks. For the night she kept the plate wrapped up in a handkerchief in the open drawer of the bedside table, and always before ringing for the nurse she would put the plate into her

121

mouth. And so, for the first few weeks, she would, when brushing her teeth, also clean the plate. No nurse was allowed into the room until she was back in her bed. This was one of her little vanities.

Once or twice also, in the beginning, she was able to walk down the corridor supported by one of the girls, and at certain times of the day she answered the telephone and made a few calls herself.

Whenever she was free of headache and not under sedation she would talk to the nurses on every kind of subject, from the most simple such as flower arrangements or the beauties of rural England, to the most difficult such as the philosophy of Eastern sages, Elizabethan music or general problems of life and death. She also listened to the professional problems and heartbreak stories which the girls brought to her and gave them sound advice. Later one of the nurses told me: 'Soon it had become an accepted fact that whenever a girl could not be found, she was with your wife. Look in at No. 116, we used to say; she will be there.'

The doctors now had to decide what to do next. They were faced with what military communiques in war time used to call 'a confused situation', invariably meaning, as many may remember, that the initiative had passed out of one's hands and passed into those of the enemy. No one seemed to be effectively in command, and there was an overall lack of co-ordination and communication. For example, Mr. P. G., the surgeon, had not been informed of the grave turn of Diana's illness and that she had been taken to a nursing home. This was all the more astonishing since he and Dr. L., the radiologist, saw each other almost every day at the hospital where Diana had had the radiation treatment. Whether Dr. L. himself knew I never learned; he did not, to my knowledge, make the attempt to find out. It was only almost at the end that the surgeon heard by some coincidence of what had happened. Being a conscientious and sensitive man who had a real affection for Diana, he was deeply distressed. He assured me later that, had he known, he would have come to see her regularly and might even have been able to alleviate her suffering by various means.

Not quite knowing then in which direction to move, having—to use the military simile—lost contact with the enemy and completely in the dark as to his intentions and from where he would strike next, the doctors decided to call in another Consultant Physician. He might have some new approach, some new ideas.

The Consultant duly came, examined Diana, listened to her detailed account of the course of the illness and ordered another series of X-ray pictures to be taken and further clinical and biological tests to be made. They proved a severe ordeal for Diana. She told me about it when I came to see her later that day. She had been taken to the X-ray department and been kept waiting there all alone for a considerable time. Then the pictures were taken; one in particular upset her very much. It was taken through the mouth down her throat; its object was to investigate the condition of the top vertebrae and the base of the skull.

'For the first time I felt discouraged,' she told me, 'why should they take all those pictures unless they felt that my condition was really very serious. When I came back into my room I had to cry a little. But I am all right again now,' she added with a smile. 'I only wished you could have been with me at the time; I felt very lonely and frightened.'

The next day I was myself present when the doctors put the pictures against the illuminated glass panel. I stood there, feeling drops of sweat trickling down from my forehead and arm pits as they examined those ghostly pictures. First came the chest. 'Perfect,' said Dr. R. after a brief silence. 'Perfect,' repeated Dr. M., his assistant. Then came pictures of the skull, from the front, from above, sideways. Again the doctors declared themselves satisfied. 'Not a sign of a tumour.' Finally the picture taken through the mouth showing the base of the skull and the top vertebrae.

This picture, it was thought, would most certainly reveal the truth if there were 'secondary deposits' (this euphemism for cancerous growths) in brain or bones. There were none. 'Perfect, perfect,' the two doctors kept repeating, 'there is absolutely no abnormality anywhere.' Other laboratory tests (the results of which were before them) seemed to bear out the findings of the X-rays: no abnormality. There was therefore every reason for hope that whatever the cause and nature of her illness there was no malignancy. 'No malignancy' meant life. She would make a slow but certain recovery. 'Malignancy', on the other hand, meant only one thing: death. There was at this stage no third alternative.

'Could there be tumours, or as you call them, "deposits", in the tissues which do not show up in X-rays?' I asked.

'There could, but let us not jump to conclusions; on the face of it it seems highly unlikely.'

Well then, there was real reason for hope or rather, as the doctors put it, 'cautious optimism'. When the Consultant arrived a little later I wanted to retire from the room, but Dr. R. said: 'I don't see why Prince Loewenstein should not stay; we have no secrets to discuss; besides, we treat him almost like a colleague.' In my presence then the findings were discussed and the same conclusions reached as before: 'No sign of any abnormality'. The four of us then went into Diana's room. Dr. D., the Consultant, sat down on her bed and said (with somewhat startling frankness, I thought), 'My dear young lady, there is absolutely no trace of a spread of the cancer to either bones or the brain; we must assume therefore that your illness is in fact entirely due to the effects of radiation. If we want to give it a name, we could say that you are suffering from a form of meningism caused by radiation and not by a virus.'

That evening, when I returned to Smith Street for dinner, Rosemary as always asked me as soon as I had entered the house: 'How are things?'

I answered: 'I really think we can all feel much happier today.' A little later in the evening, just before nine o'clock, the time when the switchboard closed down in the nursing home, Diana herself rang to tell me how happy she felt and to wish me a good night. This was the end of the second week.

Four

A few days later Rosamond asked me if I would like Mrs. M., a woman of great spiritual healing power, to visit Diana.

I confess that I have always been sceptical over spiritual healing. Though one had heard of many cases of successful healing, when probing more deeply the majority of cases had turned out to be psychosomatic conditions such as spinal troubles, obscure pains or other not clearly definable disorders. In so far as many illnesses have a psychological or rather psychic component they may yield to or improve on treatment on a non-physical level which is not necessarily the spiritual level. Psychotherapy, by elucidating and bringing into consciousness disturbances in the psyche, very often cures what appears to be (or has become) an organic illness. Whether every illness that can afflict the body has its origins on those planes or dimensions of our being which lie, as it were, behind or above or around our physical body, no one can say.

I believe that our total being or *real Self* is—to use terms of space and time—infinitely wider, greater, more enduring than our physical body which is but the visible focus and operative centre of that greater being. I also believe that our five senses are but instruments designed for this limited purpose of present space-time existence. Hence our understanding is limited also by the very limitation of the instruments through which we operate. In short: we are greater, more significant than we ourselves know. We are strangers to our *real* selves, in like manner as we are strangers to the Universe which is our abode.

Perhaps the ultimate aim and task of all human striving and endeavour in science, religion and in the pursuit of our daily life, is to find out what we are in reality and to *realize* ourselves within the context of Creation as a whole: to become *aware* on an ever-widening scale. This, in turn, may be but part and aspect of the Creator's purpose: to become aware of HIMSELF through each individual consciousness and through His Creation as a whole.

These are speculations which have exercised the minds of philosophers and mystics throughout the ages. It is not my purpose to pursue them further. But trying to clarify my own mind and to find a *rationale* for what I would have wished to believe and passionately desired, namely that she could be healed, I found myself of necessity drawn into these wider speculations. Spiritual healing, by definition, belongs into a realm which reason cannot grasp, but, I asked myself, is there somewhere in this vast sea of mystery a tiny island which faith and hope can share with reason? If man is greater and in an absolute sense more significant than he appears to be—and in this my belief (and wish) is in no conflict with my intellectual conviction—if this is so, then he must also have access to realms of being, and power over 'inner' laws of life, which life beyond the sphere of rational comprehension.

Spiritual healing must be based on some such inner laws which are beyond the grasp of reason but not beyond the range of what man can do. My scepticism over spiritual healing therefore was and is not over the possibility itself but over the fitness and the claims of the individual healers.

If all illness then has its 'psychic' component or partly originates in the 'unseen' layers or dimensions of the human being, from where it is projected on to the physical body as on to a screen, then to be a spiritual healer, one must be a person with unusual insight into those unseen realms where illness originates. Depending on the depth of this insight and on the degree of his power a healer may be able to effect cures of a minor or major kind.

A *great* healer, then, must be a person far advanced in awareness or self-realization, a person who has overcome his own limitations and attachments; in short, a 'master' or a saint.

I do not doubt that there are such people in our present age, and not only in the East. But there cannot be many. It seemed to me, hard as I tried to think otherwise, that it was not in her

126

pattern of destiny that such a healer should be guided to her. I felt that if the illness was secondary cancer of the brain, this was beyond the powers of any healer I could think of.

I told Diana that a spiritual healer, a friend of Rosamond's, would come and see her. Diana agreed. She believed in spiritual healing, but like myself was sceptical over the claims made by some well-known healers and the stories circulated about them.

Also the hocus-pocus surrounding some of the actual healing sessions: the trance, the adoption by the healer of strange voices and the ubiquitous presence of Red Indian, Chinese or Scottish spirit doctors, seemed to her to belong in the realm of primitive magic rather than of spiritual healing. 'Christ did not heal in this manner,' she said.

On the 23rd of February I met Mrs. M. at Rosamond's, and together we went in a taxi to the nursing home. I had made arrangements there that no one should enter the room while Mrs. M. was with Diana.

Mrs. M. was full of hope. She felt sure that Diana's illness was the result of the prolonged radiation which would affect someone so sensitive and delicate particularly badly. In this she voiced, but also strengthened our own hopes. Had we not just had the new X-ray findings and the clinical tests showing no abnormality; and the great Consultant's reassuring pronouncements?

Once or twice during this period of renewed hope Dr. R. gave me a lift home in his car at about eight o'clock in the evening when Diana had been settled down for the night. As we drove along the brightly lit streets from Harley Street to Park Lane, Hyde Park Corner and Knightsbridge in the exceptionally mild pre-spring weather, both relaxing after the strains of the day, we felt that optimism was justified. Dr. R. seemed confident that all would be well though he admitted that this was a most puzzling, unusual case. He had never encountered post-radiation symptoms so severe and so persistent.

I am sure that he was expressing his honest opinion, but in his heart of hearts he must have known—as I did deep down on the threshold of consciousness—that we were fighting a hopeless battle against a decision which had been made and was irreversible.

I have always been grateful for these few last weeks of illusion and self-deception, and I am grateful to the doctors if, as I suspect, they carried the deception beyond the time when they themselves no longer believed in the radiation theory.

It gave us all strength and it gave to me precious moments of happiness. Had I consciously carried with me the knowledge which had flashed in blinding clarity through my mind the moment I entered room No. 116 in the nursing home on the 11th of February—that she would never leave that room alive—I most probably would not have been able to conceal my distress from her during those first four weeks when she was still in complete mental control of herself. One cannot play-act beyond a certain point.

As I sat outside smoking endless cigarettes, profound scepticism alternated with fervent hope and faith in the possibility of miraculous healing. Perhaps Mrs. M. had that gift or, perhaps, she had been able to succeed where the doctors had failed so far, and had diagnosed the true nature of this baffling illness and established beyond doubt that it was not cancer of the brain. And if this was so, she could, even as a minor healer, effect a complete cure.

When Mrs. M. emerged from Diana's room she seemed completely exhausted. Rosamond also appeared to be under the spell of some powerful experience. 'We must let her sleep now,' Rosamond said to me, 'so don't go in for a while.'

'Will she be all right?' I asked.

'Yes, she will be all right,' Mrs. M. answered.

I was anxious to know more. I wanted to know what kind of spiritual healing Mrs. M. had applied. Was it the mediumistic type of healing in which the healer acts on the instructions of some discarnate being whom he believes to be his guide? Or was it the direct healing in which the healer becomes a channel between the source of healing power and the sufferer? I wanted to know this, not because I had any special experience of either method, but (being sceptical as I have already said) I hoped to be able to draw from Mrs. M.'s account of what had happened my own conclusions as to her powers as a clairvoyant and healer. But neither Rosamond nor Mrs. M. wanted to say much at that moment. They merely indicated that they had found themselves in a fierce contest of powers and energies which filled the room in waves and currents almost beyond their power to withstand. It was like battling through a storm. But in the end harmony and stillness prevailed and the certainty that all would be well. 'Don't worry any more,' Mrs. M. said before leaving, 'she is healed, she herself felt this and expressed it before we left.' She had been, and still was, very ill from the effects of the radiation and she would be another four weeks in the nursing home.

'Will you come again to give her another treatment?' I asked.

'It should not be necessary,' Mrs. M. said, 'but I will come once more in a month; just before she leaves the nursing home.' This was to prove true in the way the Delphic oracle proved true in antiquity; the healer came back exactly one month later, and a week afterwards Diana left the nursing home.

I prayed for the voice of disbelief which said to me: 'This was not the miracle for which you hoped' to be stilled.—'She is healed; she will be all right'—what did it mean? If this was true, the very next days, indeed tomorrow, would show.

I did not return that evening to the nursing home, but I telephoned later and was told that Diana had slept a great deal, but then had woken up with a bad headache. The Floor Sister also mentioned, without stressing the point unduly, that Diana had been sick and not been able to eat anything apart from a little consommé.

The next morning the news was much better. She had had a very good night, no headache, no sickness, and was quite cheerful. I could not come that morning but sent a message to her, saying I would be with her in the early afternoon.

I arrived at about half-past three: she was asleep. On the

coverlet lay face down her open Prayer Book. She woke immediately, looked at me and said: 'Mr. P., I think I am healed.' Then she threw her arms around me.

'We all think so, my pet,' I answered. Had the miracle happened?

'Do you know what happened today,' she continued with great animation, 'I must tell you; you'll be interested.'

'Tell me, darling,' I said, and pointing to the open Prayer Book, 'I see you have been reading.'

'That's just it,' she said. 'Do you know that today, for the first time in more than six weeks I had the desire to read—you know reading had become a great strain to me lately—and I read the whole of the Communion service; I had no difficulty at all. When I had finished, a great feeling of complete peace came over me; I knew I am healed, and I went happily to sleep . . .'

On these words, I burst into tears. She took my hand and said: 'There is nothing to cry about, Mr. P.'

'Of course not, darling,' I said, 'I was moved by your words—and happy.'

'I am really much better today,' she continued, 'and I have no pains; do you think Rose's friend has done the trick, with the help of the "boys on the other side"?' (That is how she always referred humorously to unseen powers.) I asked her if she could remember any details of the healing session. 'I could not really see much; I had my eyes shut most of the time, and the room was fairly dark, but I can only tell you there was a lot going on all around me . . .'

I remembered something Mrs. M. had told me before parting. This was to the effect that Diana, despite her great interest in Eastern religious thought and tradition was, as she put it, 'a child of Christ'. Her way was not really the Eastern way but that of the 'Imitation of Christ'.

I told this to Diana. She looked up and her eyes filled with tears. Slowly, deliberately and gravely she said: 'I have been a Christian all my life; ever since I can remember.' And she went on: 'When I was a little girl of five and went to a private day school in Kensington High Street, I and four other little girls who were Jewish, always had to wait in a room while the other little girls in the classroom next door assembled for their morning prayer. And every morning they began with the Hymn *'All Things Bright and Beautiful.'* I heard them sing, and I remembered:

> All things bright and beautiful,
> All creatures great and small,
> All things wise and wonderful,
> The Lord God made them all.
> Each little flower that opens,
> Each little bird that sings,
> He made their glowing colours,
> He made their tiny wings . . .

'You see', she interrupted, 'my memory is not so bad after all. After this of course comes the famous verse about "the rich man in his castle, the poor man at his gate . . ." etc., which Socialists so dislike, but it all makes sense; we won't go into this now.'
She continued:

> The tall trees in the green wood,
> The meadow where we play,
> The rushes by the water,
> We gather every day;
> He gave us eyes to see them
> And lips that we might tell,
> How great is God Almighty
> Who has made all things well . . .

'I heard them sing it, and how I wished that I could be with them; I knew I belonged to them. But I was told that I was Jewish and would not understand. I did not really know what it meant to be "Jewish", but whatever it was, I knew that I was a Christian.'

The Jewish religion in its institutional form had never meant anything to her. Her parents did not practise it, nor had she ever received instruction. She remembered that when she was a small girl her parents still held to certain more formal Jewish observances and traditions such as putting lighted candles on the table on Friday night, and that her father would on appropriate occasions say some Jewish prayer. In her maternal grandparents' house Jewish feasts such as Passover, Purim and the Feast of Tabernacles were strictly observed, and her most pleasant memories of Jewish religious customs were of special meals at her grandmother's house and of certain cakes and sweetmeats associated with the different feasts. All her life she retained a liking for them.

Her father's attitude to the concept of Judaism, as a religion, philosophy and way of life, remained highly ambivalent throughout the whole of his life. This is well known from his own writings and pronouncements.

As a child and up to the time he went to the University he suffered much under the narrow orthodoxy of his parents. The religious services at the Synagogue he found quite intolerable. Those interminable prayer sessions (especially on feastdays) with their repetitiousness, atavistic invocations and formalistic rigmarole, made no appeal to his imagination, failed to kindle that sense of the numinous that dwells in the heart of every child, and without which there can be no true religious experience.

But Jewish orthodoxy as practised in his parental home was not confined to religious observance: it permeated every aspect of daily life, regulating it down to the smallest details. Its taboos, irrationalities, obsessions, absurdities; its 'sympathetic magic' (which, for example, did not permit the switching on of the electric light on Sabbath because electricity is akin to fire which no orthodox Jew was allowed to handle on that day); its compulsive rituals; its dietary regulations, prohibitions, prescriptions and tribalism, formed a nightmarish maze from which he felt there was no escape.

It filled him with a passionate desire for liberty.

132

As a schoolboy he became increasingly and painfully aware of that 'otherness' and 'separateness' of his condition (the inevitable concomitant of Jewish particularism) which erected an insurmountable barrier between himself and the community in which he lived and whose interests he shared.

As an undergraduate at Oxford he turned to Christianity in which he saw the liberation from the spiritual prison of Jewish orthodoxy. Later in life he discovered, as all truly religious people inevitably must, that all the great religions teach the same truth.

He discovered that this truth was enshrined in the mystic, esoteric teaching, and here he found that Jewish mysticism rose to the same heights of beauty and had the same depth of insight as that of Christianity and of Islam. He never acquainted himself with the religions of the East.

It was in the teaching and in the person of Jesus that he saw the ultimate fulfilment and the incarnation of the Divine Principle on this earth. Yet he never took the step of becoming a Christian.

The key to the many incongruities and contradictions in this remarkable man's character, to his philosophy of life and his work can be found in the conditions in which he grew up. This, of course, holds good for most of us. Tradition and early environment or rather our reaction to them, to a large extent determine the course, at least the outer course, of our life. But it is only with exceptional people that this assumes a significance that goes beyond the circle of family and friends. With Diana's father, his whole life can be seen as a struggle for liberation from the claustrophobic atmosphere of his childhood. This struggle for personal liberation, in which he never fully succeeded, he projected on to the contemporary scene in his many campaigns against social injustice, oppression, poverty, war and numerous other less obvious evils; it found expression also in his writings, most of which had the character of public confessions and in the general frenzy of his unceasing activity.

His closest friends, his employees and above all his family saw the shadow-side of his struggle for light. He never attained to the wisdom which alone would have enabled him to reach that liberation which he so passionately desired.

Diana had inherited some of his most outstanding traits and qualities: his penetrating intellect, his love of nature and beauty, his burning quest after truth. As a young girl she was very close to him. They were both aware of the affinity that existed between them. He responded to the warmth and generosity of her nature, he loved her gaiety, her sense of fun—her sense of non-sense. And he recognized that behind that bubbling exterior, which made her into the clown of the family, there were unfathomed resources of mind and heart.

But later—such are the strange and unaccountable twists in man's mind—those very affinities which had previously linked them, those very qualities which he had admired in her, became a source of ever growing irritation to him.

As she grew up and became a person in her own right, his love changed into suspicion, distrust and jealousy. She was beautiful—the most beautiful of his daughters—she was independent, she had her own mind. She did not share his political views, nor show great interest in his causes; she became altogether 'different'. It became clear to him that she would go her own way. He could not understand it, he could not tolerate it. In his heart of hearts he must have felt that she had left him behind; that she had, in some mysterious way, always been where he wanted to go; that she had, without torment, travail and conflict reached a goal which he would never attain.

He did *not* know that the Way of Action was not the only, and not necessarily, the best way to enlightenment. There was also the Inner Way, the way of devotion and love. This was her way.

To assuage his conscience and sense of guilt over his uncharitableness towards this daughter whom he at once loved very much, and probably loved to the end of his life (which preceded the end of hers by only two months) he built up an elaborate system of rationalisation to explain to himself and others this strange antagonism. He formed the opinion and tenaciously

134

held to it, that she was 'artificial', 'superficial', lacked the sense of social responsibility and was only concerned with the irrelevancies of a 'mundane' life.

Diana suffered greatly under this estrangement, for she loved her father. Many times she tried to heal the breach, but the opportunity was denied to her. In the twenty years of our marriage she did not see her father more than once or twice a year, and every time she left depressed and disheartened.

It was only during the last three weeks of his life, when Diana herself was already desperately ill—she never knew that I had told him—that his love and tenderness for her broke through that solid block of misunderstanding and ill will as the rays of the setting sun break through dark clouds at the end of a stormy day.

After the last occasion when she saw him, towards the end of January 1967—he sat in his wheelchair partly paralysed on the right side of his body, and she herself had developed symptoms not unlike his own—she said to me: 'This is the first time in thirty-five years that my father has held my hand and has spoken tenderly to me.' A week later, on the 3rd of February, he suffered his second and fatal stroke, and a week after she was taken to the nursing home.

In Oxford, during the war as I have mentioned, she met Charles Williams who was then a middle-aged man. He was the first to recognize the religious genius and the great proud soul of this beautiful young girl whose dark eyes shone with compassion and tenderness, but whose gaze no one could meet who was not himself pure of heart.

A number of letters to her, written on odd bits of paper in an inelegant hand, and also one poem written in the form of a letter, survive. It appears from them that he had conceived a deep affection for her which he expressed in chaste and slightly self-deprecatory terms.

When in the middle of March 1967, twenty-five years after Charles Williams had come under the spell of those eyes which were now going out like stars extinguished from the sky, I said to her: 'No one could have shown greater *tenue* than you have, my love, during all those weeks; you are a true princess, a royal soul, and never mind the Almanach de Gotha.' She answered: 'It was Charles Williams who first said to me: "You have a Royal disposition . . ." '. His letter, ending with these words lies before me.

'I have been a Christian all my life,' she had said to me. Indeed, in all her life she uniquely exemplified the dictum: *Anima naturaliter Christiana,* even had she never formally adopted the Christian Faith.

Yet there was never a trace of self-righteousness, bigotry or intolerance in her spiritual quest, nor anything woolly or unbalanced. She tried to understand. The books she read, the annotations she made, the precision with which she formulated her thoughts, the logic of her arguments, all this testified to a well-balanced, mature mind.

As with her father thirty years before, Oxford had opened for her the doors of inner perception and the windows to the world outside. Unlike her father, she was ready for it; she never wore the chains which had fettered him to modes of thought, customs, sentiments which, though he rejected them, he could never quite overcome. She was free. And she could take the step which he never dared to take: she could become what she had always been: a Christian.

Had I not been divorced and therefore disbarred from marrying in church she would have taken the step at the time of our marriage. Not in order to conform or to please me, but because she was ready for it.

I never tried to urge her or to influence her. My own attitude to religion was, as I shall show later, unconventional. Born a Catholic I remain a Catholic and will die a Catholic. But in those years preceding my marriage to Diana, and in the years after, I was steeped in the study of Eastern religion and esotericism.

Diana followed me in this. We attended lecture courses and meetings, read many books on Buddhism, and its various schools,

136

and for a time belonged to a Society for the teaching and practice of Yoga.

Diana, as I have said in an earlier passage, persisted in her readings, studies and practice long after she had become a Christian; my interest turned increasingly to the Jungian School of religious thought. But we went to mass together as well as to Anglican services, mostly at week-ends in the country. When we were in France, Italy, Germany or Austria we regularly attended mass on Sunday. In those countries, with their great cathedrals and beautiful Gothic and Baroque churches, religious services, especially High Mass, seemed to us endowed with dimensions of significance which we sadly missed in England. Perhaps also the (relatively) carefree mood of holiday contributed something to this feeling.

Then the time came when Diana wanted to be baptized. To our intense distress and dismay the Catholic Church refused to baptize her on the ground that she was married to a divorced Catholic. According to the absurd casuistry of the argument, she was, as long as she was not a Christian, validly married. Once baptized, however, she would be living in sin. Therefore baptism would make her into a sinner (when, in fact, according to Christian teaching it does the very opposite, namely 'wash away sin').

Nothing, it seems to me, could be more contrary to Christ's command: *Go ye therefore, and teach all nations, baptizing them in the name of the Father, and of the Son, and of the Holy Ghost,* contrary to the spirit of Christianity, than to refuse baptism to someone who earnestly desires it.

I pointed this out to several priests with whom I discussed the matter. They showed themselves sympathetic, they were embarrassed, but they could do nothing. Here was a case where the letter of the law destroyed the spirit of the law.

Subterfuges and dodges were suggested; for example that there existed possibilities (if one took the trouble to explore them) of having my first marriage annulled; or that one might give certain undertakings (with due mental reservations) as to the mode of our married life in the future, which would enable the Church to set aside the interdict.

In those early years of our marriage, when we had very little money, Diana had a job as a switchboard operator with a small firm of architects whose offices were in Victoria Street, very close to Westminster Abbey. The job was not very strenuous for the switchboard was not overbusy. (It had the additional advantage that I could always ring her, knowing she would answer the phone immediately.) She did not earn much, yet the time was not wasted, for she could read and think to her heart's content. Almost every day, except when I met her for lunch, she spent the lunch hour in the ancient chapel of St. Faith in Westminster Abbey. St. Faith was an early English woman martyr. One day Diana said to me: 'I think I shall be baptized into the Anglican Church and I shall choose as one of my names "Faith". I hope you have no objections to this, Mr. P.'

Of course I had no objections. 'I want your other name to be Maria; you will then be "Diana Maria Faith".'

And so it happened. She was christened in the Chapel of St. Faith by Canon Edward Carpenter. I was the only witness. A year after she was confirmed by the Bishop of London in Westminster Abbey. Few people knew of it. It was her most private and intimate concern. Had her relationship to her father been a happier one she might have wanted to tell him, and he might have understood. But she never wanted her mother to know, for she was aware that this would meet with unbending hostility; not on religious grounds, but because in her mother's eyes it would have meant only one thing: that Diana had 'betrayed' her Jewish heritage.

That afternoon in February when she felt she had been healed she talked much about our life together, and she talked about life and death. The idea of death held no terror for her. There was one terror only for her: the thought of leaving me behind, alone. 'I cannot think how you ever managed before; you cannot even brush your hair properly and you always drop the soap

138

into the bath. How could you manage if I should die before you? I must not die before you.'

She had often said these things to me. That afternoon she returned to them. But she spoke with great seriousness. 'You know, Mr. P., that I don't mind the idea of dying; in fact, as I have said many times, I am rather tired of this incarnation; if it weren't for you I would be quite prepared to go. But it is my job to look after you, and when the time comes—when you are well into the nineties—it will be my task to be with you; to help you across. Then I shall follow almost immediately. For this reason I don't want to die yet.'

And she continued with deep conviction and visionary certainty: 'I know what the "other side" is like. I know what it will be like when we meet again there. It will be you and me, but there will be some differences. We shall be in a body of light, more beautiful, prototypes, as it were. The ideal accomplishment of what we are and are trying to strive for.' She spoke for about half an hour, not allowing me to interrupt her flow of thought which came with a poetic force and beauty of sentences and words, such as I had never witnessed before. I could not interrupt her; I sat—spellbound. This, I felt, was her last message to me.

When she had finished, she seemed exhausted. 'I have a little headache now,' she said; 'nothing much, but I am tired.' Then, very suddenly, she said: 'Do you think, Mr. P., that I am dying?'

'No, of course not, my love; you know yourself you are healed.'

As in a vision she continued: 'If I should die, I want you to promise now that you will never grieve for me; I shall never be away from you; *I will always be present*. This,' she clasped my hand and held it tight, 'you *must* believe; you *must* believe. And now you must leave me alone for a while; I think I want to sleep. Come back before dinner.' I kissed her soft lips and left.

139

Five

Alas, the improvement was of short duration. By the end of February we were at our wits' end, the doctors as much as I.

We could not conceal from ourselves any longer that she was steadily getting worse. The agonizing headaches had become more frequent, the intervals between them shorter. The pains began to radiate from the base of the skull down the whole length of the spine and in the legs. There was hardly a position left to her in which she could find temporary relief. If she lay on her back with only one pillow under her head this would for a short time reduce the tension in the neck and shoulders but tend to worsen the pains in the legs. She would then turn over on to her right side and pull up her knees as far as possible; often when she lay in this position I would gently rub her legs and feet which seemed to give her some comfort. To prop her up in her pillows became an elaborate operation which demanded skill and patience, for the slightest jerk would cause her almost unbearable pain. One by one the pillows had to be inserted under her neck while she was being held up by one arm in a very special way which only a trained nurse knew how to do. Often these movements would make her sick. She had not eaten a proper meal for four weeks and had lost over two stone since she had first been weighed on entering the nursing home.

Eating and being sick became two closely associated ideas in her mind, for more and more frequently the slightest stimulation of the stomach would make her retch. I remember vividly one particularly distressing incident, for it stood for so many similar ones. She had been looking forward to her consommé. She started to drink it, but almost at once an acute malaise seemed to overcome her. She pushed the cup away and cried like a little girl: 'I cannot eat my soup, I cannot eat it.' She looked deeply distressed and pleaded once more in anguish: 'Oh, why can I not eat my soup?' Then she was violently sick. The type of sickness which, I knew from what the doctors had said, was symptomatic of 'intracranial pressure'.

Then soon came the time when she would be sick for no apparent cause. She would, for example, be talking quite happily and with great animation when suddenly her face would flush, an expression of distress and bewilderment come into her eyes, and she was sick. Mostly there was no time even to reach for the bowl. The sight of these cruel, fiendish onslaughts on this inno-cent defenceless human being—for this is how it appeared to me—was almost more than I could bear. It was like watching a murderous hand plunge a knife from behind a dark corner into the back of a child playing in the sun. And each time it happened I felt as if I myself had been struck by the murder-er's weapon. When it was over, she would turn to me, trying to smile: 'I think I am all right now, give me a sip of water.' Her face would be wet with perspiration, her pulse beat rapidly. 'I can't understand why I should be sick so often. I hardly eat anything. Do you understand it, Mr. P.?'

'I don't, my love; it must be all those new pills they give you; I will speak to the doctors.'

'Oh God,' I often thought, 'why must she suffer so? What is the meaning, what is the purpose?'

In the middle of February she had still been able to walk along the corridor supported by a nurse. This now seemed al-most like the distant past. She was now only just able to leave her bed and sit in a chair while the bed was being made up. To get back into bed unaided became more and more difficult. 'I have no strength left,' she said. 'As soon as I reach the bed I flop into it like Edna.'

Edna had been her favourite doll, an old-fashioned doll dressed in home-made petticoats and skirts. Her head was made of leather, her facial features had almost completely vanished, but what was left had an expression both infinitely touching and beautiful. Total acceptance of all that fate might decree was written in that little face which reminded one of those quickly sketched faces of children from the crowd scenes in Goya's mural *'The Miracle of St. Francis'*. Edna's head rolled helplessly about when you lifted her up, her limbs were loose and floppy.

She had indeed become like Edna in her helplessness, touching beauty and total acceptance. But unlike Edna she was not a doll but a suffering human being; unlike Edna who was immortal, she would die.

One day, in the same casual manner in which, while still at home, she had told me that she could no longer get into her bath unaided, she said: 'For the first time, Mr. P., they had to make my bed with me in it; I was too weak to get up.' I did not immediately grasp the significance of what she had said. I thought: 'It will get better in a few days.' At first slowly and stealthily, but now more boldly and at an ever-quickening pace the deadly enemy took from her one by one those sovereign rights (which we take so much for granted) which make us into independent human beings: the bodily abilities and mental faculties.

The sinister process had begun in January when she had noticed that her handwriting, so exquisitely beautiful and elegant, was changing. No longer did the letters, as if directed only by the mind, appear on the paper in their usual perfect alignment and harmony. The fingers holding the pen did not seem to obey the nerve impulses that made them move.

I have since found a number of her unfinished letters to friends. In one of them she writes: 'My dear Julia, just a short note to thank you for yours. I can't write much because my right hand and arm are going through a . . .' and here the note ends. A little further down on the paper she attempts to write normally by putting greater pressure to bear on the pen, but once again the hand does not carry out what the mind demands.

142

There is another letter that was never sent, to an elderly man whom she had met at the Oxford and Cambridge Club at the end of December. This gentleman had extolled the virtues of snuff against cigarette smoking and had promised to send her some samples. This gentleman had also promised to show her the parrot which he had donated to the club. The bird lived in its cage in the bar to which women had no access. It had been arranged that Diana and I should come on a Sunday at a time when the bar was empty and relaxed vigilance would make it possible for Diana to enter this inner sanctum and see the parrot. It never came to it. In her letter, the very last of the many embellished by comical drawings, Diana acknowledges the receipt of the samples of snuff, expresses her joy at the thought of meeting the parrot and combines the two incongruous topics in a series of small sketches depicting the parrot on its perch taking snuff. The writing is only barely legible, and after several attempts to improve it she had to give up.

The last time she ever signed her name was early in March when I asked her to sign a form authorizing me to draw cheques on her behalf. She had the greatest difficulty in forming the letters. Not only had she lost command over her movements, but her finger-tips were becoming numb.

And now she could no longer brush her teeth.

Telling me about her latest disabilities, she said: 'You know, Mr. P., I soon won't be able to brush my teeth any more. You remember that even before I came here, I found it difficult to put on lipstick or use the eyebrow pencil. You know I used to say that it was a great effort; my hand would not do what I wanted. Now I cannot brush my teeth without getting into a most terrible mess . . .'

And then she told me that on that morning she had started to brush her teeth as usual by the basin, when suddenly her hand had gone wild and completely out of control. 'Instead of, say, three strokes up and down with the brush, I was making ten or twelve very fast ones, bumping the brush against my teeth. It was very upsetting, and I also nearly dropped my little plate into the basin.'

I had heard of paralysis agitans in which movement once started cannot be controlled; that must be it. 'Have you told Dr. R.?' I asked.

She would tomorrow, she said, but there was always so much to tell, and she forgot. 'I really ought to write it all down, but this is now almost impossible.'

The next day and for about three weeks, after having helped her with her supper, I rinsed the plate and helped her brush her teeth. I propped her up with pillows, put a bath towel around her neck and shoulders arranged the bowl, prepared the tumbler and the toothpaste on the brush.

'Now do it slowly, my love, just brush very gently; once or twice, up and down; forward and backward.'

She had told me that whenever she found it difficult to carry out any physical task she would sing a little song which would help her to co-ordinate her movements. And so she now tried to hum her 'little song'. 'I am sure it will help,' she said. But then suddenly her hand went wild, moving frantically and beyond control. At the same time her head rolled backward and sideways and then fell forward. She looked frightened. I was utterly helpless. When finally she had regained a measure of control she said quietly: 'You see what I mean.'

I felt as if I had received a blow into the pit of my stomach. I could hardly speak: it was unspeakably terrible, what I had just witnessed. 'My poor, poor angel,' I said. 'We must do something about it.'

'I imagine it will get better again,' she replied. 'And now I think I will just rinse my mouth and we will leave it at that for tonight.'

We tried again the next evening and the evening after, but soon she could not sit upright at all; soon she could not use the toothbrush any more; soon she only just managed to rinse her mouth. But even reduced to this pitiful state of helplessness, she took command over the procedure. She told me exactly where

144

to put the large towel and the small one, and where to place
the bowl when she rinsed her mouth. And every night I washed
the little plate with the two front teeth, and she put it carefully
back into her mouth and did not remove it until later when they
had bedded her down for the night.

Six

There were still moments, brief moments of communion and
intimacy into which we gathered the happiness of those twenty
years which were now coming to a close.

There was, for example, the little ritual of helping her to
take off the nylon pyjamas she wore during the day and slip
on the cotton ones which she liked wearing at night. 'I sleep
so much better in cotton,' she said, 'it is so much cosier.'

She had become very weak and, as I have said, every movement,
especially of the head and the neck, caused her pain. Yet she
took charge of the pyjama-changing operation and told me exactly what to do and how best to do it. 'Don't forget, Mr. P., *le
geste essentiel.*'

First we had to arrange the pillows so that her head lay as
flat as possible. It required as much care as the procedure of
inserting pillows which I have already described. Even the tiniest
jerk had to be avoided. Then I turned back her blankets and
the top sheet and pulled off the pyjamas slowly and gently, one
leg after the other. The cotton trousers had already been laid
out: 'You must get them the proper way round,' she said, 'the
back is different from the front; the back is more bulky, have
you never observed it?' (I hadn't.) This was of course important,
in order to slip them over the legs without sudden hitches.

She had become terribly emaciated; her once so perfectly
shaped thighs had lost most of their flesh. Her pelvis stuck out

145

over a belly that had become concave. Carefully I raised first her right leg and pulled the trousers over it, and then the left. This done, I laid both legs down flat and pulled the trousers over her hips.

'Now we must try to slip off the top of the pyjamas.' Pillow by pillow I propped up her body, took first one arm and then the other and slipped them out of the short sleeves of her pyjama top. She helped me by giving me instructions on every move. For a moment she lay with her shoulders and chest bare. And here I would pause. Emaciated as it had become her body was still exquisitely beautiful: like carved ivory. Her skin was silky and had the fragrance of youth. Her breasts were as perfect as when I had first kissed them by the glow of an electric fire that far away night in my 'digs' in Oxford, twenty-three years ago. They were the breasts of a young girl, except that on one of them was written indelibly a sentence of death from which there was to be no reprieve.

'Don't look at me,' she said, 'I am a terrible sight.'

'You are not, my love, you are as beautiful as ever.'

'I don't believe it,' she replied. Her hair had grown very long over the weeks and was flowing down in a dark stream over her shoulders. In the subdued light of this hospital room I covered her with kisses as I had done that far-away night.

'The nurse might come in,' she said, as she said then: 'The landlady might come in.' But this time she added: 'What does it matter; after all we are a married couple.'

What does it matter, my love, my Sweetheart. Let them see— they know—that I adore you; that I desire you as I did when I first met you, when you wore ugly spectacles and a home-made skirt; as I have desired you ever since, through all those years of struggle and happiness: that I desire you now at the end of your chaste and saintly life.

When finally we had accomplished our task of changing her for the night (there was little difference between night and day for her, and soon there would be none) she would lie back, exhausted. 'Thank you, Mr. P., that was very kind of you.'

146

Then there were the moments when I helped her to eat her supper. In the early days at the nursing home when we all hoped against hope that she would recover from her mysterious illness, it seemed important that she should take proper nourishment in order to keep up her strength. The food at the nursing home was much more varied and better than at the average English hospital. The menus were like those in a good sea-side hotel with pretensions above its station. There was a great variety of dishes to choose from: hors d'oeuvres; avocado pears, with or without shrimps, smoked salmon, consommé; in the main course there was sole, turkey, chicken, steaks, and as desserts one could have stewed fruit, various jellies, ice cream and cheese. In the morning the Floor Sister would bring the next day's menu to every patient and enquire after their wishes. In the weeks to follow I was to acquaint myself fully with the invariable sameness of that variety, for I would see the food trolleys come up from the kitchen and the avocado pears (with or without shrimps), the chicken, the turkey, the lamb cutlets, the jellies and ice creams distributed over the length of the corridor and see the empty or half empty dishes collected from the different rooms later.

But even in those early days Diana would eat very little: half a cup of consommé or vegetable soup, a little fish, chicken or turkey ('they all taste the same to me,' she said), some vegetable, and she would finish up with yogurt and some stewed fruit. The latter were the only two things she really enjoyed.

Until the very last day when she was still able to take nourishment, she always had yogurt. She often commented on it, and even when she could no longer speak, she seemed to enjoy its texture and acid taste. In the early days she wanted me to bring her what she called 'real' yogurt from a health food shop in Chelsea, because the yogurt in the nursing home seemed to her to be synthetic. I went twice a week to the shop to buy that yogurt; this gave me a deceptive feeling of continuity and normality; had we not always bought our yogurt there? And no doubt, we would continue to do so in the future.

147

But in the relentless march of the disease, the time was soon to come when this special yogurt service was no more required. 'Our yogurt is really perfectly all right, and it is real yogurt,' the nurses said to me, 'and besides, she would not know the difference.' And I stopped going to the health food shop, and, much as I hoped that she would, she never commented on the difference between one type of yogurt and the other any more.

Helping her to get through her pathetic little supper was a slow and laborious process. I propped her up in her pillows, brought the bedtable as close as possible, cut up the small amount of chicken or fish and encouraged her to continue after every mouthful in the manner one encourages small children who refuse to eat. 'Just a little more, darling, you must eat, otherwise you will lose too much weight and become too weak.'

'I know, Mr. P., but the trouble is I never seem to have any appetite.'

Her hands, that had been so steady and sure when executing those miniature paintings and flower sketches were now weak and lacked central guidance. Often she would fail to put the food on to the fork; often the food would fall off the fork in mid-air; often she would give up and say: 'You put the food on the fork and hand it to me.' She could not grip the tumbler any more; I had to bring it to her lips and hold it while she drank in small sips. But we were still together, she and I alone as we had been during countless meals over all those years. 'No thank you, my dear,' she would say to the nurse offering to help, 'thank you very much, but my husband will look after me.'

Then came the time when she no longer could hold fork or spoon; she would take small pieces of meat or fish with her hands, and when she ate vegetables, stewed fruit or yogurt I had to guide the spoon to her mouth. I would peel grapes for her, one by one and feed them to her very slowly. But still we were together talking and sometimes making little jokes. We still could have our 'discussions' which she had always loved so much: 'Do you remember, Mr. P., we always had such interesting discussions over our meals, right from the beginning. That is why

148

I love going to restaurants with you alone; one can talk so much more interestingly than when one eats with others or at home.'

'We shall soon go out to restaurants again, my darling; you and I alone as in olden days . . .'

'Yes, Mr. P., we will.'

These were moments that were happy evocations of happiness past.

Before we were married and in the early years of our married life when we lived in Chelsea, had very little money and food was still rationed, we lunched regularly at an Italian restaurant in our neighbourhood. It had a good clientèle of respectable Chelsea citizens, mostly older people. The food was insufficient in quantity, poor in quality and worse in the way it was prepared. But there was much to make up for these deficiencies. The Italian waiters, all elderly men who had never been interned during the war, still wore frock coats, greasy and frayed at the sleeves. But they went about their task of serving the unattractive fare with complete dedication and exquisite courtesy. The set lunch at 2/6 on weekdays and 3/- on Sundays consisted of three courses with two alternative main courses to choose from: invariably steamed cod and shepherd's pie. The first course was soup, and to finish up there was 'trifle'. ('Ma si, signore, è fato a casa') or a minute piece of cheese. All courses, vegetables and trifle included, were of the same greyish colour and all tasted more or less the same. Sunday lunch, however, had one distinctive feature which accounted for the extra 6d: spaghetti Napolitane. They also added the only splash of colour to the meal: the pale pink of the tomato sauce.

The headwaiter presenting the menu would stand respectfully aside while one made one's decision, cod or shepherd's pie, and would take the order with the same earnestness and professional 'know-how' as though, from a large variety of equally tempting 'Plats du Chef' one had after mature reflection decided on Suprême de Volaille Perigourdine in preference to Sole au Chablis, a choice of which he had approved.

And here we sat, almost every weekday and many a Sunday, Diana and I, facing each other over a small table by the wall, a

149

table always kept for us. She was so close to me across the table that leaning forward I could easily touch her forehead with mine. We ate our horrid little meal and then we had our coffee which was excellent and served in old-fashioned copper cans; I smoked a cigarette and we talked. This was the beginning of our 'discussions', on every topic in the world: our own problems of everyday life, our respective childhoods; politics, history, art, music, philosophy, religion, people and life in general. It was the beginning of a dialogue which never ended in all the years that followed. Here the foundations were laid to that intimacy of mind and spirit which was to grow and grow through the years until we had become, in the words of a friend who wrote to me after her death, 'one being in two persons'.

And the intimacy of body and soul, so intense, so complete that twenty years later when she lay dying before me, her body wasted and her eyes sightless, I loved her with all the passion and singleminded devotion of early love, the foundation to that union in which two persons had become 'one flesh' was laid in those early years of marriage when we lived in two furnished rooms, walked hand in hand wherever we went, travelled on buses, had practically no money and lunched at our Italian restaurant on steamed cod, shepherd's pie and the occasional 'spaghetti Napolitane'.

As time went by we were to lunch and dine in better restaurants, in England, France, Switzerland, Austria and Germany. Even at some of the best restaurants; even at the Hotel Sacher in Vienna. By then she had mastered the art of choosing from elaborate menus with a knowing air, though she always pondered unduly long and with knitted brows and then invariably made what I thought was the wrong choice.

But through all the years of our married life those meals at the Italian restaurant in Chelsea remained the archetypal reality of our 'eating out'. In later years also, when we dined out in the company of others she would always look at me across the table, and catching my eye she would seek my approval for what she chose. 'Do you think, Mr. P., I should have this?'

150

Sometimes, however, she would defy me. 'Don't eat fried scampi,' I would say (having myself an idiosyncrasy against them), and she would order fried scampi all the same. But she always ate very little, and she rarely touched meat.

'I could live entirely on fruit and vegetables,' she often said.

'You could not, my pet.'

'Yes, I could, and perhaps yogurt and rice pudding and cucumber sandwiches and tomato sandwiches and a little smoked salmon and other fish and old-fashioned cherry cake and treacle tart.'

In the last year before she became ill when some young friends of ours invited us to Claridge's from time to time, she discovered caviar. 'I must say, I like it,' she admitted, 'but I could do without it.' She could do without so much, not only in food and drink (she loved cider because it reminded her of her schooldays in Devonshire) but in most other things which people consider essential for their well-being. 'I know in one of my more recent incarnations I was a nun in a French convent; ever since I have attached no importance to material possessions.' Surrounded as we were by relations, friends and acquaintances most of whom were well off or rich, had beautiful houses, estates, antique furniture, silver, pictures, jewels; went to the opera, travelled and had and did all the other things which people of financial ease take for granted, she was free of all envy.

Now her material needs were reduced to a few articles such as dusting powder, face flannels, toothpaste, soap which had to be renewed from time to time; to some lavender toilet water, her comb (which she could no longer use herself) and to the sad paraphernalia of the sick room. Very soon, too, she would not be able to eat any solid food but only liquids which she had to take through a glass tube and a few spoonfuls of yogurt or slippery elm which the nurses or I fed her with a spoon.

One day, earlier in March, she said to me: 'Sister and I have had a talk and we decided that the little tomato sandwiches I sometimes have for tea are really rather boring. So, what I would like to have, if you can get it for me without too much trouble, are those cinnamon stars which we sometimes buy for Christmas and some old-fashioned cherry cake which you can buy at Beaton's shop in Chelsea. I know they bake it themselves. It would make my teas more interesting; also Sister would love it; she, like myself, is fond of old-fashioned things.'

I bought the cherry cake (there were no cinnamon stars to be had in March) and wrapped it up in tin foil and brought it to the nursing home. She had a small slice of it and her nurse had another.

Seven

Dr. R. came every day, sometimes twice, sometimes with his assistant, Dr. M., a pleasant, serious young man who like a boy trying to catch the rays of an uncertain sun with a mirror, eagerly reflected the slightest glimmer of hope in the darkening scene. Often the doctors would spend over half an hour with Diana while I waited outside smoking endless cigarettes.

Every day at certain hours she was given certain drugs, pills and capsules of various colours, shapes and sizes. Most of them, in the early weeks, were mild pain-killers and sedatives. But there were also a few more powerful drugs designed to prevent sickness and deal with other distressing symptoms. Maximum doses were prescribed beyond which the nurses were not allowed to go without special permission. But the time had now come when most of the drugs were beginning to lose their effectiveness (Diana began to ask for extra pills to be given at times not prescribed for them) and had to be replaced by more powerful and, no doubt, more dangerous ones.

Every day around six o'clock in the evening the nurse in charge brought a small number of perspex containers from the dispensary and put them down on the table just outside Diana's room. Each container had a tag bearing the number of the respective room and patient. The number of pills in the container destined for Diana's room seemed to be increasing from day to day. At one time I counted twelve, some small, some large, some very large ones. It became more and more difficult for her to swallow them and instinctively she was beginning to feel that they were of very little use.

'Now, what are these?' she would say, looking into the container. 'Oh, yes,' she would continue, 'these seem to be the usual ones, the green and blue ones; I know. And this, the longish red capsule? I suppose this is good for something or other. But what is this, this must be new; it's terribly large, I doubt if I can swallow it at all. Must I have it? All right, I'll try, as long as you promise that you won't give me any more cortisone.' They had tried cortisone for a few days, with quite disastrous results. Instead of alleviating her pains in the head and along the spine, it made them much worse and induced something akin to brain storms and hallucinations. She had firmly declared that she would take no more cortisone.

Not long after that came the time when she could not clearly see the pills any more and refused the lot. 'I have had enough of it all; I cannot see them, I cannot swallow them, and they don't help. Take them away.'

By now I had become a familiar figure in the nursing home. I knew most of the nurses, the cleaners, the visiting doctors, and I began to know by sight some of the patients and follow their progress. I saw people being brought in, wheeled to and from the operating theatre, taking their first faltering steps along the corridor and leaving in various states of recovery. I knew by the way the nurses and doctors entered the various rooms, which were the serious and which the less serious cases. More than once was I asked to witness the signature on a Will. I almost lived with the general routine of the nursing home, the daily menus, the moods

153

and idiosyncrasies even of unseen patients and the nurses' reactions to them.

Frequently, when I felt very dejected, I would go into the Floor Sister's office for a brief chat with whoever was there at the moment. I began to sense the growing concern of the staff for the beautiful gentle princess in room No. 116; a patient unlike any they had known before.

I also experienced their compassion for me. Often one of the nurses would stop me in the corridor and would say to me: 'Is there anything we can do for you?' Or: 'We know how you must feel; we know how we feel, we all love her.'

I came to admire and respect these girls in their exacting work. They were mostly young and some were attractive, even beautiful. Whatever the circumstances and motives that may have prompted each one to take up nursing in preference to another career or job, I came to the conclusion that all these girls had certain traits in common: a greater and more active awareness of the inner realities of life (into which belong suffering and death), a greater capacity for experience and the desire to serve others regardless of material rewards.

Having observed these girls at work, having listened to their conversations among themselves, spoken to many, I think I can sum up those traits which distinguish them in a body from say, the secretaries, office workers and many young professionals of similar social background, as the expression of an attitude to life still founded in religion. With some of the girls it was quite explicitly so.

As I sat outside Diana's room I could hear her voice as she told the doctors of the day's and of the night's happenings and tribulations. She still had a complete grasp on everything. Her precise and methodical mind marshalled and presented the facts clearly and in proper sequence and distinguishing between those aspects that were essential and those that were incidental. On the basis of the facts she developed her arguments and proceeded to the conclusions. Never have the symptoms and the progression of

154

an illness been more intelligently and illuminatingly expounded. The doctors should be grateful to her for her valuable contribution to the symptomatology of the disease. Mercifully for her, for the doctors and for myself, neither she nor they nor I knew up to that time (the first week in March) what caused the symptoms which she described with such accuracy and mastery of detail. We were all still caught up in the illusion that hers was a case of an unusual and unusually severe post-radiation sickness which presented the picture of acute meningism. 'If only we knew of another similar case,' Dr. R. said to me one afternoon. 'As it is, we have nothing to go by, nothing to guide us.'

We all searched for a similar case. There was one. I had known of it for quite some time but I had not up to now mentioned it to Dr. R., probably because I was afraid he might demolish the argument for the similarity too quickly. A woman, much older than Diana, of whom I knew through a business friend, had undergone the same radiation treatment at about the same time and had developed similar symptoms some weeks after the end of the treatment. Her doctors could find no evidence of secondary cancer.

I had kept in touch with my friend who regularly reported to me on the condition of Mrs. X. At first I had derived real comfort from what he told me. Mrs. X. had speech disturbances, violent headaches, numbness of the hands and had been quite unable to walk. But her condition improved, and by now it had become stationary. There was every hope, so Mrs. X.'s doctors had told her husband, that she would be completely restored to normal health. But as I told Dr. R. I myself began to be sceptical. Maybe I had not been told the full story; maybe also Mrs. X.'s doctors had not told the full truth to her husband, maybe they also did not know.

An even greater thought occurred to me: maybe the two cases were in fact identical, but the conclusion to be derived from this had to be the very opposite of what I had hoped. What if Mrs. X. was as gravely ill as Diana, but being much older the progression

155

of the disease was much slower in her case?* Finally, Diana's condition was not stationary.

Dr. R. shared my misgivings. I then contacted one of the greatest experts in the field of radiotherapy who after listening carefully to my detailed account expressed the view that radiation damage could not directly be responsible for these symptoms. However, he agreed that radiation might indirectly set in train some other pathological processes. He also promised to study the case and to look up some of his own case histories and consult the latest literature on the subject. We had reached the point where the expert was as baffled as the layman.

Thus hope alternated with despair. But looking back I know hope was like a thin layer of surface soil, from which springs, from time to time, a fragile flower, but that underneath there was the solid impenetrable rock of despair. Hope, as I knew all the time, was the hope for some miraculous intervention; despair was based on the sheer logic of events. And in between hope and despair there were these merciful interludes of euphoria: 'Of course she will be well again.'

In the end, when the last rational foothold to which hope might cling had crumbled and we stared into the abyss, illusion still persisted.

'What do we do now?' I put this question to Dr. R. one afternoon as he came out of Diana's room looking particularly distressed.

He, in turn, asked me: 'What do you suggest, I am open to any suggestion.'

Perhaps, I suggested, we could call in yet another neurologist. There was one name that had kept recurring for some time: Dr. K. Two or three friends had mentioned him, and I had heard recently that Mrs. X.'s doctors were also thinking of calling him in.

But why call Dr. K.? We had the considered opinion of Dr. B., equally famous, who had examined Diana and had found 'no neurological lesion'. And there had been the Consultant Physician,

* The woman died three months after Diana.

156

Dr. D., who only a fortnight ago had ordered that second series of elaborate X-ray tests which again had shown nothing abnormal and who had quite explicitly stated that there was nothing in the clinical picture that pointed to a secondary cancer. But her condition belied the findings of the clinical tests.

'Please get in touch with K.,' I told Dr. R. At that moment I knew I was taking a step which I had so far dreaded to take. I knew that this time we would obtain an answer, and I was almost certain what it would be.

Eight

Dr. K. arranged for Diana to be taken to the Middlesex Hospital where a series of tests was to be carried out, one known as the E.E.C. (electro-encephalogram), and the other a brain-scanning test. The latter consisted of injecting radioactive isotopes into the bloodstream and tracking their progress through the body with the help of Geiger counters. If they encounter obstructions they accumulate and bunch up, and this makes it possible to locate the position and size of tumours within the tissues. I believe, once the main points of obstruction have been established with the help of Geiger counters, X-ray pictures are taken which show up the pattern formed by the radio-active particles around the obstructions. This makes it possible to arrive at a diagnosis.

I am not absolutely certain if my description is quite correct, but I did not have the heart to enquire into all the details; but, by and large, I think this is what happens. These tests were made at the Middlesex Hospital in the department which bore the sinister name, 'Department of Nuclear Medicine'. The date for the tests was Wednesday, the 8th of March.

An ambulance took Diana from the nursing home to the hospital. The journey, though short, proved a terrible ordeal. She

157

was sick all the way, and the jolting of the ambulance gave her excruciating pains. She wore dark glasses to protect herself from what was to her an intolerable glare: the greyish light of a dull March day.

I had wanted to accompany her, but when I arrived at the nursing home at eleven o'clock, as arranged, I found that the ambulance had arrived an hour too soon and that she was already at the Middlesex. The Floor Sister told me I could go to the hospital at about 12.30 when the first test would have been completed.

It took me a considerable time to find her. In the best of circumstances it has never been easy for me to find my way about in large public buildings. In a huge hospital with its many departments, endless corridors, signs and arrows, steps up and steps down, swing doors, doors marked 'No Entry' and the general confusion of visitors, patients in wheelchairs moving in all directions; of nurses, porters, doctors, messengers, I was absolutely sure to go wrong. Information and directives, reluctantly sought by me and freely given by officials and people wandering about equally lost as myself, did not quickly yield the desired results.

Finally I was directed to the Casualty Department which I entered with my heartbeat pounding in my temples. There in a small cubicle I found Diana lying huddled up and covered by blankets, on a trolley. The special nurse whom we had engaged to accompany her sat beside her, with a cup of tea.

Diana had been here for a considerable time. She seemed only half awake. 'I had to give her another injection against sickness only half an hour ago,' the nurse explained.

I said: 'Hullo, darling, how is it?'

She answered: 'Hullo, Mr. P., I am sorry, I must look terrible; I have been sick so many times, and I haven't brought my comb to do my hair.' And then she added: 'I assure you, Mr. P., this is no picnic . . .'

Two porters came in to take her to the 'Department of Nuclear Medicine' for the next two series of tests. At once she took command of the situation. 'Before they wheel me out,' she said to the

158

nurse, 'turn me over on my back; it will be more comfortable; also the way I am lying now, my knees stick out over the edge of the trolley and I would bump them against the frame of the door.' It was quite true; the door was very narrow, there was just enough space for the trolley to get through. What amazed me was that she should have noticed it on being wheeled in and have remembered it now two hours later. As the porters were about to move the trolley she gave her final instructions: 'Nurse, please give me my dark spectacles; I think they are on the chair, and put the bowl within reach, in case I should be sick—I don't think I shall, but just in case.' She turned to me and smiled: 'See you later, darling.' Then, with utmost care and gentleness the two big men wheeled the trolley out.

I followed, but the little group disappeared behind a corner. A moment later, however, as I crossed the central hall, I saw her again. She was lying on her back in her pink dressing gown, the blankets covering her up to her chest. Her hair was open framing her pale face. She wore her dark glasses which hid much of her features, but her lips on which someone had put a touch of lipstick (for she could no longer do this herself) were as full and as delicately curved as ever. I kissed her, and then they wheeled her into the lift. I made my way back through the anonymous milling crowds. One more reminder that we were nearing the point in our journey where our ways would part. Already she lived in this strange and remote world of the sick.

She was then taken back to the nursing home in the late afternoon and put under sedation.

That evening I dined with friends, and during dinner the phone rang. It was Dr. R. It gave me a shock, but he merely wanted to tell me that he had seen Diana and that she was quite comfortable. I asked him when the results of the tests would be known. 'Perhaps by tomorrow evening,' he answered and added, 'Don't worry, enjoy your dinner.'

'Perhaps,' I thought, 'she is all right after all . . .' A short-lived euphoric fantasy.

The next day Diana described the ordeal, of which she could

not remember many details, with great good humour and detachment. She even repeated some little jokes which had passed between her and the doctors who had all been very kind and considerate to her. I heard later, how, racked with pain and frequently overcome by sickness, she had co-operated in the tests and never for one moment had lost her composure and dignity.

'It was not very pleasant,' she said to me, 'when during that strange test in the afternoon they wanted me to turn over on my tummy and I was sick immediately. I apologized, I could not help it . . .'

On Friday, the 10th of March, I spent most of the afternoon with her. I helped her as usual over her dinner consisting of a cup of consommé, a little stewed fruit and yogurt. Then once again we went through the elaborate procedure of changing her into her cotton pyjamas and preparing her for the night. But contrary to her usual attitude, this time she did not want me to leave; 'Stay a little longer with me, Mr. P., unless you must go; let's have a talk.' We talked for a while but then the nurse came with the sleeping tablets and a number of other pills of different shapes and colours. This was the moment for me to leave. 'Good night, Mr. P.,' she said, 'and thank you for staying so long. It has been a very nice evening.'

As I passed the Floor Sister's office I was given a message from Dr. R. asking me to come to the nursing home the next morning at 9:30 when Dr. K. would meet me to discuss the situation with me. I knew then that the results of the tests had reached the doctors and I also knew that they would be bad. Had they been satisfactory Dr. R. would have given me the news at once. But he had not even come to the nursing home, nor had he telephoned during the day.

The next day was Saturday, the 11th of March. I felt I could not face the coming ordeal alone. Rosemary had gone away for the week-end; close friends were also away; my son and daughter-in-law were in Egypt. Finally I found a woman friend whom we had not known for very long but who had taken a great liking to Diana. She at once agreed to accompany me.

We arrived at the appointed hour and had only waited a few minutes in the entrance hall when we saw Dr. K. followed by Dr. R. come down from the first floor. Dr. K., a tall, big man, looked impassive; Dr. R. when introducing us avoided my eyes.

We were shown into an unoccupied room on the ground floor. Joan* sat down on the only available chair. Dr. R., still avoiding my eyes, placed himself on the low wide windowsill in the bay window. I sat on the bed, and Dr. K., holding some papers, remained standing.

The moment of truth had come.

Dr. K. broke the silence. Without preliminaries he said: 'As you may already have suspected, this is a grim picture. There are at least three tumours in the brain and secondary deposits in the tissues right down the whole of the spinal column.'

Dr. R., now for the first time, looked at me. Tears were running down his cheeks. We had all hoped together. He, the doctor, had hoped until quite recently that the illness would, after all, turn out to be benign. Had not all the tests pointed to it? I had hoped too, but I had hoped for the miracle. In truth, I think, he also had been hoping for just that. I could not cry, I could not speak. The doctors, Joan, the room itself, all looked infinitely small and far away. For a brief moment I felt I was not present. The room and the people in it had vanished. I, too, had vanished.

I knew that this particular sensation was sometimes a symptom of an acute psychotic disturbance: rejection of reality. After a few seconds I returned from my mental fugue and said: 'Is there no hope, Dr. K.?'

'I am afraid there is none.'

'So what can we do now?'

'Do you mean,' answered Dr. K., 'what can we do to prolong life or to reduce suffering?'

'Both,' I said.

* Joan Woods.

'An operation might achieve both ends.'

Before he had finished the sentence I had already rejected the idea. And so I passed on to my next question: 'How long could she live without an operation?'

'Difficult to say; perhaps one month, perhaps even two or three.'

'And with an operation?'

'If the operation is successful,' he answered after a pause, 'it might prolong life for perhaps another year.'

'Under what conditions?' I asked.

He made a gesture as if to say: 'Don't ask such questions.'

I pursued my examination and said: 'What is the operation you had in mind?'

'I propose that both ovaries should be removed.'

There, for the first time the fatal link between the condition which necessitated the hysterectomy the year before and the subsequent cancer of the breast was openly mentioned.

At the time of that first operation I had been surprised to learn from the surgeon that the ovaries had not been removed, not even partially. Diana had expected it because she had suffered such frequent discomfort and often pain in the region of the right ovary and I, thinking of the general imbalance in her menstrual cycles, had felt that it would be done. The surgeon, however, had explained that there had been no need to remove the ovaries. They were perfectly healthy. 'Everything as clean as a whistle,' as he put it. But he had removed the appendix 'whilst he was about it'; it had been awkwardly placed and it had been quite a job to dig it out.

I said to Dr. K.: 'Why then were the ovaries not removed a year ago?'

'You appreciate,' he answered, 'I knew nothing of this until I was called in on the case and you may be right in hindsight, but it would be bad gynaecological practice to remove perfectly sound ovaries.'

'Why?' I asked.

'It might have brought about a catastrophic "change of life". . .'

'Even if only one had been removed?' I persisted.

162

'Not if only one had been removed.'

'Why then do you now at this late hour suggest the removal of the ovaries?'

'Because the removal will inhibit or slow up the further spread of the cancer.'

'In other words what you are saying'—I was determined to press home the point—'what you are saying is that there is a link between the over-production of female hormones, which once the womb has been removed have no natural outlet, on the one hand, and the cancer of the breast on the other; is this not so?'

'It would appear to be so,' he answered, 'however this does not mean that the hormones cause the cancer.'

'This I understand,' I replied, 'but if there is a link at all, why was the operation not done at the time, even at the risk of a catastrophic change of life; would that not have been preferable to what we are facing now; would not anything have been preferable to this?'

'I can only repeat,' said Dr. K., 'that you may be right, speaking from hindsight; again you may be wrong. I am merely giving my views as to what should be done now.'

My suspicions that Diana had for years suffered from a hormonal imbalance, a suspicion which I had ever since I had seen a link between the findings on 'Nasal Reflex Neurosis' published by Freud and Fliess in 1897 and Diana's peculiar menstrual troubles, were now clearly shown to have been justified.

I cannot judge whether timely removal of the ovaries would in fact have made a difference to the course of events, for if, as many research workers and specialists believe, cancer—any form of cancer—is due to a virus, the hormone theory must fall to the ground, except in so far as hormone imbalance may favour the sinister work of the virus or inhibit the counterforces, the antibodies.

But I still hope now as I did on that fateful Saturday, the 11th of March, that no element of neglect or lack of vision or overall grasp of the situation on the part of the doctors, had contributed to the fateful turn of the disease. The thought—might she be alive today if only this or that had been done in time?—is too terrible for me to contemplate.

If the thought of the hormone imbalance had been at the back of my mind even at the time of the first operation, it had become a very definite and explicit worry after her second operation and the beginning of the radiation treatment. We both wanted to know what steps should be taken to prevent a repetition of the process that had led to the cancer after the local treatment had come to an end or even while the local treatment was being carried out. More than once Diana said to me: 'What is the good of curing the present cancer if the root cause, the basic condition which led to it, is not also eliminated?' But every attempt to come to grips over this problem with the doctors failed. Each time Diana broached the subject, the doctors would discourage her from pursuing it.

'Well, I think we need not go into this just now,' Dr. L., the radiologist would say. 'What we are concerned with is to cure the present condition and in this we are doing very well. We can leave all these other questions until later. Meanwhile it is best for you not to worry your head too much over such hypothetical questions.'

But the later opportunity never came. Twice a week Dr. L. saw his private patients at the hospital to examine their general condition and satisfy himself on the progress of the treatment. He worked under great pressure. Nurses kept coming and going; messages were handed in; patients buttonholed him, and frequently he would be called to the house telephone to answer some urgent query. However hard he tried, he was always behind schedule.

Diana, who was very methodical in all things and looked at her own illness with almost scientific objectivity, had prepared three large sheets of notes in which she gave a complete medical history of herself and a full description of the symptoms and general changes in her health which had led up to her present illness. The account was headed: 'Notes for Dr. L.' I am certain that this comprehensive and lucid exposition would have been

164

useful to any of the doctors concerned with her case, for it showed that there was a general background of ill health and a significant link between the particular condition from which she had suffered for a considerable time and the cancer.

I remember that towards the end of the radiation treatment Diana said to me: 'The only thing to do if Dr. L. refuses to discuss things with me, is to write it all down and send it to him. Then he must read it.'

But he never saw the notes intended for him, and I only found them after her death.

I reproach myself for not having insisted more strongly on a special interview with Dr. L. However, I doubt if it would have produced the desired results. English doctors in general and specialists in particular do not encourage their patients to take too close an interest in their own case or to have any views of their own on the illness or the manner of treatment. They know that the vast majority of their patients lack any insight into their own condition and are quite content to think that the doctor knows what is best, and this they feel is as it should be.

In a general sense and from a statistical point of view this attitude is probably justified: the patient is ill, and that is on the whole all the patient knows or suspects; the doctors know more; it is his business to know more and to act accordingly.

But it is not always so. I have found over and over again that when a condition or illness does not conform to an established and clearly definable pattern the doctor soon begins to guess and surmise. In this age of specialization in medicine there are few great diagnosticians left. Intelligent co-operation on the part of intelligent patients who are able to think for themselves ought therefore to be welcome to doctors and they should encourage it. But very few do.

Dr. L. certainly did not; he did his part of the job to perfection; the rest, as he himself said to me, 'was not his province', and therefore he never had wished to know more than the barest facts of the case.

The only one among the doctors who really listened to what

165

Diana had to say, listened attentively and later spellbound, was our own private physician, Dr. R. He had known Diana for some years, but it was only during her illness that he began to realize that this beautiful, delicate and sensitive young woman also had a powerful, precise and well-disciplined intellect which could never be fobbed off by half-truths or generalities. He listened with ever growing admiration bordering on awe as she, almost to the last week of her life, kept an iron control over her fast dwindling mental powers, always trying to understand what was happening, trying to give the doctors any bit of information which she thought they ought to have, trying even to make suggestions—often absolutely sound in themselves, had the illness been anything else but cancer of the brain—on problems of nursing, the giving of drugs and injections, sleeping hours and matters of hospital routine which needed improving.

But, alas, all our combined brain power, the careful nursing, the doctors' professional skill and experience, all this could not, in the words of one of the doctors, 'avert the inevitable'; not in the present state of medical knowledge, both as regards the cause and the treatment of cancer.

Some weeks after Diana's death, Mr. P. G., her surgeon, wrote to me: 'It is such a tragedy that this can happen for no apparent reason; perhaps one day we shall know the answer. . . .'

When Dr. K. had finished I said: 'Is there an alternative to the operation?'

'There is, but it may not take effect so quickly: injections of male hormones.' This treatment had been tentatively suggested once or twice before by Dr. R., but each time he had dismissed the idea on the ground that the possible beneficial results might be outweighed by certain unpleasant side effects; in particular it would play havoc with her complexion and change her facial features, at a time when she was still conscious of her appearance. At this late stage, however, if the injections could help to alleviate her suffering—I did not think that they had any chance of pro-longing her life—considerations of an aesthetic or psychological

166

kind could no longer stand in the way. But I was determined that there should be no operation. Even if she were to come through, and this I doubted, for her strength was ebbing fast, she would have to suffer all the post-operative pains and discomforts on top of the never-ceasing pains and discomforts caused by the illness itself.

She was utterly helpless; she was perplexed and unable to make any decisions. She would be frightened; she would (rightly) feel that something terrible was being done to her which she could not understand and had no power to prevent. It would be an outrage against the sanctity of the personality, and an outrage too against her poor afflicted body. I could not bear the thought of this renewed psychic assault and physical mutilation, just in order to satisfy Medicine at its wit's end, that all had been done that could be done—yet knowing that it would be of no avail.

They were known as 'heroic operations', these desperate attempts to gain a short respite from the inevitable outcome. In the case of advanced cancer of the brain, the removal of the ovaries was sometimes followed by the removal of the adrenal glands and ultimately by excision of the pituitary gland or its destruction by radioactive needles.

She had suffered so much, and she would suffer more: not only physical pains but mental anguish and distress. Let everything be done to reduce her suffering, but as she was to die, let everything be done to uphold her human dignity, and this included the dignity of her body. Let her die with all the comforts that love and spiritual ministration can give to her soul and care, gentleness, delicacy and respect to her body, for her body is her incarnate presence on earth. No more operations. Let her die in dignity and in beauty.

'Under no circumstances will I give my consent to a further operation,' I said to Dr. K.

Dr. R., who had been anxiously watching me, nodded his approval. 'You were right,' he said to me later.

'As you wish,' said Dr. K. 'I will discuss the matter of the injections with Dr. R.' At this our sad little group dispersed. On

167

taking leave Dr. K., shaking my hand, said: 'It has been a pleasure to . . .', but quickly realizing the inappropriateness of these words, corrected himself: 'I wish we had met under less tragic circumstances.'

This was Saturday, the 11th of March. She had exactly three more weeks to live.

After the doctors had gone I went to see Diana. To my surprise I was completely composed. Time and space seemed to play strange tricks on me. What had just happened on the floor below seemed infinitely remote and not connected with her.

She brought me back to reality.

'I have really had enough of all these tests,' she said, 'what did Dr. K. tell you?'

'The tests at the Middlesex proved that you are suffering from the very severe after effects of the radiation treatment. Now that they know, you will be given new medicines . . .'

'None of these pills I have had so far seem to do any good, let's hope they know what they are doing. There are moments when I think I shall never come out of this place alive . . . I am certainly not getting any better.'

'You will, my love.'

'Do you really think so, Mr. P.?'

'Of course, I do.'

Nine

The following Monday, March the 13th, was my birthday.

Undimmed by the passage of time and the cares of life, my delight in Christmas, in birthdays and other festive occasions of giving and receiving, shines as brightly today as in those distant days of childhood when the candles on the birthday cake or on the tree, the gold and silver stars, the chains of tinsel, the Christmas angels sparkling in their insubstantial fabric, the coloured wrapping papers and ribbons, the wishes (whether fulfilled or not), the surprises and the sense of mystery, were part of the central reality of life.

These irrational delights are perhaps amongst those 'childish' things which St. Paul enjoins us to 'put away' when we become men, and many people do in fact put them away—to their great and irreparable loss. The gift of understanding 'as a child' is most precious; it opens the doors to the treasure house of the soul in which are stored the wonders of the universe. From the tinsel glittering in candlelight to the stained glass windows of the great cathedrals, all things that evoke in us that sense of the extraordinary are symbols of those wonders and mysteries which reason does not comprehend, but are the very stuff which we are made of.

Diana had never known the joys of Christmas and of birthdays. Christmas was altogether ignored in her parental home, except for a Christmas dinner bare of all significance. Birthdays were disposed of by small useful presents and later by cheques just sufficient to buy a small useful present.

Her sisters had all adopted the same rational, disenchanted view. But Diana had retained the gift of understanding the world 'as a child'. Nothing was commonplace to her, and what was commonplace she transmuted, as I have said, into the exceptional by a process of spiritual alchemy. Christmas and birthdays for her, though they lacked that dimension of meaning which can only come from childhood memories, quite early on in our married life gained a special significance as days of love and dedication. Their extraordinariness and regular recurrence became symbols, at once of the uniqueness of our relationship and the constant renewal of this relationship in our journey through life. As the years went by and those 'behind' us grew in number and those 'before' seemed to diminish, these special days became milestones as well as centres of recollection to which we would cast back our mind: points in time that had not been lost.

When the 13th of March 1967 came, 'Mr. P.'s birthday', according to that final solitary entry in her pocket diary, I knew it would be the last she would experience and that for me it would be the day on which I would receive her very last present.

A few days before, when as usual, I opened her letters, I came across a bulky envelope. I opened it. I wish I had not done so. She could not turn her head, but she noticed my sudden hesitation.

'What is it, Mr. P.?'

'Something came for you,' I said, 'something private. Take it and put it in your drawer.' It was the present for me which, unbeknown to me, she had asked Rosemary to buy for her. As I handed her the envelope, she showed distress. 'Don't upset yourself, my angel,' I said, 'I have not looked at it.'

When on Monday morning I came into her room, she groped for a moment in her drawer (her vision was beginning to fail) and then handed me the present.

'Here, darling, is a present for your birthday; it is only a tiny present. It would have been difficult for me to get anything else, and you will forgive that it is not nicely wrapped up and that there is no little card. But you know I cannot write, and cannot see very well. But you also know how much I love you and that my one wish in life is to make you happy.'

The present she gave me was a tablet of *Roger Gallet* toilet soap: *Oeillet Mignardise*. It still fills the drawer of what was her dressing-table with its strong scent.

I did not keep a diary during the first four weeks when Diana was at the nursing home; I could not write while I was with her, and on coming home in the evening I was too tired to put pen to paper. I made the first entry on Saturday, the 11th of March, and from then on I made brief entries every day.

The events and reflections recorded under the consecutive dates that follow are linked to these dates, for this is how I recalled them later. The dates, however, are merely vantage points from which the events leading up to them are reviewed, fountainheads also, where the feelings and reflections that belong to the events emerge from the depth of the heart into the light of consciousness.

This book was not written as a biography in strict chronological sequence. It was composed rather, like a symphony in main themes and their variations. This is the reason why certain events are referred to more than once: they are variations of a theme.

This applies especially to the last part of the story, when, as I put it earlier on in a different context, the main themes are gathered up and move towards their climax and final resolution.

Ten

March 14th. The doctors having admitted their impotence in the face of what they now called the 'inevitable'; having admitted also that they had not the faintest idea of how long she might live, the question arose whether it might be possible to bring her home. 'If we had round the clock nursing,' I asked Dr. R., 'do you think she could come home?'

He said he saw no reason why this should not be possible. He warned me, however, that if the illness were to take a rapid turn for the worse, it might not be easy to get her back into the nursing home. Not even the most expensive private nursing homes—and this was one of them—liked to admit the dying.

The problem of how to meet the ever-mounting costs began to loom before me. The weekly bill was never less than a hundred pounds, and in addition there were the pathology tests, the X-rays, the outside consultants, private nursing, drugs and extras which brought the weekly expenditure to nearly £150. Of this my insurance would reimburse about one-third.

However, there were certain limits to the insurance benefits; partly they had been reached already. Moreover, the benefits payable on the basic cost of the room were restricted to thirteen weeks a year. What would happen after that? My business venture was not paying yet. Financial help could not be expected from anywhere.

Yet all this did not seem to matter. I felt that somehow the financial problems would sort themselves out. My one thought was to be with her as much as possible and for her to know that I was with her. This was of course not possible in the nursing home. I spoke to her about it: 'Darling, Dr. R. thinks it may be possible for you to go home in about two weeks' time. What do you think about it?' I said it in the cheerful voice of one who brings good news.

She appeared puzzled and not quite able to grasp the idea. 'Do you think I will be well enough by then?' she asked. She continued: 'I discussed the idea the other night with my night nurse—she is such a nice girl; you ought to meet her—I asked her if she would come to me as a day nurse when I go home because I thought I would need a nurse for some time, and she immediately agreed.'

'Of course, my darling, we shall ask her to come,' I replied, 'as soon as you go home; in fact you will need a day nurse and a night nurse for quite a while.'

She did not answer for several minutes; she was pursuing her own thoughts. Then, disregarding what I had just told her, she said: 'In fact I made her promise to stay with me until the end; she promised she would . . .'

This startled me. I asked: 'What do you mean by that?'

'Nothing special, Mr. P., I mean she promised to stay with me until the end of the illness.'

Whatever she may have meant, it was obvious to me that she was still sufficiently aware of her condition to realize that she could not face the change from the established hospital routine to the uncertainties and possible responsibilities of being ill at home. She also understood that this would impose new and terrible strains on me. Also she was beginning to realize that her sight was rapidly deteriorating. 'I'll think about it,' she concluded

172

the conversation, 'but what good is it if I am at home and cannot see?'

(I could not say to her what I wanted to say: 'Even if you were to go blind, my love, it would make no difference; I would love you all the more—if only you would live.')

I soon realized, what I had of course known all the time, that it would have been impossible to bring her home, even had the progression of the illness been less rapid. It was not the kind of illness in which life gently ebbs away over a period of months. It was an illness unpredictable in everything except for the outcome: violent, brutal in its onslaughts one moment, deceptively quiet, working by stealth, the next. But always restless.

But she was not weakened by age, her body ready to die. She was still young, and, strange to say, healthy. Her heart, the doctors told me, her lungs, all the vital organs were unimpaired, refusing the order to surrender, unwilling to die, resisting to the uttermost.

And so, as the illness gathered momentum towards the 'inevitable' outcome, it became a fierce struggle between the forces of death and life. She had to be where doctors were available day and night and the whole armoury of modern medicine: the drugs, the injections, the oxygen, the artificial aids to failing physical functions, which though they cannot save life, can alleviate pain, suffering and mental distress.

When she went into hospital for her first operation in May 1966, flowers arrived the very first day; indeed were there to greet her, and the following two or three days huge bunches of spring flowers, of roses and carnations of all colours arrived. Also potted plants and most elaborate arrangements in bowls, baskets and trays covered with moss; complete miniature rock gardens which carried instructions on how to tend them. The gifts were accompanied by the usual messages such as people send to patients whose recovery is certain.

The average time people spend in hospital after a not too

173

serious operation is from two to three weeks. Relatives and friends send flowers usually only once (and usually the day after the operation). By the time the patient leaves most of the cut flowers have gone or what is left of them has been re-distributed in fewer vases. The potted plants last longer and present a problem.

During the seven weeks of Diana's last illness I often watched the awkward procedure of taking home potted plants that were still flowering, though no longer looking their best. When Diana left the hospital two weeks after the first operation we decided to leave the potted plants and miniature gardens behind. They had done their job.

It was all quite different when she had to enter the nursing home on that Saturday, the 11th February 1967. No one, at first, knew of it. Few friends knew the exact nature of her illness and those who understood that she was gravely ill were hesitant at first to send flowers. What was the message to be? But after a few days the flowers began to arrive; the little cards pinned to them expressed hope and love, but also anxiety. Again Diana read the messages (soon, however, it would be I who would have to read them to her), but this time she could not write the message of thanks. She could not sit up; her eyes had become too sensitive to light, and the room was darkened. Writing itself soon became impossible. She put the cards into a tray: 'We must make a note of them all, so that we can answer them when I come out.' Later she said: 'Mr. P., have you thanked everybody who has sent these beautiful flowers? I shall not be able to do it myself.'

This time friends sent flowers more than once. As some faded—and they faded rapidly in that overheated room—new ones took their place. But there was a pause towards the beginning of the third week; the week patients normally go back home. About the same time Diana began to take a little less interest in flowers: 'I don't really see them properly. I have my eyes shut practically all the time, and when I open them, you know how short-sighted I am.' I put some of the most beautiful flowers and plants on the table closest to her so that she could see them more clearly. She looked at them, spoke lovingly to them, but seemed a little

174

unhappy over some strongly scented plants; hyacinths for instance. 'They make my headache worse.' Also she found it increasingly difficult to turn her head. 'Tell people not to send flowers,' she said.

'But people want to send you flowers, darling,' I said. And flowers arrived again.

The cards attached to them did not speak of immediate recovery. They were messages of love and concern. She began to hand them to me. 'What does it say, Mr. P.? It is difficult for me. Describe these flowers to me.' Her vision had began to fail.

I have never known the names of certain species of flowers or flowering shrubs. As with so many other things I experienced and enjoyed them through her. She knew them all. She knew where and when they flowered, their habits, their variations, their botanical names, the exact shape and structure of every petal, leaf or grass. There was no need for me to know. In her parents' house in the country there had been a conservatory enclosing two sides of the building. As a young girl before and during the war she had helped her mother in tending the flowers, transplanting them, pruning them, watering them.

And then there were the wild flowers in Devonshire where she had been at school. She often spoke of them and it had been one of her most ardent wishes to revisit that school where, at the age of thirteen, lacking love and affection at home, she had experienced a sense of liberation which released the springs of her generous and romantic nature.

In Devonshire amidst the wild flowers, the farm animals, the fields, the woods, she discovered and developed her profound communion with nature. This was to become one of the main sources from which she drew her inner strength for the whole of her life. Whatever the difficulties, adversities and worries which beset us, her communion with nature enabled her to operate from an inner centre of stillness and harmony and to distinguish with unfailing clarity true values from those that were false, artificial or shallow. Nothing could ever cloud or sway her judgement.

This unerring sense of quality and of what was fitting in all situations of life became one of her most outstanding characteristics. The *geste essentiel* to which I have already referred, which she applied to whatever she did, sprang from the same inner certainty.

But if her judgement was unclouded and her sense of values uncompromising, she never criticized others or tried to convert them to her views. Her integrity of mind was tempered by true compassion and a love for all living things. She loved people, and no one could resist her love. She loved animals, and they responded to her. I was amazed at her fearlessness which seemed in such contrast to her delicate physique. She would go to any horse, however frisky, stroke it, pat its head, even put her face against its face.

I would watch these moments with apprehension and would keep my distance. 'Be careful,' I would urge, 'how do you know it is not suddenly going to jerk its head or bite you; horses do such things.' She would answer laughingly, assuring me that there was no danger and would caress the horse all the more tenderly.

Any dog, however fierce looking or furiously barking would, when she approached lovingly and unhesitatingly, submit to her at once.

She spoke to cows and heifers, blowing air down their nostrils; they seemed to enjoy this, for once she had started, more and more beasts would come around her, eager to take part in this strange ritual. I feel sure that she would have had the same power over wild animals. Had she been a Christian in the days of Diocletian, the lions and tigers in the arena, instead of tearing her to pieces, would have lain down by her side.

(My own relations with animals, especially with dogs, have always been formal and cool, and they in turn ignored me. After Diana's death it happened more than once at the house of friends that dogs that had hitherto taken no notice of me, would greet me with demonstrative joy and friendliness; almost as though they had seen her in me or through me.)

To her there was nothing that was inanimate in the whole of creation. She loved flowers in the mystical way of a St. Francis.

They were little sisters to her; she spoke to them, she understood them. They spoke to her. A woman friend wrote to me after Diana's death: 'She had so much to give, that rare quality of universal love seemed to shine from her towards every form of life. I remember going round the garden with her and saw she picked out for tender admiration not the prosperous protected flowers, but the wild ones and the tiny leaf-hidden weeds. For me this will remain typical of her.'

In her many flower paintings she painted the spirit, the idea of the flower, leaf, or plant; she conjured up an intimation of the all-pervading consciousness held still for a fleeting moment in the form of a tulip, a rose, the tiniest blossom and most delicate leaf. Her flower drawings and paintings had the ease, the freedom and certainty of the great Masters of Zen. She put her pen or brush to paper, and as by magic her hand would be guided to establish what *was* there, as it were, underneath (as in those 'magic' paint-books for children)—the flower, the whole of the flower, with petals, leaves, stem, seedpods, pollen. It had been there all the time. Only oneself, one had not seen it before.

I framed a coloured sketch which I found tucked away in one of her sketchbooks depicting a half-opened tulip on which a butterfly is just alighting. Every time I approach the picture I tread softly for fear it might fly away. I can almost feel the vibrations of its wings as it touches down on the flower.

Alas, the trip to Devonshire was among those of her wishes which were never to be fulfilled. I blame myself for it; I had always put it off, and whenever I put it off, she said: 'Never mind, we'll do it next time.'

But now everything was beginning to recede from her, and the flowers she loved so much and had painted so lovingly were beginning to recede too. The day was now fast approaching when she would no longer see them.

One afternoon Stella brought her a bunch of camellias, the first from her garden. Four deep red glowing camellias. She held them up quite close to her to touch and to see. 'I can see them,'

177

Diana said, 'they are beautiful,' and she touched and stroked them with loving hands. I think she was only just able to see them, but whether she could make out their colour I never knew. The next day she said: 'Tell people not to send any more flowers; I cannot see them.'

One Sunday I went to the country to the house of friends where we had spent many week-ends in the past, the last about ten days before she entered the nursing home. Every week-end, summer or winter, she would pick some flowers and her first concern when we reached home was to arrange them carefully in vases and distribute them in the flat. On that Sunday, early in March, I picked some branches which I knew she had always liked, and some others of which I was not quite sure but hoped they would appeal to her. I gave them to one of the nurses and asked her to put them into a vase. When they were brought to her, she hardly took any notice of them and said: 'I don't know what they are; put them over there on top of the TV set; I don't like their pungent smell.'

Some elaborate flower arrangements came from acquaintances who did not know her intimately. She would ask me to describe them and then give them to other friends. The flowers began to leave her room; faded ones were not replaced; new ones were given away: 'Give them to Rosamond, give them to Rosemary, with my love.'

As darkness began to envelop her, everything in the room beyond the reach of her hands ceased to exist. The carriage clock which had been with us always and had accompanied us on every journey and been placed on the table on the left side of the bedhead, my photograph which stood on the right side, the many brightly coloured 'Get better soon' cards, had all lost their meaning; they had become as remote to her as if they were millions of light years away. And, strangely, they had in fact receded. In the early weeks everything: flowers, photographs, postcards, bottles of scent had formed a circle close around her; now they were no more part of her life; they had become mere onlookers who kept a respectful distance.

178

Almost all the flowers had gone; the room began to look very bare. But among the flowering potted plants there were two or three which defied all attempts to remove them. Someone continued to water them and bring them back into the room every morning. There was one in particular that caught my attention, an azalea plant of the brightest red. At one moment it had shown signs of dying, but then suddenly it revived. It stood there quietly, firmly, radiating light: 'I will stay and watch over her till the end,' it seemed to say.

I understood its message and said to the nurses: 'See to it that it never lacks water; I want it to remain here.' And then, mysteriously, other flowers began to make their appearance. No longer were they the flowers we send to a patient on the way to recovery. They were the flowers that carry out the task allotted to them by the wisdom that dwells in the soul of man from age immemorial: the flowers that prepare the way for those who are about to reach the shore beyond.

The azalea which had stood, a solitary sentinel, for several days, was no more alone; one by one new bunches of flowers ranged themselves alongside.

In the many hours she spent alone, especially at night or in the limbo between night and day, her mind dwelled on happy memories and on plans for the future. She thought of journeys abroad and on trips by car in England. One of the places she had wanted to visit had been the Lake District. She had long talks with one of the nurses, Sister Edwards, who had taken her into her heart and always found some excuse to be with her as much as possible, about the beauties of the English countryside and her wish to go with me to the Lake District. Sister Edwards knew the Lake District; her parents lived near it.

When I arrived one afternoon I found the Sister sitting on her bed. Diana was in a happy mood. 'I must tell you something very exciting,' she said. 'Sister knows the Lake District very well and she has promised to come with us on a trip. She can drive a car, so you don't have to do all the driving, and she can take us to all the most beautiful places, won't you, Sister?'

'If your husband has nothing against it, I should love to come with you,' the nurse answered, looking at me with an expression of infinite sadness, for she knew the verdict of the doctors; she knew there was no hope. And so we sat there, the three of us for the next half-hour planning in great detail our trip to the Lakeland.

'Sister Edwards says that June is perhaps the best season when the weather is usually very fine.' (More than once when Diana had proposed that trip I had said I thought it was always raining in the Lake District). 'So you see, Mr. P.,' she continued, 'it is not always raining there as you thought; perhaps I will be well enough to go in June.'

At this point the nurse made an excuse and left the room. 'I'll be back later,' she said, 'when I have finished preparing the dinners.' I saw that she could not contain herself any longer, for the last few minutes she had been fighting to hold back her tears.

When we were alone, Diana holding my hand, said, half anxiously, half reassuringly: 'I am sure you will like her; she is a very pretty girl and she is well educated. You would probably quite fall for her if you saw her not in her nurse's uniform.'

I did see her—some weeks later—not in her uniform, when she came to my flat to talk to me about Diana. She was a beautiful girl. She said to me: 'Your wife was a saint; we all wanted to be with her. We were drawn to her as one is drawn to the light. If ever I am in a bad mood or want to give a snappy answer to anyone, I think of her and all bad temper vanishes at once. That Saturday after she had died, I spent every free minute in her room looking at her wonderful face. It gave me a feeling of peace such as I had never experienced.'

180

Eleven

'For where is any author in the world
Teaches such beauty as a woman's eye?'
(*Love's Labour's Lost*)

March 18th. Diana is blind.

As darkness had begun to descend on those beautiful tender
eyes the room had gradually brightened, until towards the end
she lay with the curtains drawn back in daylight or by the full
light of the bedside lamp shining directly over her head. But she
lay in darkness. It is only those who are totally blind who
experience neither light nor dark, for where the sense organ has
been completely destroyed, there are no impressions to be carried
to the visual centre in the brain. But with her, at least when
she first became blind, it was different. Her sight had gone,
the light had gone, but the opposite of light still registered: she
was conscious of pitch black darkness.

It did not happen all at once, but it did not take very long once
the tumour had begun to encroach upon the optic nerve; perhaps
five days from the moment she could no longer make out the
colour of flowers, until all colours, all shapes, all movements had
been swallowed up by the night from which she was never to
emerge in this life.

That Saturday, the 18th of March, at nine o'clock in the
morning, she rang me—it was the last time she ever used the
telephone, and she could not replace the receiver—and said: 'Mr.
P., when you come to see me today I must discuss with you a very
serious problem. You know I can really not see any more. We
must discuss this and decide what we should do.'

When I came into her room, immediately after lunch, the

181

curtains were open. Two days before I had found her for the first time lying in daylight; she had not commented on it, nor had the sinister significance of this regained light immediately struck me. And even that very day when she had told me clearly and unmistakably that she knew that she was blind, I did not link the two together: the new daylight with her night. I did not wish to recognize the brutal irreversible finality of it all. Somehow I thought: this is a passing phase.

And so I said, when I entered her room that day: 'Would you like me to draw the curtains a little? The room is very bright.'

She answered gently: 'No, leave them as they are, I don't mind.' As usual, when she wanted to talk, she had turned on her right side. This position was more tolerable; it put less pressure on her spine.

'Where are you?' she said. 'Sit close by me and hold my hand. And listen carefully to what I have to say.' Her eyes were closed. I was grateful for this, for later she was mostly to keep them open, wide open, the pupils dilated to their maximum and not reacting to any change of light: sightless.

She spoke slowly, deliberately, often searching for words, battling against the inner darkness that was relentlessly pushing back to its innermost sanctum the shining light of that wonderful, precise and balanced mind. 'Listen carefully,' she repeated, 'and don't interrupt me; this is a very serious problem. If one goes blind gradually, one can adapt oneself to it. Your mother did in the last two years of her life, and in fact she never went totally blind. She could not read any more or watch TV, but she could see colour; she could see shapes, she could see movement—and she could see light. All this I cannot do any more. And it came on very suddenly.' I pressed her hand in mine. The tears were streaming down my cheeks; she could not see. 'Now this is the problem,' she said. 'If one goes blind suddenly, the way it has happened to me, one must be very careful not to go off one's head.'

Not all secondary cancers of the brain lead to blindness. I have been told of cases since, in which the sight remained unimpaired

182

until the end; it depends on the location of the tumour. But nothing was spared her.

As I have mentioned, the first symptoms that all was not well with her sight had come early in December, about three weeks after the end of the radiation treatment. We could not go out often in the evening in those days; she was too tired. And so we often watched TV. But she began to notice that it strained her eyes too much and gave her headaches. Later, in January, when the first serious symptoms of her illness had appeared, she could not tolerate strong daylight or even artificial light. She had to wear dark glasses, especially when lying in bed during the day as the bed faced the windows. We put it all down to the 'after-effects of the radiation treatment'. She also had to give up reading. But she could still paint.

As the symptoms became more and more alarming, when the headaches became severe and the vomiting started, Dr. R. made certain neurological tests and also examined the inside of her eyes with an ophthalmoscope. There was nothing abnormal to see. However he noticed a tendency to nystagmus (unsteadiness of eye movement). He asked her in my presence whether she had experienced double vision. She had not. 'That's very reassuring,' he said.

She did not ask him why it was reassuring. Later he explained to me that double vision could be an indication of the presence of 'intracranial pressure'. The very delicate mechanism of vision could be easily disturbed through some undue pressure.

'I know,' I said, 'it happens to me when I have migraine. I get visual disturbance.'

'Exactly,' he replied, 'this is the kind of thing I mean.'

'And what could be the reason?' I asked. 'Could it be a swelling of the brain tissue? And would this be consistent with the diagnosis of post-radiation effects? I mean, if she had double vision, could this be due to radiation?'

'It could be,' he answered, 'but anyway, she has no double vision, and there are no other symptoms pointing to pressure in the brain.'

'Except the headaches and the vomiting,' I said.

183

He looked at me gravely and nodded his head.

Soon after that, I think it was two days before we had to take her to the nursing home, she complained of double vision. 'Only for a few minutes,' she said. This, Dr. R. explained, was undoubtedly due to the effects of certain drugs which he had given her to stop the vomiting. 'It has no particular significance.'

'I thought you said that this was a definite sign of intracranial pressure, and this could be due to . . .'

'A number of causes,' he interrupted me. 'At present, these are purely subjective symptoms.' But the double vision came back, together with those other symptoms; above all the numbness in the fingers of the left hand, the weakness in the right arm; all these the doctors called 'subjective' symptoms. But one day during her second week in the nursing home, Diana had said to me: 'I really *have* double vision. When Sister brought in a pot of cyclamen this morning I thought she was carrying two pots, and I could not see them very clearly. And when Dr. R. sat on my bed this morning, there were two Drs. R. sitting there.'

'Did you tell him?'

'Yes, I did, but he said he attached no particular significance to it. He thinks it is probably all those strange drugs.'

'Have you double vision now?' I asked.

'Come close to me,' she said, 'let me have a look at you.' She looked at me with infinite tenderness. 'You are just my one and only boy,' she said, 'I don't need two . . . and you have scurf on your collar, you dirty boy. One can see that no one is looking after you.' She paused and added: 'What really would you do, if I were not with you?'

'I don't know, my love, what I would do.'

Two days later she told me that she could see two ties on me. 'I also find it a little difficult sometimes to make out the exact shape and colour of flowers, unless they are very close.'

'Well, you know the light is not very good; I also find it difficult to see properly,' I said, 'and you are very short-sighted and never wear your spectacles.'

'I don't mean that,' she answered.

184

The neurologist had come again on a Saturday. Throughout, Saturdays had stood out as signposts on her via dolorosa. He had spent a long time with her while I was waiting outside in the corridor.

Dr. B. was a man of few words, and these he uttered with great hesitancy. He did not wish to commit himself. On that Saturday he had observed 'a slight swelling of the optic disk, nothing of particular significance, still within the limits of the non-pathological'.

'What could it be due to?'

'Difficult to say. Some slight pressure.'

'Perhaps a swelling of the tissues of the brain?'

'Very likely.'

'And the causes?'

'These things are difficult to determine.'

Something had prevented me from probing further.

Two days later Diana told me that she now had double vision all the time and she added: 'There is certainly something very peculiar about my sight. I cannot really say that I am very pleased with it.'

'Darling, let's make an experiment,' I suggested. 'You say you have double vision now?'

'Not when you stand quite close; I see you in one piece.'

I stepped back.

'Now you begin to divide and at the same time you are getting blurred. There is no doubt about it.'

'Now I want you to put on your glasses,' I told her, 'and try again.' 'Excellent idea' she immediately agreed, ready as always to put subjective experience to the test of objective observation. She put on her glasses and after a while she said: 'I still see you double; less blurred, but double.' And she repeated, imitating the voice and emphasis of those housewives on TV who declare, when asked what had struck them about the results of a particular detergent: 'Definitely whiter'—'definitely double.'

She now had double vision, the very symptom the absence of which had so delighted Dr. R. only a very few weeks ago. When

I spoke to him the same evening he said: 'There is undoubtedly intracranial pressure which is affecting the optic nerve.' Again, I probed no further.

One afternoon when I arrived, Sister Edwards met me in the corridor. 'We have a surprise for you today,' she said, 'your wife has been hoping that you would be coming soon; she has asked many times. You can go in to her now.'

As I opened the door, she said: 'Is that Mr. P.? Look, I am sitting up.' She was sitting upright in a chair, propped up by many cushions. The room was still in semi-darkness. As I walked towards her, she said: 'I was fed up with lying in bed, and so I asked Sister to put me into this chair. We wanted to give you a surprise.'

I kissed her on the mouth and on her forehead. I gently stroked her hair; I held and kissed her pale hands. She sat very still and upright. She said: 'I mustn't move too much; otherwise my neck hurts.' I noticed that she was looking straight ahead, while speaking, and not looking at me. Her eyes were open but there was little expression in them.

'How is your sight today, my pet?' I asked.

'Not too good, my angel-boy,' she answered, 'not really very good.'

The next day, about the same time in the afternoon when, as usual, the bedside lamp was dipped low, she said: 'You can bring the lamp a little higher, if you want to see better.' She then asked did I think there was something wrong with the light; had they put in a weaker bulb or switched on the night bulb by mistake. I told her there was no change. 'Strange,' she said, 'the room used to look different. It used to have such a warm orange glow. Now it seems to have lost its colour. There is certainly something not quite right with my sight.'

Relentless, the darkening cloud swallowed up the light around her. The room had lost its colour; she was no more able to distinguish the colour of the nurses' uniforms. Everything seemed to her shadowy, greyish-black.

She asked me to raise the lamp high so that it shone fully on the bed. The effect was that of switching on the headlights of a car. The whole room emerged, brightly lit.

'How does this look to you, my pet?' I asked.

'If you really want to know,' she answered, 'it looks as dark as a large Victorian drawing room, lit by one solitary candle.'

I realized then that never would she see my face again, nor the colour of my hair, nor my photograph which stood close to her on the table. It was her favourite photograph taken some years ago in Italy; only two or three days earlier she had been discussing it lovingly with Sister Edwards.

It was this photograph which was always to be with her to the end of her life. She would, she had told me, when the time approached, gradually give away most of her material possessions and retain only what was the absolutely essential and those things which reminded her or were symbolic of what had truly mattered in her life: certain books and paintings, letters, certain small treasured objects such as the two ivory Netzuke which she always carried about with her, one or two pieces of jewellery and the photographs; above all this photograph. She often talked to it when she was alone in the flat, and she would always talk to it— talk to me through it—when I had gone. 'This will not happen for a long, long time,' she used to say, 'and by then I myself will not have many more years in this incarnation.'

And now this photograph will be with me until the end of my life, and its only purpose will be to remind me of the inscrutability of human destiny; it was never meant to be looked at by *me* after *her* death. And what will happen to it after my death? Maybe my son or maybe someone else will look at it; maybe it will even pass to a new generation. 'This was my grandfather (great-grandfather?) in his early fifties . . .'

But what is certain is that she, the only person for whom it had true significance, will never see it again.

Only a few days before she had said to me: 'You must have your hair cut; it is getting too long.' But now when I asked her: 'Can you see my face?' and came quite near to her, she answered: 'Only a pink blur.'

187

'Can you see your own hands?'

She moved them close to her eyes and said: 'I can see something moving.'

Unbelievable, ungraspable, grotesque, outrageous and totally unacceptable as it was, there could be no doubt any more: she was rapidly going blind.

In January she had still painted those delicate miniature pen and wash pictures which so uniquely expressed her vision of reality. Shortly before the crisis which took her away from home, never to return, she had brought eight of her latest oil paintings to the framemakers. It must have been about one week after the fateful incident of her mental disturbances and temporary incapacity to speak normally. I was afraid she might not be able to explain how she wanted the pictures mounted and framed. However, she had regained all her faculties. She considered each painting carefully, selected from scores of samples the mounts best suited in colour, shade and texture to each painting, decided on the type and size of each frame and gave the most detailed instructions on how the work was to be carried out.

I sat there, every now and again agreeing or disagreeing with a suggestion, but mostly just watching with amazement and admiration this extraordinary human being so totally absorbed in her creative task and apparently completely oblivious of the sinister powers that had declared war on her and were at this very moment working at her destruction. Or was it that she did know and wanted to use what precious time there was left to her to complete what could still be completed?

She was able to see her pictures in their frames, and she was happy. 'This,' she said, 'has given me new confidence in my work, and as soon as I am well again I shall work hard to have enough pictures for a one-man show.' This was two days before she entered the nursing home. We had not time to bring the pictures home. But she often spoke about them and of her new-found confidence: 'I know now that my paintings are good. I must be well soon. I want so much to start painting again, and also I must complete my anthology.'

188

She was never to see her paintings again. Even had she lived, she would not have seen them again. But so powerful is the (merciful) urge to deceive oneself even in the face of overwhelming evidence that a few days later, when she had gone blind completely and irrevocably, I asked Dr. R.: 'Do you think that if the growth of the tumour could be arrested' (we were then trying out some new French preparation which had been specially flown over from Paris), 'her sight could come back?'

'I very much doubt it,' said Dr. R., 'the optic nerve which is most delicate, is being compressed by the advancing tumour; it is literally being squeezed to death.'

Her sight—what she saw and the way she saw the living world around, had become my way of seeing: seeing the world in depth, in colours, in shapes and dimension I had not known in all the years before I had met her. I realized that I had seen the world through her eyes. Nothing ever escaped her. For example, having once seen a room she would remember it in photographic detail. She would immediately on entering a room notice even the slightest change: a new chair—or a chair, ornament, rug in a different position. Once seen she could describe the arrangement of the furniture, the pictures, the colour and pattern of the wall paper, the material of the curtains and the way they were hung, with complete accuracy.

She could distinguish every type and make of porcelain and pottery; every make and period of silver. She was never content with a cursory glance or superficial examination but always gathered as much detailed information as possible, studying characteristic designs and patterns, looking up hall marks and factory signs. Again, though she had little formal training, she would always recognise the quality of a painting and know whether it was a work by an important or a lesser master, and she would always recognize the quality of a painting and know

She had the same critical understanding and discrimination for furniture, carpets, jewels, architecture; in short, everything fashioned by the skill of man. Here her extraordinary powers of observation were supported by her scholarly application to detail

189

to which I have referred earlier on, which enabled her to accomplish to perfection every task she had set herself.

She also had a never failing sense of space and orientation; what is called 'a bump of locality'. But it was more than that. She remembered every turn and twist of the road, every house or landmark and would guide me unfailingly to our destination. 'Don't you remember,' she would ask with surprise when I hesitated which road to take or did not know exactly where we were. 'Don't you remember'—the church, the clump of trees, the pub at the corner or merely the familiarity of the landscape as a whole. But she also found her way in places we had never been in before; she knew because what she perceived externally was supported by an inner vision which was pure, detached, compassionate, unbiased and true. Localities as well as features of a landscape and man-made things in it were arranged, patterned according to some inner law or necessity of their own which she understood: they were as they were and where they were because it could not be otherwise.

And now she was fast going blind. During those twilight days— they were not many—she mostly kept her eyes closed. I longed for her to look at me, to smile at me, perhaps just once more. I was seized by a kind of terror at the thought that never would those infinitely tender loving wise eyes see me again. 'Smile at me, my love,' I said; she opened her eyes, but how can eyes smile if they no more reflect the impact of instant recognition. There was but a fleeting flicker as she opened her eyes. 'I cannot really see, Mr. P.,' she said, 'but I expect it will get better.'

One day before she had gone totally blind Joan brought her a little egg made of highly polished serpentine. She had always loved these polished stone eggs; some had delicate and intricate designs that were projections, on to their polished surface, of their innermost structure. Many of Diana's miniature paintings resembled the surface patterns of those stones. Joan put the egg into her hand. 'You hold it, darling,' she said, 'I brought it for you.'

190

Diana held the egg quite close to her eyes. 'What colour is it?' she asked.

'A kind of mottled brown, pink, grey and white,' I told her. 'Is it stone or polished wood? I cannot quite get the feel of it.'

I knew that of late the fingers of both hands had become increasingly numb. Now she was obviously beginning to lose her sense of touch completely. One more faculty mercilessly destroyed by the enemy. I had so often played with her hands, opened and closed her fingers in turn, passed my tongue over them, kissed the tips gently, caressed them and let them caress me. The play of hands between lovers is like an intimate dance in which can be expressed the whole wide spectrum of love from passion to worship. I could never tire of this play. Her hands, like every part of her body, were part of a secret world open to me alone, for me to explore and to enjoy at leisure and at will.

This world was closing now.

With the progression of her terrible illness and the ever widening area of her body over which the pain spread in concentric waves from the afflicted centres of her brain, there was little left of that precious body for me to caress. I could still kiss her gently, but I dared not put my arms around her for fear of causing her pain. I could still stroke her forehead and her hair, I could still hold her hands and play with her fingers, opening and closing them as I had done in happier days, and I could still kiss them. 'Can you feel my lips?' I would ask her. 'Of course I can,' she would answer.

But lately when I had kissed her fingers she had made no comment, and I had not asked any questions. (The increasing numbness in her hands, the failing muscular control, the steady deterioration of her sight, all of which the doctors had until recently called 'subjective neurological symptoms' had now become 'objective symptoms,' meaning they could be related to definite clinical findings. At the stage which we had now reached they confirmed the general hopelessness of the picture.) But she could still hold my hand in hers and press it gently, though the pressure became weaker from day to day.

And so, when she held that little polished egg, she could neither see it nor feel it properly any longer. 'Woud you like to hold it a little longer?' I had asked her when Joan had left.

'No, my angel,' she said, 'put it in the drawer.'

And now she was totally blind. 'To me this unfortunate thing has happened; I have gone blind suddenly.' And she repeated: 'When one goes blind gradually, one can adapt oneself to it, but if one goes blind suddenly, one must be very careful not to go off one's head.' She spoke quite calmly and deliberately as though discussing a purely theoretical case.

'Listen carefully,' she repeated, 'it is difficult for me to explain; I have thought it all out but I cannot always find the words, so you must help me by retaining everything I say, and you must repeat it to me if necessary. Also because I cannot hold on to ideas for very long.'

After a pause she continued: 'You know there are people who have to pass certain tests which show whether they are ready and fit to take on certain jobs. Do you know what I mean?' she enquired anxiously as I had not said anything. I was not quite sure what she was leading up to, but I realized that she had great difficulty in marshalling her thoughts.

'Go on, my love, I follow.'

Imitating a friend of ours who, whenever she explained anything that was self-explanatory, interspersed her stories with frequent expostulations of 'Are you with me', she said: 'Are you with me?' and gave a short little laugh. Then she resumed: 'The people in America who go into space, they are the ones who undergo these tests; now hold on to that idea for me.'

'Yes, darling, you mean the astronauts.'

'Exactly, the astronauts; they are being trained under simulated conditions in order to get used to the weightlessness and the solitary conditions they will encounter in space.'

I sat amazed at the precision and clarity of her embattled mind. I said: 'You don't have to worry about your thoughts not functioning properly; you make everything perfectly clear.'

'If these people, these Americans,' she continued, 'were not

192

trained carefully and systematically before being shot into space, their personality would disintegrate—you and I have often talked about it—they would go off their heads once they found themselves in space.' I wanted to say something, but she pressed my hand and said firmly: 'I am like a spaceman shot into space without training; I don't know where I am; this is the serious problem which faces me. I must not go off my head.' Her face was flushed, her forehead damp with perspiration; she was feverish, weak and in pain; engulfed in darkness; but she was in complete control of herself.

Who was she, this extraordinary human being, my wife and companion for so many years? Who was she really? What great spirit was incarnate and spoke in and through this frail, suffering, dying body bound and fettered by the rules of incarnation, yet sovereign, free and glorious? Who was she? I knew that barring a great miracle she would never see again, even should she live— which by then we knew she would not, save for an even greater miracle—the Christ miracle of instant healing; did she not also know it? Or could it be that she had believed the doctor's explanation that this was a temporary blindness due to the action of a particular drug and that she would see again in two or three weeks.

'I am like an astronaut in orbit without having been prepared for it, and so I don't know what is happening. I wanted to discuss this with you.'

'What shall we do, my sweetheart?' I said.

'The most important thing is that my day should be properly structured,' she replied. 'That is what I want you to tell the doctors. I mean I must always know the date, the day of the week and, above all, the time of the day. I must know what happens at, for example nine in the morning, so that I know it is nine in the morning, and what happens at ten, at eleven and one and so on, so that I know what time it is. This is the only way I can retain my sense of orientation because, since all is pitch black around me, I don't know what time it is and whether it is night or day. So what you must do is to impress upon the doctors and on the Floor Sister that the times when they do my room, the times when I get my various pills, the times when they take my temperature, the times of my meals, should not be varied; otherwise I fear I might go off my head, lost in the darkness and infinity of space.' She paused and then concluded as she so often had done when explaining something to me: 'Have you understood this, Mr. P.?'

'Yes, my sweet girl, I understand and shall talk to Dr. R. and to Sister later this evening.'

During the early days in the nursing home and up to almost the middle of March, her one and only pleasure was to listen to me when I told her what I had been doing between the times of seeing her. She wanted to know all details—whom I had been seeing, how people were, what we had been talking about, whom I was going to dine with; what kind of dinner I had had or was expecting to have, how the 'boys' were, whether I was driving carefully, whether our daily woman had washed the curtains and done all the things she had to do to keep the flat in perfect order.

She would listen to all the smallest details of actions, events, thoughts and preoccupations, so utterly familiar but ever new, from which was woven like from so many coloured strands the rich tapestry of our happy married life. For far from breeding contempt, familiarity in a true marriage is a constant source of renewal and enchantment. It was as important to me to be able to give her these daily reports as it was to her to receive them. It gave us both the feeling—the illusion—that our daily life continued and would continue as before, once her health had been restored. That is why I also encouraged her to give me instructions on household routine and sometimes even invented little contretemps and grievances: things not having come back from the cleaners, the kitchen sink being blocked again, the daily woman having a slight cold, etc. I wanted her to feel and I wanted to feel myself that she was still part of my life, still on this shore.

But I knew she was a voyager departing. And like the voyager

194

on the ship making for the open sea, the familiar landmarks of her life were becoming less distinct to her. Slowly they faded from view, and she herself began to turn away. The nursing home and the routine of illness, her ever increasing dependence on the nurses for even the smallest actions and necessities of daily life, the visits of the doctors, the pills, the injections, the problems connected with eating, drinking, sleeping, washing; the many hours of the day and of the night when she was alone with her suffering and her thoughts, and above all the inexorable progression of her illness, more and more engaged her fast ebbing vitality.

For this was no ordinary illness. It was the end of a life. And so I had begun to notice of late that she asked fewer and fewer questions about my daily activities. There still remained a core of interests to which she clung, all questions directly concerning my own health and well-being, but all less important details, so important to her even a little while ago, began to vanish from her purview.

On this fateful day, after she had told me about the structuring of her day, I said to her: 'I think it is important also that I should tell you every day, as I have done all these weeks, about all the things I am doing, the people I meet, the "boys", my business and all that. Don't you think so?'

She did not answer at once. She lay quite still, her eyes shut. I could see that one of her eyes was slightly twitching behind the closed lids. After a long silence she answered, and her voice sounded hard: 'I am sorry, my darling, but I am not interested any more in what you are doing. I am sorry. But this is of no concern to me any more.'

These were terrible, doom-laden words. They fell on my head like rocks. I sat still, crushed, unable to speak. This was the point of no return for her; and for me the point beyond which I could not venture much further. Soon, I knew, I must fall behind, leave her to continue her via dolorosa to the end—alone. And I like Orpheus must return and not stop to look at her any more.

For the first time I was seized by a kind of terror. For over twenty years I had lived under the gaze of her dark, infinitely tender, wise and all-seeing eyes; she perceived me and I lived. This was to be no more. I suddenly felt that like Bishop Berkeley's famous tree I would cease to exist if I were no more perceived—no more perceived by her.

According to Bertrand Russell, Berkeley's proposition that all reality is mental and thus nothing exists unless it be perceived may be of doubtful metaphysical validity; however, it is real enough psychologically. It is in the 'I-and-Thou' relationship of one person to another that the true ontological reality of each as an individual resides and is experienced. The lonely and unloved and all those who for one reason or other are deprived of or are unable to form this relationship, suffer a diminution of their personal reality, often with far reaching and devastating results. Shut a person up in solitary confinement for a long period, and his personality will disintegrate, which means he will cease to exist, unless he be a person of quite exceptional inner strength who is able (as for example the Indian Rishis) to form this 'I-and-Thou' relationship to a transcendent idea.

In bereavement, as I said earlier, the closer the union that existed between two people, the greater the danger also to the psyche of the survivor. It is as if a partial exchange of souls had taken place in those who are united in a strong and abiding love. Therefore the death of the one deprives the other of part, perhaps even a larger part, of the reality of his own 'self' thus mutilated and diminished. In terms of Jungian psychology, the lover has projected his *anima* (the female aspect of his own psyche) on to the beloved who has become the personification of it and through whom the lover experiences and expresses his own female faculties. When the beloved is taken away from him irrevocably, something dies in him almost in a literal sense. To come again into the fullness of his own personal reality he must re-integrate his anima, regain, take back into himself that which he had entrusted to her whom he loved. This is a very

196

difficult task, and it may happen, in great and passionate love, especially if it has lasted over many years, that the task is altogether beyond accomplishment. Life then may no longer appear worth living.

That afternoon in the nursing home when I received the shattering revelation that my daily life was none of her concern any more and felt that the reality of myself as an individual entity would vanish with her death, would vanish like Bishop Berkeley's tree if no one was there to perceive it, I was not merely giving way to some irrational or neurotic fantasy; I was experiencing a basic truth of psychic life. Berkeley may not have proved his thesis that all reality is mental; that therefore material objects exist only through being perceived. But he made out a convincing case that what we perceive are not the objects in themselves but certain qualities and that qualities are relative to the percipient, that is, exist primarily in the mind of the one who perceives them. In terms of psychological reality, and especially applied to human relations, this is particularly true. It does not mean that qualities (good or bad) have no objective existence, do not exist in their own right; but it does mean that they come to life only in the mind of the perceiver, and if there is no one to perceive them, they might as well not be there at all.

Diana had the supreme gift of perceiving and of recognizing qualities in things and in people, and in doing so bringing them to life. She perceived, discovered and thus brought to life the true significance of anything or anybody she came into contact with: she created life.

If she was to be extinguished and cease as a sovereign centre of consciousness, that creative source of perception would be no more, and I (this was my fear) would suffer this catastrophic diminution of my personal 'beingness'. I did not think all this out so clearly that afternoon, but I was stunned and dismayed, and for the first time in all those weeks I showed my distress.

'Darling,' I said, 'what am I to do; I cannot bear the thought

197

that you are not interested any more in my life; there can be no meaning in my life any more if you withdraw from it.'

She answered, and the tone of her voice was severe and determined: 'I am sorry, Mr. P., you must just be tough; you must accept it.' And in a gentler voice she added: 'You must understand that your reality is not my reality any more. Come close to me, my darling; kiss me.' I put my face close to hers, touched her forehead with mine and kissed her parched lips. She flung her arms around my neck and hugged me close: 'You mustn't be a silly boy,' she whispered; 'you know I love and worship you, my blessed boy; but you must understand that what has happened to me is something very serious; and so let's be sensible about it.'

She stretched out her right hand and touched the portable radio which stood on the bedside table, always on the same spot. She had never once switched it on, but it had served her as a relay point for the bell-push which she had hitched on to its handle. Right from the beginning she had fixed the bell-push which hung from the wall on a long flex to the portable transistor set because it hurt her to stretch out her arm. Now that she was blind it was the only way for her to find the bell. This was very typical of her not to put objects to the use for which they were intended, but to some other use which seemed to her more appropriate. It was quite a standing joke between us. Whenever she did anything of the kind, for example use strips of Japanese silk wallpaper to paint on, wear a blouse the wrong way round or use discarded dentist's tools for her stone carving I would say: 'This is typical Diana.'

So this was 'typical Diana'. I could not help saying it even at this tragic moment, and she laughed. Her fingers were groping their way over the surface of the radio set to make sure that the grill—the loudspeaker—was turned in the right direction. Only thus could she be sure to find the bell. 'My reality,' she continued, 'is to know where the bell is; where the bowl is when I am suddenly sick and where the tumbler with water stands.'

'I understand, my darling.'

And then I said very tentatively: 'Perhaps it might help if you listened to the radio from time to time, for example at nine in the morning, you could get the news; or perhaps at one; you might even listen to music from time to time.'

'This is not a bad idea,' she replied; 'I will think about it.' And she added: 'Switch it on.' I switched on the Home Service of the BBC in the middle of an American newsletter by Alistair Cooke. He was talking about Texas. After a while she said: 'I don't understand what he is talking about; switch it off. But it is a good idea; I will think about it.' It never came to it.

Later the same day she said to me: 'There is something I want you to do for me. It is very important that it should be done now, tomorrow afternoon if possible.' I knew from the way she spoke that it was something which mattered to her very much. She spoke firmly. She wanted me to take away the few personal things which she had with her in the nursing home and which she treasured greatly: an antique ring—a yellow sapphire mounted in gold and surrounded by seed pearls which I had give her on our tenth wedding anniversary; a gold chain bracelet, interspersed with grey pearls which I had bought for her the year before in Portugal; the two Japanese Netzuke delicately carved in ivory. One was a mouse, the other a mythological beast. They had been given to her by an old friend many years ago, and she always carried them about in her bag wherever she went. They had become her inseparable companions. At home they had their place on her bedside table and when we went away for the week-end or abroad, her first concern on arriving was to find a suitable place in the room for her two little guardians. Then there was the small egg of polished serpentine which Joan had brought only two days before and which she had not been able to see any more. I tried to dissuade her but she insisted: 'I don't need them any more here; they might get lost or one of the cleaners might take them. I would not know because I cannot see. Now will you do this for me, Mr. P.?'

The following afternoon, Palm Sunday, the 19th of March,

she said: 'We must do these things now, before the nurse comes back to take my temperature. We must do it today; there might not be another chance.' She was determined; she had thought it out carefully as she did with all matters that were important to her. And so, at about five in the afternoon we started on this sad procedure. She pulled open the drawer of the right bedside table and carefully, delicately, relying on touch only, she took out of a zip-bag which also contained hairpins, coloured ribbons for tying her hair, the nail-file, eyebrow pencils and other odds and ends, one by one the treasured objects. She held each one for a brief moment in a parting caress and then handed them to me: 'Here is my ring; now fold it in one of my handkerchiefs and put it on the bed. Here is my beautiful bracelet; fold it properly—here is another handkerchief.' Then came the two ivory animals, the small mouse and the dragon. 'Take care of them until I come home.' Finally the egg of polished serpentine. 'And here is the exquisite little egg which Joan brought me the other day.'

'Darling,' I said, 'would you not like to keep it; you can hold it in your hand and play with it?'

'No,' she answered almost harshly. 'You must understand, Mr. P., that I cannot see things at all and that I cannot feel them properly any more; the tips of my fingers are numb.'

Then she gave me further instructions: 'Get a piece of tissue paper from my suitcase on top of the wardrobe, put all the little objects together, wrap them up carefully and take them home.' When I had accomplished this task she said, 'There are a few other things I want you to take home. First take the beautiful nightie which Jackie brought in yesterday, and put it on the bed. Describe it for me.' When I had done so most inadequately, she said: 'All right, I knew it was beautiful. And now take the bedjacket which Marie-Thé brought from Paris and put them into a carrier bag.'

'What about the pink shawl which Eileen gave you and which you have not used yet? Would you not like to keep it and put it around your shoulders when you sit up?'

'Open it for me,' she answered, 'tell me the exact colour and the pattern.' I told her. 'Now give it to me.' She held it for a while, measured it, passed her delicate white hands over it so that she could feel the pattern. 'It is lovely, I can feel it; please thank Eileen when you see her next; tell her I love it. And now fold it and put it away together with the other things; I shall not need them . . .' she paused, 'I shall not need them for a while. And now, my darling, sit by me and let's have a little chat.'

She was systematic and tidy in everything she did, right to her very last conscious act and sentence. She was now about to close the book of her life and put it away with the same meticulous care and reverence with which she had always completed every job; there were no loose ends.

But it was her life itself which she was to leave unfinished. I thought of all the many things which she had never attained, all the things I had always wanted to give her, the places I had wanted to take her to. She loved music, and I had never been able to buy a gramophone (yet she had bought records for the day when we would be able to buy one); I never could buy her a proper watch. She had only possessed one in the whole of her life: a small cheap silver wristwatch which must have been given to her when she was a child. She always said that it kept excellent time. But finally it gave out and was found to be beyond repair. 'We will get a new one, a proper grown-up watch soon . . .' We never did.

She never saw Amalfi, Sorrento, Naples; she never saw Florence, Ravenna, Perugia, Assisi, Venice; she never saw Rome. We always had to postpone these journeys: 'Next year,' and next year we said 'Next year.' After all, she was still young; there was time.

Now time was ending for her with so many things not done, so many beautiful places in the world not seen. But did it matter? She who had derived infinite delight from a leafy lane in Surrey in the spring; who had painted imaginary landscapes and cities of unearthly beauty, did it matter that she never saw any of those places? Was her life unfulfilled for that? Unfinished, yes, but perhaps not unfulfilled.

While she had still been able to see, when I fed her, her pale elegant hands would make the attempt to hold the glass tube through which she drank her consommé or water or she would guide my hand. Later I had to guide her hand. But now, when I gave her a few spoonfuls of yogurt or stewed fruit, each time I brought the spoon close to her I said: 'Another spoonful coming, open your mouth, darling.' It happened frequently, especially when her sense of co-ordination began to fail, that she would open her mouth before I had had time to fill the spoon again; as a small bird opens its beak before the mother bird has reached the nest. 'Not yet, my angel,' I would say, and then: 'Coming now.'

She was reduced to infancy trusting like an infant the hand that fed her. But unlike the infant who can recognize the hand and the face of the mother, she trusted the hand that came to her unseen in the darkness.

Yet we could still communicate; this we could still take for granted. But not very long after, when I said: 'Open your mouth,' she would no longer understand. Soon she would no longer be able to swallow anything except a little water.

Our meals in the Italian restaurant in Chelsea seemed as distant as her incarnation as a nun in medieval France.

Twelve

March 21st.

Easter was early in this year of early spring. Easter Sunday fell on the 26th of March.

A little over a fortnight before Easter the Floor Sister asked Diana if she wanted to receive Communion during Holy Week.

We had already talked about it towards the end of February, but Diana had not expressed any definite wish, and I had not insisted. I was afraid I might not be able to control my emotions and betray the fear which was haunting my mind: 'It will be the last time . . .' However, for this very reason I could not let matters drift. I knew how deeply she felt about the sacraments and that she shared my own profound conviction that it is a sacred duty to give strength, comfort, and peace of mind to those who are about to pass through the gates of the Unknown. Not for nothing is the Eucharist given to the dying called the *viaticum—sustenance for the journey.*

She must not leave without it.

I was glad therefore when she herself broached the subject that morning, after the Floor Sister had spoken to her.

'And what have you decided?' I asked her.

'I told Sister that she should not bother because we would arrange it all ourselves.'

'You do want to receive Communion, darling?'

'Yes,' she replied with great emphasis, 'I do.'

'And who would you want to give it to you?' She took a long time to answer as she always did when there was some conflict she could not resolve. Then she said: 'Of course I would like Edward*
to come, but I have decided against it. I cannot expect him to come during Easter week when he is already overworked at the Abbey.'

I tried to make her change her mind: 'I will go and see Edward; I am sure he will come, however busy he is.'

'No,' she replied firmly, 'he does not even know that I am so ill; it will come as a shock to him.'

'It is exactly for this reason; because you are ill that he should come and see you . . . and give you Communion.' I paused. Could she read my thoughts?—'*Edward Carpenter has baptized you: nothing in the world would stop him from giving you the last sacraments*'.

She said: 'I don't want him to think that I am *in extremis;*

* Canon Carpenter.

I will get in touch with him, when I am better—after Easter.'

I could not insist further, and we agreed that I would ask Gerard Irvine. I had not seen him since that fateful day in January at his house when I had told him that I must take Diana home because she was ill; I had hinted to him then that her illness might be very grave, but he did not know that it had been on that very day and from the precincts of his church that she had set out on her via dolorosa.

There was one thing that troubled her mind. She said: 'You know, Mr. P., my memory has become rather bad lately; I cannot remember the prayers; especially the prayer of the general Confession which is very long and difficult; you know the one which begins: *Almighty God, Father of our Lord Jesus Christ, Maker of all things, Judge of all men. We acknowledge . . .'* she faltered. 'Now you see, I get stuck, I just cannot remember.'

'Never mind, darling, I don't know the prayer either; we'll manage somehow.'

I do not remember the exact date of this conversation; but it must have been a few days before she was taken to the Middlesex hospital for the final tests.

I could not see Gerard Irvine immediately, but when I saw him on the 14th or 15th of March, what I had feared, had now become almost a certainty: her Easter Communion was also to be her last.

Not only had we had the doctors' verdict of doom but the progression of her illness was racing ahead of their prediction.

We fixed the time for the Communion for noon, Tuesday, March 21st.

But time was running out.

The speech disturbances which had been the first messengers of her deadly illness in January did not return until about the middle of March. But from the beginning of March on she experienced certain difficulties in retaining ideas, and at times also in following conversations. It would happen that when I told her about some event or talked about matters on a more abstract level— conversations which she always enjoyed and to which she had

204

always contributed so much—she would suddenly say: 'I don't understand what you mean.' She had always spoken slowly and developed her arguments in a very methodical way choosing her words with utmost care, but now she had to make great efforts in formulating her thoughts and expressing them in a manner which satisfied her, for she still retained her own exacting critical standards.

'She has difficulties sometimes,' the nurses told me, 'but her mental control and the beauty of her sentences amazes everyone.'

In those days when speaking had become difficult and very tiring to her she said to me: 'You talk and I'll listen, but instead of answering you and saying "yes" or "no" or "I see", I will just lift one finger from time to time, so that you know that I am listening and that I have understood; do you mind, Mr. P.?' And thus we would converse.

Later, when she had become too weak even to lift her finger, I would hold her hand and talk; from time to time she would, almost imperceptibly, press my hand. There came the day, very soon, when I would hold her hand in mine for long periods, but she could no longer press it.

This had not quite happened yet. But by mid-March I began to notice a slight slurring of her speech, and soon after she started again to mix up and jumble her words as she had done in January. She herself had been the first to notice it: 'My speech is again becoming faulty,' she remarked.

'Not at all, darling,' I tried to reassure her, 'I think it is perfect.'

'Don't talk nonsense,' she answered severely, 'I know it is; so don't contradict me.'

The days when she was fully lucid were coming to an end. She was still fully lucid on Palm Sunday, the 19th of March, when she made me take away her precious belongings. But she had said: 'There might be no other chance.' And she never made statements on insufficient grounds.

205

The next morning when I telephoned as usual to enquire how the night had been, the Sister said: 'She was wandering a little this morning; she talked a great deal about a journey to Italy, but it did not make much sense.' We had reached yet another point of no return.

'How is she now?' I asked.

'Oh, she was quite lucid when I went into her room just now,' the Sister answered.

When I went to see her later in the morning she appeared quite normal, but she spoke slowly and with some difficulty. She said: 'I don't know what I was talking about this morning; it must have been the injections and all these new drugs.' I was told that she had been sick several times and had had two injections of Pethidine to alleviate her pains and general discomfort. She was very much worse; quite frighteningly so. For a moment I doubted that she would be able to receive Communion the next day. I reminded her of it and she told me that she had made all the necessary arrangements. Before leaving I said: 'Darling, if you can do without an injection of Pethidine tomorrow morning it would be better; after all, you don't want to be asleep when Gerard Irvine comes.'

'Of course not, Mr. P. I am sure I will be all right.'

However, they had to give her an injection the next morning (March 21st). When Rosemary and I arrived at 11.30, the curtains were open and the room was flooded in sunlight. I drew the curtains and reduced the light to a warm yellow glow. Diana was only half conscious. Her eyes were open and she was agitated.

Rosemary came to her side: 'Darling Diana,' she said; 'I am here—Rosemary; we are both here.'

Diana clutched Rosemary's hand in both her hands: 'Rosemary, Rosemary,' she called out, her voice rising almost to a shriek like the voice of someone entombed at the bottom of a pit from where he hears his rescuers but cannot reach them and fears they cannot hear him. 'Rosemary, Rosemary, I am so happy

206

you have come. I have been feeling quite mad all morning; now for the first time I feel normal again. Rosemary, darling, stay with me . . .' She held on tight to her.

I put my hand on her damp forehead and said: 'We are both here, my sweetheart, and in a moment Gerard Irvine will be here and we shall all have Holy Communion together.'

As a Catholic who had been divorced and had re-married I was excluded from Communion by my Church. But long before, many years ago, I had ceased to go to Confession and Communion.

My religious upbringing had been of the narrowest and most unimaginative kind. The greater part of my childhood had been spent in remote country places—at least they were remote in those pre-motoring days—or in provincial towns in Austria. The priests who came to our home as well as those who gave us instruction at school were for the most part men of poor education, primitive and literal in their religious understanding. Their teaching was confined in the main to lurid descriptions of the punishments awaiting the sinner in the beyond—and sin was equated with sex.

My memory of Divine Service was one of unspeakable tediousness and physical discomfort. Even the beauty of the Baroque churches with their richly carved altars, their guilded columns, angels and saints, could not fill the yawning spiritual void of those interminable sermons or give deeper meaning to the automatism with which the celebrants went through the ritual of the mass. In short, the sense of mystery, of the numinous: the heart, the quintessence of religion was missing, as it had been missing in the synagogues which Diana's father had attended as a boy.

Nor did we receive guidance or inspiration at home. My father had no deep religious convictions. Correct religious observance was to him part of the established order of life—and a tribute to its hierarchical structure—which, provided one stood at the top, one had no cause to question. He was not a seeker after truth, though perhaps in his heart of hearts he may have been different from what he appeared.

For me the result of this spiritual starvation in childhood was indifference to religion plus a strong anti-clericalism which lasted well into my adult life, until I became acquainted with the teachings of the East and with Jungian psychology. It was only then that I discovered in myself a powerful longing for the realities of the spirit and step by step found my way to the perennial truths underlying all the Great Religions. In other words, I found the way to my own psyche.

Religion, I began to understand, is not a contrived system of beliefs and observances but a spiritual *awareness,* an awareness by man of the relationship between the Divine Ground and himself. Religion in an historical and institutional sense has always been the specific revelation of this relationship appropriate to a particular phase in the evolution of man's consciousness. This evolution of consciousness has not come to an end; indeed, we may only stand at its beginning. Therefore, as awareness widens, so revelation must continue, and with it also religion must evolve. Dogmas, articles of faith, anthropomorphic interpretations, liturgy, rites etc., in short all those aspects of established religion (East and West) which modern 'rational' man finds increasingly difficult to accept because they do not seem to fit into the scientific picture of the Universe, must be regarded as symbolic renderings of an ineffable truth, a truth which by its very nature surpasses rational understanding and conceptual definition.

My new understanding of religion which began from about the age of thirty became a living faith through my life with Diana, for she uniquely exemplified the basic message of all religion: that man stands in the Divine Ground, that he has, in truth, 'his being in God'.

She had often said to me: 'All I know, I know through you.' My answer to her, which perhaps I never put explicitly into words is: 'All I have become, I have become through you.'

She had become calm again. 'You know,' she said softly, 'I cannot remember the prayers very well.'

'Don't worry, my love, we shall all say them together.'

Not only was she blind, but it seemed to me that she was

losing her sense of spatial relations. When one spoke to her she did turn her head in the direction of the sound, but one felt that the mental co-ordinates of three-dimensional experience had gone. She was indeed the spaceman shot into and *lost* in the fathomless vastness and loneliness of outer space where it merges with time in an infinite continuum, and she had *not* been sufficiently trained.

I had always admired her will power and mental stability; she never under any circumstances lost her head or sense of proportion. She always calmed and reassured me when she saw me fidgety or anxious: 'Don't panic, Mr. P.,' she would say to me when I had one of my attacks of claustrophobia in a full underground train or in a lift whose doors would not open immediately. 'Don't panic, just breathe deeply and relax.'

Now it was only this extraordinary mental control rooted in her spiritual certainty which kept her sane where others (I know this certainly applies to myself) would long since have 'gone off their head' . . .

She said: 'I now want to pray silently.' We had propped her up just a little and placed her special pillow in the nape of her neck to give greater support to her head. She remained in silent prayer, the palms of her outstretched hands lightly touching as in Dürer's famous 'Praying Hands'; the tips of her fingers reaching to her lips.

She was not in pain.

Then Father Irvine arrived. He spoke to her, enfolding her praying hands in his hands. I said: 'Darling, Gerard has arrived to give you Holy Communion.' She did not respond immediately but suddenly she became aware of his presence, and once again as when Rosemary had first spoken to her, her voice rose in anguish and in hope: 'Gerard, Gerard, I am so happy you have come.'

The priest lit two candles and placed them on the table to her left. Rosemary stood at the head of the bed on the right, and I stood a little further down on the same side facing Father Irvine across the bed.

209

As I stood there ready to receive Communion in the Anglican rite, I knew I was partaking of a great and holy mystery: the transfiguration of the physical into the spiritual body in which life is everlasting.

She lay with her eyes closed, her hands still joined in prayer, seemingly unaware of what was happening around her, remote and—transfigured. Rosemary and I now knelt at the side of the bed. We spoke the prayers on her behalf. Father Irvine broke the host into three parts, but as he was about to place the smallest of the three fractions between her lips, she woke from her trance-like state and said: 'This is not correct.' She was used to receiving the host into her hands and now could not understand what she was supposed to do. 'No,' she repeated several times, 'this is not correct,' and she refused to open her mouth. She was blind, she had lost all sense of orientation; she probably at this moment did not know where she was. The words: 'The body of our Lord Jesus Christ which was given for thee preserve thy body and soul unto everlasting life' must have reached her as if from very far away. But in the fading light of her consciousness she was aware of the solemnity of the moment.

We spoke to her, tried to explain to her. Suddenly her face lit up with a smile that must have come from the days of her childhood. (I recognized this smile from a photograph of her as a little girl.) She smiled and said: 'Just tell me what to do, and I shall do whatever you think is right.' She opened her lips and received the body of our Lord Jesus Christ. She sank back into her pillows. Then Rosemary and I received Communion; I for the first time in thirty-five years.

I had often been with Diana at the Communion Service at Westminster Abbey and had always been deeply impressed by its solemn beauty. Once or twice Diana had tentatively said to me: 'You know, if you want to receive Communion here at Westminster Abbey, it will be perfectly all right. I have spoken to Edward Carpenter about it . . .' I could not make up my mind. 'Why don't you, Mr. P.? I would like it if you did.'

Was she aware that it had now happened?

Before leaving, Father Irvine gave her Extreme Unction.

That same day, late in the afternoon when I came to see her she lay motionless as in a coma; I said to her: 'Darling, do you remember that you received Holy Communion and that Rosemary and I also received Communion?'

She stirred and answered in a voice that was as clear as a bell: 'Of course I do; one does not forget such an experience.' I took her hand, and she held on tight and said: 'My blessed boy, I love you.'

After her death Father Irvine wrote to me:

'. . . There always seemed to me, and increasingly so, about Diana a kind of spiritual radiance and certainty of one whose inner eye is single. It did fill her body with light almost visible. I felt this especially on the last occasion when I saw her, only partly conscious, when she received the sacraments. There appeared then to be a metamorphosis, a peace and tranquillity, of one far gone on the way to God. I will not easily forget the last image I have in my memory of her lying there with her arms crossed on her breast, unable to see but in a kind of rapture which was not just the effect of sedation . . .'

Thirteen

March 22nd.

For the past week I had, whenever I left the nursing home, given every telephone number where I could be reached during the following twelve hours in case of emergency or if there was a marked deterioration in Diana's condition.

The result was that whenever the telephone rang in Rosemary's house or when dining with friends or even at a restaurant, my heart jumped: the call could be for me.

This permanent state of alert made it almost impossible for me to sleep, and often in the small hours of the morning I would mistake some distant sound for the ringing of the telephone or, waking up from an unquiet dream, think that I had been woken up by an urgent bell. I hardly dared settled down in my bath in the morning for fear of not hearing the telephone ring while Rosemary was preparing breakfast in the kitchen below.

At nine o'clock I made my telephone call which I came to dread more and more every day. My question: 'How is she this morning?' now had come to mean: 'How much worse is she this morning?' But trained hospital staff have a way (quite rightly so) of parrying or deflecting direct thrusts by over-anxious enquirers, and one learns oneself to control one's emotions (at a cost) and to play the game of question and answer with due restraint and in conformity with established etiquette.

On the 22nd of March, the day after the Communion, when I made my morning telephone call there was a short pause at the other end, and then I heard a rapid whispered conversation. Then came the well-known crisp voice of the Floor Sister: 'The Princess is quite well now; we had some little difficulties this morning, but these have now been satisfactorily resolved.'

'What kind of difficulties?'

'I'd rather not discuss this on the telephone, come and see me before you go into her room this morning.'

When I arrived at about 11.30, I was told that Diana had had difficulty in passing water in the morning, and that this had upset her. A catheter had since been applied and all was well.

This was an objective description of a clinical condition. It did not take into account the human drama behind it.

This was clear to me as soon as I entered Diana's room. She was no more in full command of her reasoning power and of her speech. But she was agitated. It had all been an appalling traumatic experience to her.

She tried to explain to me that something quite awful had happened to her: 'A very terrible experience,' she repeated over and over again, but she could not find the words to describe it. But bit by bit she was able to tell me how she had lain for hours in growing discomfort after waking up but had been unable to

212

make herself understood; how finally, when the night nurse had realized her condition and brought the bed pan she could not 'spend a penny'. She had tried every method (she had successfully used on previous occasions) of relaxing, autosuggestion and 'singing a little song' to herself, but all was in vain. The discomfort mounted to a pitch of agonizing pain. She could not understand what was happening, nor was she able to formulate questions. Then the catheter was applied; probably clumsily. It caused her even worse pains, but, above all, it caused her terrible distress for, though her mind was drifting, she must have experienced it as an outrage to her body and her sense of modesty. How could the nurses who hitherto had been so considerate, so gentle, indeed so affectionate, how could they do such an appalling thing to her?

So there was yet another faculty knocked out, one more stronghold of personal freedom surrendered: her bladder could not function any more; the central control had been destroyed.

As in a beleaguered and totally encircled fortress, the perimeter of her defences steadily contracted; one position after another fell and she had to retreat further and further into the inner recesses of her mind from where communication became increasingly difficult, and finally had to cease altogether, because one by one, the communication centres were being isolated or knocked out. Her distress and mental anguish must have been intense. 'I cannot understand what is happening,' she kept on saying.

She was being told that she was getting better; I told her, the doctors told her, the nurses told her. But how could 'getting better' be compatible with feeling steadily worse, being less able, from day to day, to communicate or to receive impressions from her senses; with being pushed back into an ever narrowing land where she could still exercise her rights as an independent human being? What was the meaning of it all? Was she being deceived by all, including her beloved husband? Was there anybody left whom she could trust? After that terrible experience with the catheter she seemed to have completely lost faith in the people around her.

I think we were alone at first that morning, but when she reproached me, she whispered into my ear so as not to embarrass me in case there were witnesses present. She said: 'It was very wrong of you, Mr. P., to bring me here; you did so under false pretences.' And immediately to make good the offence she might have caused me, she added: 'Now let's go home together; we have been here long enough . . .' She was terribly thirsty (she was suffering from constant thirst) but now she refused to drink a drop of water. Again, whispering into my ear, she said: 'They are playing tricks on me . . . I know they are . . .' I tried to reassure her. 'I know they are,' she repeated earnestly. But suddenly she smiled angelically and said: 'I shan't press the point any further just now.'

The nurse came in and we tried to persuade her to have something to drink, a little lemonade, real lemon juice in water with some sugar, she was very fond of it. She resolutely refused, and she tried to explain that, not being able to pass water any more, it would cause her great distress: 'It can't come out any more,' she said. (She had always firmly held that what goes in one end, must come out the other.) 'It is only logic is it not?' She spoke of the 'upper' and of the 'lower' stomach, and though she had studied anatomy in the course of her art training, she seemed to visualize the inside of the human body from the 'upper' stomach down as a series of well defined layers, very much like geological strata or a series of trays that intercommunicated and passed on the solid food and liquids put into the top tray. Now in the growing confusion of her mind and after the experience of the night, she clung on to the idea, that what goes in must come out.

I spoke gently to her and tried to tell her that all would be well and that she need not fear that she would be in discomfort. She listened and then said with great emphasis: 'Will you swear to me as a husband who loves his wife and would not wish to cause her suffering; will you swear to me that it will be all right if I drink something?'

'Yes, my pet, I swear it; it will be perfectly all right for you to drink.'

'In that case,' she answered with a deep sigh of relief, 'I would like to have three big glasses of hot sugared lemonade.'

The nurse prepared the lemonade and then helped her to drink it through the glass tube. She could only swallow in tiny short little sips. The nurse asked her: 'Do you like the lemonade?' Diana paused and then she said in her most gentle voice: 'I don't want to make you jealous; but the lemonade which the night nurse made for me was very very good. This one is also good, but perhaps not quite so good; but please don't be offended.' (In fact the lemonade was rather bitter.)

After a few more sips—more than half the glass was still left— she said: 'This is enough.' I eased her back into her pillows.

Before leaving that morning I said to her: 'Darling, don't worry too much about not being able to spend a penny; you will soon be able to do it again; this is only the temporary effect of the new drugs.'

'Well, darling,' she answered, 'I don't think I can trust you completely in this; you also said the blindness would pass in a few days; yet I am still blind.' (It had been agreed between the doctors and myself that she should be kept in the belief that the blindness was temporary and due to the treatment, and after the house physician had given her his explanation, she had said to me: 'What Dr. F. told me about my blindness made good sense to me.') But now she was beginning to have doubts.

'I did not say that the blindness would go in a few days, my sweet,' I replied, 'I said a couple of weeks or so until it had completely gone.'

'Did you say that? I must have forgotten, but one does lose track of time when one cannot see; you understand that, don't you?' She spoke clearly, her logic was faultless, her dignity supreme.

I asked her once again: 'Do you remember that you received Holy Communion yesterday?'

'Of course I do, Mr. P.'

As I went to my car parked around the corner in Harley Street I suddenly realized that I could not trust myself to drive back to Chelsea in the midday traffic. I went back to the nursing home and asked Dr. F. to look after my parking meter until my return in the afternoon. Then I took a taxi. It was the first time that such a thing had happened to me in forty years of driving.

When I came back at about three o'clock in the afternoon I stopped for a moment at the Floor Sister's office. I had to order some more Malvern Water, for right from the beginning I had not wanted Diana to drink the tap water which had a nasty taste of disinfectant. At first I had ordered six bottles, then twelve at a time (they were supplied by a near-by wine merchant). Now the Sister asked me: 'How many shall I order? Shall I order, say, four bottles?'

I looked at her angrily and said: 'Order twelve.' Of these, six were never opened.

Diana had only just woken up after an injection of Pethidine. 'Please explain something to me,' she said. 'You say, I am lying in a chair . . .'

'No, my love, you are lying in your bed.'

'Well, all right, I am lying in my bed . . . and *where* are you?'

'I am sitting by your bed.'

'What does it mean, sitting by my bed; please explain it to me, I don't quite understand.' I tried to explain that I was sitting in a chair drawn up by the side of the bed, my elbows resting on the cover. She listened carefully and then said: 'I understand what you say, but to me it is all quite different. I am not lying on the bed. I am floating above the bed, and you, you are far away below . . .'

The sensation she described may have been due to the after-effect of the injection or part of her increasing mental disorientation. Yet, she spoke with such complete clarity and authority that I decided I must not, as it were, 'bring her down to earth'.

I answered: 'Darling, you know all about the etheric body. When one is ill it may happen that the etheric body and the physical body are not quite in the same place. At the moment your centre of consciousness has shifted to your etheric body

216

which may well be floating above your physical body. Does this make sense to you?'

'Yes,' she answered, 'this does explain it.' She seemed completely satisfied.

The same afternoon she said to me: 'As my body becomes less material I become more sensitive to sounds, smells, emanations, vibrations and atmospheres.'

I had noticed it. Quite often recently when I came in from the street and sat down on her bed, she would take my hands and say: 'You dirty boy, go and wash your hands.' They were usually quite clean, but to her they carried some disturbing smell such as petrol or tobacco or simply the emanations of the outside world which were to her gross, vulgar and material.

She knew at once when one of the nurses had been smoking a cigarette, even if that had happened an hour or more before the girl came into her room. Now that she was blind she recognized her women friends by the scent of their perfume or soap, however faint; or simply by the natural scent of their skin.

Her sense of smell and hearing remained unimpaired until the end; she would respond to voices or shrink back at any unfamiliar smell.

The moment had now come when she could no longer be left alone, day or night, because of the difficulties she was experiencing. She was blind, she had lost all control over her movements; she could no longer ring the bell, call for assistance, make herself understood. Also, she was in danger of injuring her head against the edges of the bedside tables or of falling out of the bed during one of those frequent attacks of near frenzy when she struggled with all her remaining strength to escape from the grip of the monster which, like the Minotaur of the Cretan myth, held her in its deadly embrace. She struggled in the dark; the reassurance of the visual world was no more. Where could she turn to? There was only one place where she knew she would be safe: home. She wanted to flee.

'Take me away, please, take me home.'

She was now in need of constant watching, and this could not be done by the regular nursing staff. But perhaps more than physical care she needed a Loving Presence. She was rapidly moving beyond the reach of verbal, conceptual communication; her mind was withdrawing from her physical body. Someone must be with her who could communicate *directly,* heart to heart, spirit to spirit. She needed someone who, like herself, had the charismatic gift of love.

Where was she to come from?

In the afternoon I told Diana of our decision: 'We have come to the conclusion, darling, that you must have your own private nurse until you are able to see again. I don't want to leave you alone at any time.'

She replied reasonably and calmly: 'But that will cost even more money.' 'Never mind, my pet, there is enough money—for the moment.'

'Never mind,' she repeated quite gaily, 'you are right; let's not worry too much about money just now.'

It was essential to find a nurse that very day, and there was no possibility of interviewing anybody beforehand.

At four o'clock in the afternoon a girl arrived, sent by an agency. She was shown into the room and introduced by one of the staff nurses. Diana who had been lying back, her eyes closed and seemingly far away, stretched out her hand in welcome and said: 'How do you do; it is very nice of you to come . . . yes, thank you very much, I am quite well . . .'

I did not like the girl; she looked efficient but impersonal. It was clear to me that she had none of the qualities I was looking for; above all she lacked love.

Before leaving ('I must be off punctually at 6,' she said, 'I have an appointment') she informed me that she would not be returning the next morning.

I went to the Sister's office and rang the agency: 'You must send us someone quite exceptional; this is not merely a question of nursing; what we need is a ministering angel.'

'I think,' said the voice on the other end of the line, 'I have exactly what you require . . .'

The next morning, March the 23rd, when I entered Diana's room, there was Elizabeth. She was sitting on Diana's bed combing her hair which had not been combed for many days and had become tangled and matted. She was combing Diana's hair strand by strand, laying it out around her head until it covered the white pillow in a stream of dark burnished amber.

Elizabeth had returned from a holiday in Ireland only two days before. She had not yet made up her mind on the kind of nursing job she wanted to do next, but it had not been her intention to do private nursing. But when the agency had rung her to ask if she would accept the assignment of looking after a young woman dying of cancer, she had at once agreed. 'I knew this was what I had to do,' she told me later. 'I knew I could not act against what Providence and my own destiny demanded of me at this moment.'

Elizabeth had hair the colour of pure gold; it surrounded her head like a halo. With her high, clear forehead, her large topaz eyes under long lashes and perfectly shaped eyelids, the soft, still childlike contours of her cheeks and chin, she reminded me of the Madonnas by the Lombard masters of the 16th century.

Her voice was soft and it was low-pitched, very much like Diana's.

Never before had I witnessed a scene that so poignantly illustrated both man's helplessness in the face of his mortality and the transcendent power of his spirit which lifts him above his own mortal nature.

Here were two young women, each in her own way exquisitely beautiful. One was dying an untimely and cruel death, the other ministering to her with infinite tenderness and respect.

This was what I had asked for, hoped for, when I had rung the agency the previous day: someone who would take care not of a 'dying patient' but of a living person who, though deprived of most of her physical and mental faculties was still *present,* still aware of and responding to love; who could still be given comfort, peace of mind; perhaps even happiness.

In that most tragic hour of my life this scene of touching beauty and of sorrow filled me with gratitude and with something akin to—joy. If only I had been able to tell Diana; she would have understood, and she, too, would have loved Elizabeth.

There were still moments of recognition. Later that day, the 23rd of March, she suddenly said to me: 'I am aware that you are here.'

I asked her: 'Are you in pain?'

She answered: 'Do you mean that I have no pains or that I am not aware of them? I think this is the truth—the pains are covered up.' After some time in which she seemed far away, she said: 'It is marvellous. Is it that I am being given a holiday after a very serious illness?'

'Yes, my love, that is what it is.'

She was silent and then she said: 'I could of course weep and weep if I wanted, but I don't think I shall.' At this moment I felt she *knew.*

As I was taking leave of her at about eight as usual, she asked me: 'Where are you dining?'

'With Rosemary, darling.'

'Tell Rosemary,' she answered, 'I would very much like to come to dinner, but, unfortunately, I am too exhausted . . .'

'I shall tell her, my sweet, I am sure she will understand.'

'Thank you, Mr. P.'

220

Fourteen

As I have said, Diana had no real vanity. But it was part of this sense of perfection which she applied to any task, from the most menial household chores to her painting and carving as well as to the task of life itself, it was part of this sense of perfection that she took the greatest care of her appearance. She used little make-up, but pencilled her eyebrows and even made some concessions to new eye fashions by applying shades of green or blue to her eyelids. Choosing the correct lipstick gave her great pleasure and was done with the same earnestness and professional expertise with which she would select paints for her work.

She never had much money to spend on cosmetics, and her dressing-table was not lavishly appointed compared to that of some of her women friends. She never had a good mirror nor silver-handled brushed nor many of the paraphernalia of beauty care which most women consider essential. But she had a number of pretty cut-glass Victorian containers with silver tops which we had picked up here and there in antique shops, and she kept them always beautifully polished. She had a few small porcelain boxes and trays and one or two antique scent bottles.

As she had never inherited anything or received any presents from her parents or relations, every little object, ornament, trinket she possessed had been collected over the years during our married life; each one had been chosen with unfailing taste and love. I am still surrounded by many of these—not particularly valuable—objects which she treasured so much.

Nor had she inherited or ever been given any jewellery; there were no diamond pendants, clips, brooches, rings, necklaces, bracelets, no sapphires, rubies, emeralds; no pearls, not even cultured

221

ones. She did not mind except for the pearls: 'One day, when we have a little money, I would like to have a double row of cultured pearls; one can get them for as little as £25 one row; and they must have a really good clip.' It might have become possible—had she lived—perhaps even that year. But not even the cultured pearl earrings we had hoped to buy materialized. When she was half way through her radiation treatment she said: 'When I am quite well again, *we* must buy *me* a present, because I have gone through so much; perhaps earrings, if we cannot yet afford the strings.' I promised that I would; it never came to it.

She was not without jewellery. Over the years she had acquired or I had given her, mainly from one shop that specialized in antique jewellery, and where she had been known ever since as a young girl she had bought trinkets for a few shillings, some bracelets, rings—mostly semi-precious stones in antique mountings; some Renaissance pendants in silver set with tiny rubies and pearls. She also had that beautifully worked Portuguese bracelet in gold with grey pearls, two Victorian brooches in gold, enamelled and set with small stones which my mother had given her and—her latest acquisition—a piece of modern jewellery: a bird in gold and enamel and set with small pearls and rubies which she had found in the grounds of Stella's house in the country where it had been lost over a year ago and had lain half-buried in the gravel ever since. Stella gave it to her. She wore it in her lapel the day when the last photograph was taken of her at the end of January.

On her elegant wrists and beautiful strong hands precious jewellery such as diamonds, emeralds and rubies would have looked wrong; but one antique bracelet, one or perhaps two rings such as she wore enhanced and high-lighted the gracefulness of her sensitive gestures. Her jewellery, like the dresses she wore, her movements, her voice, her smile were all expressions of one and the same harmony.

She always kept her nails in beautiful condition: long, oval and polished. She never used nail varnish, but a polishing powder and an old-fashioned 'buffer' for polishing. The only other important implement for her manicure was a long nail-file of flexible steel. I called it our 'universal' tool, for its pointed end could be used for tightening small screws on electrical switches and plugs; its other end which was flat and broad served as a spatula for taking digestive powders out of a tin and stirring them into water. She took the nail file to the nursing home but was never able to use it there.

At first she still put on lipstick and powder; then she had to give this up, too. I often combed her hair at that period; it had to be done very slowly because the slightest pulling immediately increased her headache. Her nails of which she had been so proud grew very long, and she could do nothing about it. At first she minded; then, as the illness progressed, she seemed to mind no more. When her movements and gestures had become erratic and unco-ordinated I began to fear that she might injure her eyes with her long nails. Finally, Elizabeth cut her nails effectively but with little regard to shape and beauty. Elizabeth told me later that Diana, though blind and with very little sensation left in the tips of her fingers, had protested at her nails being cut with scissors and not filed as usual, but finally had resigned herself to it. But it was I who grieved over the destruction of one more of her characteristic features: her well-groomed nails which crowned her long, pointed fingers . . .

She who had always been in such perfect command of herself and so meticulous about her appearance, she had had to abandon one by one all those little cares and ministrations which women devote to enhance their beauty in their own eyes and in those of men.

A narrow streak of grey hair which, growing from the top of her forehead, divided her dark hair and which for some months past she had been hiding by a dark rinse, had now become visible again. It was to me a deeply moving sight, this narrow streak of grey hair—a reminder of her little vanities, a symbol of things not accomplished.

March 24th, Good Friday.

One of my standard questions in the morning, on arriving at the nursing home was now: 'How lucid is she?' for the periods of mental confusion (or what seemed mental confusion) were becoming more prolonged every day. I now spent practically all day at the nursing home, mostly in her room, but every now and again walking up and down the corridor or smoking a cigarette in the small ante room just outside her door. Now that she had permanent day nursing, I did not watch out, as I used to before, for the red light to come on above the door, indicating that she had rung her bell.

When I went into her room on Good Friday, she was asleep. I sat by her and held her hand. When she woke up, she knew at once I was with her.

I asked her: 'Are you happy, my love?'

She answered: 'Yes, very happy, darling . . .'

Then she resumed her soliloquies which as I gathered from the nurses she was now pursuing intermittently day and night during all those hours of twilight consciousness which followed hours of deep sedation. That morning she was preoccupied with problems of geometry, with circles, squares, sections, cubes. They seemed to correspond to a vision of reality which she was trying to grasp and to convey to us. As she had never been interested in geometry and had no sense for mathematics of any kind, this seemed to me of extraordinary significance. These must have been true visions of reality on an archetypal level. I noted with amazement, the first time on that day, that the themes of the fantasies which occupied her embattled mind were as pure, and all in their own way as significant, as anything she had ever expressed.

There was a human being *in extremis,* the intricate mechanism of the brain with its millions of pathways and associative connections and centres of intelligence damaged beyond hope. Only those deeper layers of the brain, where the primitive, vital functions are located, were still working (to a certain extent), but without control from the centres of higher intelligence with their moral code and 'feed-back' from memory and from impressions which impose an orderly and 'reality-orientated' pattern on our thought, speech and behaviour.

Thus freed from the restraint of reason the deeper, more primitive but also collective contents of the psyche are given free vent, and as we know from dreams or from states of intoxication or drugs, these deeper contents reveal aspects of the personality which are often suppressed and almost always modified in normal waking life. They reveal if not, as has been said, our 'true' personality ('in vino veritas') but certainly an aspect which is as true as and complementary to our normal waking personality. Aggressiveness, resentments, fears and traumatic memories reside in these layers of the psyche where they live their own secret life to break through to the surface of the mind openly or disguised only under conditions of reduced control. But together with these primitive individual or collective contents of the 'Unconscious' dwell the *Archetypes,* those basic configurations of the mind through which from ages past the human psyche has become aware of the innermost realities of life. Here are the sources of revelation that reaches our conscious mind in the hieratic language of symbolism.

It had always struck me that Diana had dreams of two very distinct kinds only; neither lent itself to Freudian symbolic interpretation in the sense of conveying, in symbolic form, repressed sexual or aggressive complexes, fears or frustrations or childhood traumata. The first kind were simple straight-forward wish-fulfilments or desires not very different from the type one might have in waking life, and barely disguised. It has been said somewhere, perhaps even by Freud himself, that if a child dreams of strawberry ice-cream, it simply means a desire for strawberry ice-cream. Most of her dreams belonging into this category were of the 'strawberry ice-cream' type: when she dreamt of eating it meant she was hungry, when she dreamt of travelling it meant just that; when she dreamt of a string of pearls it was because she would have liked to have one; no hidden meanings could have been discovered here by the most or-

225

thodox Freudian analyst; never was there an element of guilt or shame in these dreams, never anything that might have caused her embarrassment on the analyst's couch.

The other type of dream was the profound archetypal dream or the dream of inner knowledge that showed how her conscious search for truth and spiritual perfection sprang from an inner vision and necessity. In other words, there was no conflict between the 'without' and the 'within' of her personality; it was all of one piece; the conscious 'visible' aspect merely the controlled and harnessed aspect of the inner, invisible one, as the jet and play of a fountain is the controlled aspect of the source that feeds it.

There existed complete harmony between the conscious and unconscious levels of her mind. She could well afford the 'strawberry ice-cream' side of her nature, for she combined it with extraordinary maturity of mind. She was the most fully integrated human being I had ever known. Her dreams were merely a confirmation of what she expressed in her painting, her writing, her everyday activities and her relations to others.

It should therefore not have surprised me that in her fantasies and ravings in the last days of her life she again expressed these two aspects of her personality: the 'strawberry ice-cream' aspect of innocent childlikeness which she had always expressed in her comical drawings, poems and in her illustrated letters to adults and children and in the never-ceasing bubbling stream of her humour, on the one hand, and the visionary quest for truth to which her life had been dedicated, on the other.

And so in her final, apparently confused soliloquies, confused not in basic meaning but only because of their lack of reasoned control and language; she talked complete 'non-sense', the wonderful, 'Alice-in-Wonderland' and Edward Lear type of nonsense which had been a source of never ending delight for me in all those years, or discussed the ultimate nature of reality. It was like the end of a brilliant firework display, before the last star of the last sheaf of the last multi-coloured rocket has spent itself in the darkness of the night.

On coming home in the evening of that Good Friday I wrote into my pocket diary: 'Never have I understood the significance of this day more fully: the divine spirit crucified in the suffering flesh.'

I suffer anguish, unspeakable anguish for you, my beloved, you gentle, tender, noble human being: to see you suffer in your body, to see you perplexed, puzzled and anguished in your mind. And I cannot help. And we cannot even 'discuss' together, and I cannot explain to you.

'Mr. P. must know the answer,' you had said so often. 'We'll just ask Mr. P.; he knows.' You cannot ask him, and he does not know. In the ever more impenetrable darkness that has descended on you and with all the strange and terrible things that have happened to you which you can no longer understand, you have surely wanted to ask Mr. P., but he now seems so very far away from you, even as he sits by you holding your hand or kissing your brow; he seems so far away; your voice cannot reach him.

In the earlier days when you could still see and were still in command of your senses and your mental faculties you could still ask Mr. P., 'Why do you think there is this numbness in my fingers?' And he could explain: 'Migraine often produces this kind of sensation; Rosemary invariably gets it when she has migraine.' Or, when your headache would not get better after taking the various pills: 'Do you think we might tell Dr. R. that Panadol does not stop my headaches any longer; could we not try something else?' Or, 'Why do I suddenly get sick, without any warning, even if I have not moved at all, nor eaten anything?'

One could still talk to Mr. P., compare things, take comfort from his words, keep a sense of proportion. Now you could no more get through to him, and yet it was so urgent, so desperately urgent, that you should be able to ask certain things. You felt there were important problems to be solved; there were totally unexpected sensations for which you could not account but which

227

surely could be explained if only Mr. P. were within reach. There were these terrible nightmares, and if one called, surely Mr. P., sleeping soundly by one's side, would wake up and would comfort: 'It is only a dream; look, we'll switch on the light. There—you see, all is cosy and normal again.'

But now one called and no one answered; one struggled in the darkness and there was no one to help. Where is Mr. P.?

A few days earlier when she had still been able to communicate in moments of lucidity, she told me one of her nightmares. 'I dreamt that we were sleeping in the flat. It was a very dark night. I was woken up by a noise at the front door, someone was trying to break into the flat. You were fast asleep; I tried to wake you. I heard them come into the hall and then towards the bedroom door . . . I called and called to wake you, but you did not answer. I gave up and thought: if it has to be, let it be. There is nothing I can do. But I was very frightened. But I needed you so much when I had this dream. Why did you not answer?'

'I was not here, my love, when you had that dream.'

Her mind wandered a little, and she said: 'Why not, darling?'

'You are at the nursing home, and I don't sleep by your side.'

'Could you not come and sleep here with me?'

'I wish I could, my sweet . . .'

One could still talk. But now, when one had one of those nightmares and one opened one's eyes, it was pitch dark; one did not know what time it was. And if one heard voices one did not know from where they came.

But there was a gentle hand touching one's forehead; that was real. And then there was a voice quite close, the voice one knew, Mr. P.'s voice saying: 'My darling, my beautiful girl, I am here with you; I shall never leave you; I am always by your side.'

How could I fathom what went on behind that white damp brow as she lay there sometimes quite still, sometimes tossing about; sometimes softly moaning, sometimes with her eyes shut, sometimes with her eyes open. 'Close your eyes, my love,' I

would say to her, 'close your eyes'; those eyes that once had
been pools of enchantment to me, now wild, staring, sightless,
I could not bear it; it struck terror into my heart, a kind of
agonised suffering which shattered me completely.

Why should she who had at all times been prepared to take
on other people's burdens, to listen to other people's troubles,
to come to their aid, why should she be overwhelmed by a
catastrophe beyond all possibility of help or comfort by those
who loved her? How did she experience it, this incapacity
or even seeming unwillingness of others to come to her rescue?

This 'mystery of inaccessibility' to the quality of her experience and suffering was to me almost the greatest torment,
not only during those last weeks of her life, but also long after
her death. Only she could have relieved it; she was the only
one with whom I could have discussed it intelligently in order
to bring some sort of sense into it. She would have understood
all the nuances of my own terrible distress. She would have
thrown just the right kind of light on it and would have made
me understand and accept it. But this could not be. And so
the mystery and the torment must remain.

Often as I sat by her bed or when driving through the
streets of London with its milling crowds of ugly people, its
vulgar newspaper posters and general tawdriness, I asked myself:
Can God permit, let alone want, such beauty and perfection
to perish and allow the mediocre, the ugly, the gross and vulgar
and the evil to flourish? It makes no sense; in terms of reason
(or in any other terms I could think of), it makes no sense.

And every night I prayed: O God, it cannot be Your will
that she should die, and die so terribly, her life not yet fulfilled.
She has so much to give—to me, to others and to—You.
Perhaps You do not know that she is dying of cancer of the
brain. Perhaps You have not been informed and yet, is it not
written that 'not one sparrow shall fall to the ground without
your Father', and is she not of more value than many sparrows?
Or perhaps You are not particularly concerned with it. But
I am. And I am informing You now. This is what is happening

229

to her, to her who is one the most perfect flowers of Your creation. Will You not intervene, now, immediately, while there is life? I cannot, I will not say: *fiat voluntas Tua,* for this would be admitting that it is Your will that she should die . . .

Or I addressed myself to Christ: The Church enjoins me to believe, and You, Yourself have told us that You always dwell amongst us . . . Nothing about Your life and short ministry on earth would make sense if it were otherwise. You must therefore be with us *now;* with her and with me. If You healed the sick then and listened to the entreaties of those who sought Your help then, why can You not do it now? Credo in unum Deum . . . et in unum Dominum Jesum Christum, filium Dei unigenitum . . . is this what I believe? I want to believe, but *heal her now.* . . . Perhaps it was wrong to address my direct to the Father. And so I address myself now, as You commanded, to the Son. *Heal her now.*

Childish supplications, but can prayers be sophisticated? Is there a right way and a wrong way of speaking to God? How must one pray to make one's prayers effective, or is it like a game of chance, like filling in football coupons with the odds seven hundred millions to one, against?

Yet I persisted in my prayers. I felt that if I could keep this one-sided dialogue going there was still hope. Something new, some new idea or event might suddenly arise which would change the fatal course of the illness or at least change my attitude to it. I might in these moments of intimate converse with my own inner self come nearer to an intuitive understanding of the great mystery of evil and suffering in a world created and ordered by a God Whom we hold to be infinitely good and all-powerful.

As I prayed, trying to penetrate the mysterious ways of God, what I really wanted was to discover the error in our thinking that makes us seek an intelligible explanation within the framework of religious belief.

Somehow, I felt it must all be utterly different from what we imagine, beyond the power of our dualising mind to grasp, yet ultimately startlingly simple. There was no answer, no explanation. Yet there might be some form of comprehension granted by sudden flashes of illumination. I resolved to give up all attempts at arriving at a consistent philosophy and to yield to the existential experience of each moment, however irrational the experience, however inconsistent the experience of one moment with that of the next.

Childish and unreasonable though my prayers were, they had not been in vain. They finally made it possible for me to say: *Fiat voluntas Tua,* but without meekly accepting what was to me unacceptable and incomprehensible. By ceasing to probe into the mystery I knew I would be able to bear whatever sorrow was yet to come, with my faith in the supremacy of the spirit over all outward appearances and the tribulations of the flesh unimpaired.

Saturday, March 25th.

'We must reduce her level of consciousness,' Dr. F., the house physician had said to me two or three days before, 'because we are entering the most distressing phase—for her and for you.'

I pleaded with him: 'We are still able to communicate; this is all that is left to us; there are still moments of happiness; could we not wait a little longer?'

He answered: 'If we do not reduce her level of consciousness soon with drugs, the illness will do it, and this will be much more distressing as it will be uncontrolled.'

'What do you propose to give her and what will it do?'

'A mixture of gin and heroin.'

This, I knew would be another point of no return, another door of life slammed shut. 'No,' I said, 'I cannot bear the thought of it.'

'Don't you think,' said Dr. F. gently, 'it would be better also for you to know that she does not suffer any more, physically and mentally, even if this meant that communication would be reduced?'

231

'Does this mean,' I replied, 'that she would be in a kind of coma?'

'Not necessarily; she would be in a slightly euphoric state.'

'Please, wait another two or three days.'

'As you wish.'

I knew if at that moment I had said the word, the drugs would have been stepped up beyond the dosages necessary to alleviate pain and suffering. The doctors, all conscientious and humane men, would have, by bringing to an end this suffering in a situation which was past all remedy and hope, acted in accordance with irreproachable humanitarian standards. But are these standards really the ultimate standards of judgement? I, for my part, cannot accept it. Whilst I am against prolonging life at all cost in an utterly hopeless situation—this is why I rejected the idea of a desperate, 'heroic' operation which had been suggested to me on the 11th of March—I am profoundly convinced that it cannot be right deliberately to bring life to an end. We simply do not know enough of what is involved in the mystery of death.

Whether we regard death as final: as the extinction of the individual or as a door through which we pass from one state of existence into another (this is my belief), one thing seems certain to me: it is a most solemn, perhaps the most solemn event in our life, the event for which our entire life is a preparation.

Into the hour of our death we bring everything we have been, everything we have made of life, everything we have been to others—for this also is part of our reality as individuals—everything from which we may be reborn into a new life.

That is why death, the moment of death, should be regarded with awe and treated with deep respect. Though the state of mind of the dying must remain a mystery, my experience at the death of Diana convinced me that they are *present* at the moment of death—and beyond.

By deliberately bringing a life to an end we may be taking a law which is God's alone into our own fumbling hands, and we may do untold psychic and spiritual harm to the dying and to those who loved them.

I did not argue the case when Dr. F. spoke to me that day on reducing her physical pains and mental suffering by reducing her level of consciousness; all I knew was that she was living, that she was still aware, essentially aware that is, of my love for her and her love for me, and that we could still communicate. All I knew was that under no circumstances would I allow any drastic interference with her appointed span of life.

I also knew that much suffering and anguish was still before me; suffering and anguish in proportion to hers, perhaps even in excess of it. As Dr. F. put it, the 'most distressing phase' was still to come.

'You may if you think it necessary, to reduce her suffering, increase the potency of the drugs somewhat,' I said to Dr. F. on parting, 'but bear in mind what I have said, we can still communicate and that is all that is left to us . . .'

It was exactly four weeks to the day that Mrs. M. had said she would come to see Diana for a final healing session. 'So that the prophecy, or rather the oracle, might be fulfilled,' I thought.

I found Diana very agitated in the morning, desperately trying to explain to me and to Elizabeth why it was essential for her to leave the nursing home. She kept on repeating: 'Please, please, take me away; I must go home; don't you understand, I must go home . . .'

At midday Mrs. M. came accompanied by her husband and Rosamond. She remained with Diana for about half an hour. On leaving—I did not put any questions to her—she once again expressed the belief that Diana would recover. I knew she would not.

When I returned in the afternoon Diana was asleep and peaceful. She woke up at about six o'clock and at once became terribly anguished and agitated. Eileen, who had arrived a little after me, tried to calm her. It was of no avail: 'Take me away, take me away,' she cried, 'I must leave.' She began to struggle. She gripped the bars of her bed above her head trying to pull herself

233

up. Her face was contorted, her lips trembling. Then she spoke rapidly and incoherently. She desperately wanted to get away. It was as if she had suddenly realized that this was the last chance given to her to leave her bed of suffering alive. She pleaded for our help and could not understand why we could or would not help her. She was in profound distress. With her last strength she threw aside her bedclothes, baring her emaciated body, still beautiful and graceful in its agony.

We held her gently and covered her up. 'Lie quietly, my love, you are not well enough to leave just yet.' Her head rolled back, her mouth was open, her eyes turned upwards showing only the whites. She seemed in the very throes of death.

I rang for Dr. F. who could not be found immediately. I spoke to her, and suddenly she calmed down, put both her arms around my neck and said: 'My darling boy, my blessed angel.'

In my diary for that day I wrote: 'Is this the last time she recognizes me?' Dr. F. came after about a quarter of an hour and asked us to leave and wait outside. He was with her for a very long time while we sat in the ante-room watching nurses entering and leaving the room carrying trays with medicines, syringes and cotton wool.

When Dr. F. came out at last he said: 'She is quiet now; I gave her a strong injection.' I knew this was the heroin of which he had spoken two or three days before. I knew that the process of 'reducing the level of her consciousness' had now begun.

A few weeks later the chemist who supplied the nursing home with medicines told me: 'We knew from the progression of the drugs—they were steadily becoming more terrible—that your wife was dying.'

That evening, after the doctor had left, I spent another half-hour with Diana. She was peaceful and seemingly asleep. I spoke to her and I think she understood. Her eyes remained closed, but she smiled, and she nodded her head. At one moment she began to conduct with her right hand an invisible orchestra. Her expression became intense, absorbed in the music that

234

came to her from within. She repeated over and over again: 'How beautiful, how very beautiful . . .' Then again she subsided into sleep.

I kissed her on the forehead and tiptoed out of the room. Just as I reached the door, she said in a clear voice: 'Good night, Mr. P.!'

March 26th, Easter Sunday.

She now had entered the last stage of her journey where there were no recognizable landmarks, no friendly passers-by from whom she might ask the way. Elizabeth and I who were watching her every movement, listening to every sigh and breath, were helpless to give her comfort. She did not know us. She spoke earnestly and with great emphasis on matters that must have been of desperate importance to her, but to us it seemed only a jumble of unco-ordinated words and sentences. At times it sounded like an unknown language. Mostly her eyes were open. I kissed her, stroked her hair, held her hands, knelt by the bed in disconsolate dismay.

Elizabeth, seeing my distress, silently left the room for a few minutes. I spoke to Diana, softly in our most intimate private language, hoping the words would penetrate the walls of her besieged brain and bring a message of love and hope to her imprisoned spirit. And every now and again they did. Suddenly her mutterings would cease, and she would fling her arms around my neck, pull my face close to hers and whisper: 'My darling boy, I love you; don't leave me.' Then again she would fall back into her pillows and lie still or continue her earnest deliberations on the nature of reality. Her face was still flushed, not waxen as I was told the faces of the dying are. Her lips were still delicately red.

'My love, my beautiful girl, please stay with me; don't leave me. Please, live. Oh my darling, if only I could perform a miracle; if only a miracle could happen. My precious one, I am with you, your husband, your lover. I am with you; I will be with you to the end and beyond . . .'

235

When Elizabeth came back into the room she told me that there was a message from Canon Carpenter, asking me to ring him urgently. He had heard that Diana was gravely ill, and when he could not obtain a reply from my flat, he had rung several hospitals and nursing homes until he had found the right one. He seemed to know without having been told that she was dying. He came the same afternoon and prayed silently over her, commending her spirit to God.

She woke up later, and I told her that Edward Carpenter had been to see her, but as she had been fast asleep he had not wanted to wake her, but he sent her his love and would come again. 'Yes, I must have been asleep,' she said, 'but at one moment I thought I heard a voice, like someone saying a prayer.'

I sat quite close to her. I put my head close to her chest; she stroked my face and passed her hands through my hair. She asked: 'Is this your head, darling; is this your hair?' I confirmed that this was so and she was happy. (Some days before when she had held my hand she had examined it closely by touching the palm, the fingers and the back of the hand, and then she had asked: 'Is this your hand?' I had then realized that she could no longer co-ordinate perception with sense impressions. She also could no more place a voice in space unless one sat quite close to her.) But she was still present, fully present, even on Easter Sunday when she asked me 'Is this your head?'

At about seven o'clock in the evening I sat as usual outside her room when the nurses were tending to her, carrying out all the pathetic ministrations of which her body, over which she had no longer any command, still stood in need.

For one moment she was left alone with the door half open. I went into the room which was brightly lit, both from the ceiling and the bedside lamps. She was lying on her back, her eyes open, but to all appearance only semi-conscious. I don't know what possessed me to say to her as I went in: 'Darling,

236

can you see anything?' (Perhaps it was the desperate desire to maintain the illusion that all would be well again.)

She smiled and answered: 'I am sorry, Mr. P., as you know I haven't got my specs on . . .'

When the nurses came out a little later, one of them said: 'She is quite extraordinary; while we were doing all the things we had to do, she suddenly said to us: "All this seems quite foolish to me; fancy two grown up girls like you wasting their time over such silly things" and then she laughed. She is really all there . . .'

This was the day after they had begun to 'reduce her level of consciousness'.

March 27th, Easter Monday.

She was asleep when I arrived in the morning. I had brought the two Christmas angels, the golden and the silver one, which had been with us for so many years. I placed them on the bedside table, quite close to her at the head of the bed. They were to hold permanent vigil over her.

A few days before, the night nurse on the orders of the doctor had removed her small dental plate, for she restlessly moved her mouth and was in danger of swallowing the plate. (They also wound some cotton around her wedding ring, because she kept on pulling it off and placing it into her mouth.) She lay there with a gap showing between her front teeth, looking like a little girl who had lost her milk teeth. She did not know. Or so I thought. On that morning, when she suddenly emerged for a brief moment from what was more a coma than a sleep, and became aware of my presence, she pointed to her mouth with an apologetic smile and said: 'They have taken away my little teeth.'

In the afternoon she was awake for longer spells and very restless. She who had been so skilled with her fingers was now reduced to tying, or rather trying to tie and untie the pretty ribbons that adorned the neckline of her nightie. Restlessly her elegant hands passed to and fro as if to find a resting place.

237

This strange fluttering of the hands seeking a place where they could alight, I had already observed some weeks back when we were still able to talk together. I had asked her one day why she was doing it. 'It gives me some sort of comfort,' she had replied. 'I like to feel my body; it reassures me that I am still here.'

Several times, when I spoke to her, she recognized my voice, put her arms around my neck, kissed my face and tried to stroke my hair. I said, 'Darling, say something to me, something funny, something quite nonsensical, then I shall know that you are getting better': I had said this to her many times during the past weeks, and often she had complied with my wish. But now even her soliloquies had ended. The problems had been solved. Her agitation was of the body only. Her mind was entering into peace.

March 28th.

She was awake when I came in the morning. She recognized my step as I entered the room. She recognized my voice. She put her arms around my neck and said: 'Mr. P., I love and worship you.' She kissed my face, stroked my hair and held on to me. She whispered: 'Take me away, please. Take me away. I want to be with you, I love you . . .'

Elizabeth tried to make her drink some soup, but it was very difficult. She tried to swallow, but she could not really swallow any more. She knew all the time that I was with her.

In the afternoon she slept; her face was now smooth, waxen and peaceful. She was gently slipping away from this life.

My Love. This is the end of our happiness.

I made this entry into my pocket diary:

'How often had she said to me: 'I don't mind being alone when you are away from me, for I am never really alone. I think of you and sing a little song for you.'

'Her whole life had been a song of love. The words she spoke to me today, perhaps the last words she will have spoken, were words of love. Now she is silent.'

238

Nothing more could now be added to our relationship; nothing could be taken away. She had given me everything. Had I given her enough? If there was anything I had neglected to do, I could now do it no more. If I had failed in anything, it was now too late to make amends.

The books were closed. The accounts were made.

I spoke to her: 'My love, did I do all I should have done to help you in your suffering and in your anguish? Did you feel that you could confide in me or did I give you the impression at times that I was impatient when you tried to tell me how ill you felt? I know that once or twice when I sat by you and you were in pain and you moaned a little I said to you: 'Darling, please don't moan; it upsets me so terribly.' And you stopped immediately and suffered silently. 'I must not upset Mr. P.' you thought. But I, instead of thinking of myself, I should have helped you to bear your pain. I should have held your hand, talked to you, encouraged you. No one can take another's physical suffering upon himself—how often in those weeks I wished that I could have done it, for as you know I can bear pain more than others. (You often teased me about my 'heroism' in the dentist's chair.) But perhaps there were other ways in which I could have helped you more when you needed help most. But in some of those moments you could not let yourself go. (You even said to me one afternoon: 'I wish you weren't here when I am in such pain; I am only making a nuisance of myself.') You dared not moan for fear of upsetting 'Mr. P. who hates to hear me moan because he cannot bear to see me suffer, and also because he thinks that to moan, to complain about pain, to *jammer,* as he puts it in German, is to lack *tenue.*' My love, the real reasons why at times I appeared less understanding and was less patient in the face of your distress; why I said: 'Don't moan; I cannot bear it', was not because I thought you lacked *tenue*—you showed the fortitude of those who belong to the very small élite of mankind, those who draw their strength from the depths of a purified self. The real reason was because I felt, quite irrationally, that if I adopted an attitude of making

239

light of your illness, the illness, by a process of sympathetic magic, might become less serious. In short, I could not face the truth.

'My love, of all the gifts you have bestowed on me, the most precious was the power to love which I had not possessed before; or if I had possessed it, it must have been in early childhood. Feelings, as you know, were frowned upon as manifestations of weakness by my father, and so I must have discarded them as burdensome and useless a very long time ago.

'Not that I had been unable to fall in love, before I met you; I had been in love, or what I thought was being in love, several times. But I always had received more than I had given. I had never fully yielded to love, never allowed myself to surrender. Thus I did not really know love.

'Have I loved you enough?

'Tell me that you love me,' you would often say. 'I love you, darling.' 'Say it again . . . no, wait a moment . . .' You would take up a new position in your chair, upright, your hands on your knees, your head lifted up and assuming an expression of mock-earnestness, like someone about to receive some important yet not quite unexpected piece of good news. 'Now I am ready, we are all ready; now you tell: do you love me?' 'Yes, my sweet, I love you very much.' 'How very much?' 'Very, very much.' This little game repeated itself many times over the years. Looking back I wish I could have expressed my feelings more convincingly. There can be no greater bliss than to be asked the question 'Do you love me' by the one whom one loves. I loved you very much; you were everything to me. Then, why this lack of conviction in my voice—for I could hear my own voice; why this slight awkwardness when I replied to your question?

'And why did I not tell you more often how beautiful you were? I thought you—you are—the most beautiful woman I had ever known. I did not know there was so little time left; otherwise I would have told you more often. But whenever I did tell you, you would not believe it; you used to say: 'I am not beautiful at all; my nose is too big, my eyes are too deepset. I have a funny sort of face.' And you really believed that it was so.

'Perhaps I should have spoken with greater insistence and emphasis as young ardent lovers do in the rapture of first love. How I wish I had told you more often, more insistently; every day, every hour, every moment. How I wish I had brought you flowers every day, had sent you little notes of love (as you sent to me), had looked more often and more deeply into your beautiful eyes. I must have thought that time was unending and that I need not hurry.

'Time has ended now.'

She had given me the power to love, and I never loved her more than in those last weeks of her agony.

March 29th (Entry in the Diary.)

My beloved is leaving me. She still seems to be aware of my presence when I speak to her, but she is too weak to give any sign of recognition. I spoke to her again: 'My love, we never thought you would die before me. You did not want to die before me, not because you feared death but because you had made it your vocation to look after me.'

'What would become of Mr. P. if I died before him? Who would look after him?' This was the one agonising thought to you. The thought you could not think. You said so one day in the nursing home. In your many hours of lonely suffering when I was not with you this dreaded thought must have been with you often: 'What will become of him if I die?'

But from the 11th of March, when the great specialist said to me: 'This is a grim picture, there are at least three tumours in the brain . . .' I knew that you were dying. Did you know it too? And did you know that I knew? We never mentioned it. I did not mention it because I knew of your unthinkable thought: 'What will become of Mr. P.?' You did not mention it because you must have felt that I could not have denied it any longer, and you did not want to put me to this torture.

241

And so we both pretended, but we knew that we knew. It was better that way. But had you asked me in those last brief moments of lucidity when your mind broke through the ever tightening encirclement of the disease: 'Mr. P., am I dying?' I would not have been able to keep up the pretence any longer that you would be well again. I would have said: 'My sweet love, my adored wife, you are dying. You are leaving me behind, for I cannot follow you now.' And now that you are standing at the gate, I say to you: you are about to enter the greater life. I cannot follow you now, but I shall be with you and you will be with me again. You said so yourself only a few weeks ago . . .'

I then read her the whole of the Communion Service. She was too weak even to press my hand, but her eyelids flickered almost imperceptibly, and she looked serene.

Thursday, March 30th.

Once again the protective fog had come down on me. I could no more clearly grasp what was happening before my eyes.

She was dying. Her heartbeat had become very rapid.

'What is it?' I asked Elizabeth who had just taken her pulse.

'A hundred and sixty,' she replied.

'And why is this?'

'Because to keep the circulation going, the heart must make ever greater efforts; it begins to race. Very probably she also has developed pneumonia.'

'This cannot go on for long, can it?'

'I am afraid not.'

'How long then?'

'A day or so only.'

She was dying. I saw it quite clearly, yet it had the reality only of a nightmare from which one might escape; even while dreaming it one might say to oneself: 'I can wake up any moment I choose.'

My mind was dreaming, but my senses registered every detail as I watched her living out the last hours of her life. Her hands were moving restlessly, folding and refolding the top edge of her bedsheets and blankets. At moments she would pass one hand or both over her forehead or rub her nose. 'This is typical of this kind of brain affection,' said Dr. F.

Her mouth, so delicately curved, so perfectly proportioned, so infinitely tender in its smile, had begun to change. The left side slightly drooped (as it had on that first day in January), the upper lip receded showing a little of her teeth. The lower lip had sunk in because the plate had not been put back. Her expression had become severe, remote, impersonal. Her eyes were sightless, far, far away.

Her breathing was changing; deep breaths following long intervals. Her chest was heaving under the effort.

'This is the Cheyne-Stokes breathing,' commented Dr. F. 'It heralds the beginning of the end.'

Is it right that one human being should watch another in the agony of death? There were moments when I felt it was wrong. No, it could not be wrong. She would have been present at my agony with the same all-conquering love with which I was present at hers. Love sanctifies.

Friday, March 31st.

In the morning before leaving the house in Chelsea, I wrote into my diary: 'This, I am certain, is the last day of her life.' There was no need that day to ring the nursing home at nine o'clock to ask how she was as I had done every morning in the past seven weeks. I knew she was still alive, for had there been a sudden crisis, I would have been told.

At about 9.15 I entered the familiar corridor on the first floor. The cleaners were still there, and the nurses went about their morning business. It was not the hour when visitors are normally present. The nurses' silence as they saw me was eloquent beyond words. The two cleaning women bent over their polishing cloths on the floor made way for me, and one of them said: 'We are terribly sorry, Sir; we all love her.'

They all loved her. I had known this for a long time, for love

243

cannot be concealed. The way they used to speak to her, look at her, hold her hand, were constantly around her; their mounting concern as they began to realize the full gravity of her condition, and their open distress when the end came near; by all this and by the touching solicitude they showed for me I knew that they all loved her. They felt drawn to her; they felt safe with her and happy. None could resist the power of *her* love.

In his autobiography my brother Hubert, writing about Diana, says: 'It was she who enriched those who shared her agony.' This applied not only to the nurses and the doctors but also to the visitors, especially to those who came to see her regularly in the last three weeks of her life. During the first weeks at the nursing home, when Diana, though in constant pain and discomfort was still in full mental command, she did not want to have many visitors. It required too great an effort; also she did not want to cause distress to others. She answered telephone calls and once or twice a day she herself rang up friends: 'Come and see me when I am a little better.'

It had been my duty, often painful, to tell people not to come. But as her condition relentlessly and at an ever growing pace deteriorated, the whole picture changed. The level of communication changed, the purpose and the meaning of visits changed. I encouraged, indeed, asked people to come.

What was now required was not friendly bedside conversation giving comfort to the patient by engaging his interest in the affairs of life and giving comfort to the visitor by the thought that all will be well with the patient. What was required now was *Agape,* selfless Christian love, the love that '. . . beareth all things, believeth all things, hopeth all things, endureth all things . . .'

It meant seeing another human being suffer, witnessing the havoc wrought by a terrible disease on body and mind; watching helplessly; suffering with her and for her without hope and comfort. It meant facing ultimate things. Not many people are capable of that. A number of our friends and members of her own family failed in this test.

Among those who came, who had the fortitude to bear the distress and the agony, because they had *agape,* were three women: Rosamond, Rosemary and Stella.

Rosamond came every day until the end. When Diana had gone totally blind she still recognized Rosamond as soon as she entered the room by the scent of her toilet water: *Le Dix* by Balanciaga. Diana loved it and would happily exclaim: 'There is Rosamond; I know the scent . . .' And, even after her mind had all but withdrawn from this world she would still be aware of and respond to Rosamond's presence.

And there was Elizabeth. Though she had never been able to communicate with Diana in a reciprocal way, she established from the first a deep rapport with her. Diana, as far as her ebbing strength permitted, would do anything Elizabeth asked her to do: she would turn over to one side, hold out her arms, let her hair be combed, take nourishment and drink. None of the other nurses succeeded in making her do this. And she would smile when Elizabeth bent over her and spoke to her.

I have likened the face of Elizabeth to that of a Madonna by the Lombard masters. But behind that beautiful face there lay a deeper secret. It came to the surface and communicated itself in an enigmatic smile that played around the upturned corners of her mouth.

It was the 'archaic' smile of the *Eternal Feminine,* the 'embodiment of the everlasting and all-embracing, the healing, sustaining, loving and saving principle.' Elizabeth was already with her when I came into the room. The whole morning she never left her bedside. She stroked her hair, dabbed her forehead, moistened her lips and from time to time took her pulse and listened to her breathing. 'One cannot feel the pulse any more,' she said. For the last few days I had wanted to ask Elizabeth to cut off a strand of Diana's hair, but I had put it off for fear that she might be aware of what we were doing. But on that last Friday Elizabeth cut off a strand and placed it into my hands. It was silky, alive, shining—the hair of a healthy young woman.

I sat opposite Elizabeth on the other side of the bed; I talked to

Diana; she was quite still, not really unconscious. Her eyes opened from time to time. I think she was aware that she was surrounded by love.

Her breaths came very faintly; no more the Cheyne-Stokes breathing accompanied by the heaving of the chest as on the previous day, but hardly noticeable shallow breaths interspersed with noises in the throat known as the death rattle. But it was not nearly as frightening as I had imagined. Indeed, in those last hours of her life, all the dread, the agony had gone.

According to Hindu teaching everyone has an appointed number of breaths, and it is this which determines the length of the individual's life. Breath control, an essential part of Yoga, aims at regulating the flow of vital energy (prana) in such a way that life may unfold on the physical, mental, and spiritual level to the individual's maximum capacity and fulfilment.

In the main all breath control means breathing rhythmically and slowly, thus reducing the number of breaths per minute, and thus ultimately prolonging life according to Hindu teaching.

Diana had acquired an extraordinary degree of mastery over her breathing. As I have mentioned she and I, some years back, had attended a course of lectures and practical instruction by an Indian Yogi. Breathing exercises, some even of a very difficult kind, were part of the course. Diana continued some of the simpler, basic exercises ever after and also studied certain Japanese methods of breath control which especially appealed to her.

This may account for the fact which so surprised the doctors that though she had hardly taken any nourishment for many weeks and despite the catastrophically rapid spread of the cancer, which one by one destroyed the centres of the brain, her heartbeat remained strong and regular for so long, with the vital functions of the body almost unimpaired until the end.

To me who saw her those last days and on Friday, the 31st of March in the translucent, indeed luminous pallor of her face, her features composed and now of classical beauty, physiological

246

explanations had very little meaning. She was dying as she had lived: in the radiance of the spirit.

I had read only a short time before Simone de Beauvoir's account of the unrelieved and unredeemed horror of her mother's death from cancer, an account that seemed to make a mockery of the idea that any transcendental significance could attach to man's life. Diana's death was different. In the very act of dying she seemed to be conquering death.

She had accomplished the task to which her life had been dedicated: the transmutation of the impermanent into the permanent; of the physical into the spiritual; of the body of flesh into the body of glory.

My sister-in-law, Helga, was expected from Germany at about five o'clock in the afternoon. She had kept herself in readiness for the whole week. My brother, Hubert, could not come because he was about to leave for India on a lecture tour.

Helga's plane was delayed, and she arrived at the nursing home only at about half-past six.

Diana was still alive, but it was clear that the 'appointed number of her breaths' was very nearly reached. Helga and I sat in silent prayer by her bed. She had a very high temperature, her forehead was moist with perspiration. 'It is most probably pneumonia, almost inevitable at this stage,' said Dr. F. who came into the room at regular intervals.

Dr. F., the young house physician, had been urging me for the last two weeks, and with greater insistence during the past few days, to take certain drugs to alleviate anxiety and tension and also to enable me to sleep. He feared that I would have a nervous breakdown and said so to me quite openly. I reassured him that there was no such danger. The nature of my suffering was of a different order and in a different realm of my soul, which could not be reached by tranquillizers or pep-pills. Neither in the weeks before Diana was taken to the nursing home, nor at any time since had I taken pills of any kind though I allowed the doctors to write out the requisite prescriptions. It is true, I could not sleep and I smoked far too much, but on the physiological level I seemed to make up for lack of sleep as well as for the quite frightening expenditure of nervous energy—I almost felt it rushing out of my body from morning to night—by a Gargantuan appetite. Psychically I never suffered—contrary to what I had feared—a catastrophical decline in sense of personal reality; psychically, I remained intact.

However, towards the evening of Friday, the 31st of March, I began to subside into a state of exhaustion, more mental than physical. At about half-past eight Dr. F., who had been watching me, said: 'You must go now and have some food. You are too exhausted. We will keep you informed should there be any change, so that you can come back immediately.' In his view, 'Diana might live through the night but not much longer.'

And so I said my last farewell to her. I kissed her pale, burning forehead again and again. I kissed her dry, half-open and inert lips. 'Goodbye my beloved, my sweetheart. In this life we shall not meet again . . .'

And then we left. We had dinner at my son's house, and all during dinner and after we expected the telephone to ring to summon us back to the nursing home.

After dinner, at about 10.30, Helga suggested that we go back to the nursing home. I felt I could not do it; mentally and physically I felt I would not be able to stand the strain. 'Dr. F. has undertaken to let us know if there should be a change for the worse; we must rely on that, so let us go back to my flat.' (I had moved back into my flat that very morning.)

I was fast asleep when the telephone bell woke me. I put on the light and looked at my wristwatch.

It was 1.45 a.m., the 1st of April.

I lifted the receiver. It was the voice of Dr. F. 'I am sorry to have to tell you that your wife has just died . . . there was no time to let you know; it all went very quickly. About a quarter of an hour ago the night nurse called me. Your wife's breathing had suddenly become very rapid and ten minutes later she died . . . you could not have been here in time . . .'

248

All I could think of saying was: 'Thank you for letting me know . . .' After a short pause I added: 'Shall we come now?'

'No, please don't; there is no point in it; come in the morning.'

'Thank you,' I repeated, 'thank you for everything, you have been very kind . . .'

I put down the receiver. Helga stood by my bed. 'She has died,' I said to Helga, 'ten minutes ago she died . . . and I was not there . . . there was no time to let me know. It was Dr. F., the young house physician; you met him earlier in the evening; yes, he is very nice; he did all he could . . . there never was a hope . . . but a few hours ago she was still *alive;* now she is dead; she is no more. Diana has died . . .'

It is not easy now to recapture exactly what I felt at that moment, a moment which, I had known for a long time, would be coming. It was as if a trapdoor had suddenly been sprung under my feet and I had plunged into a great void, a void of which I myself was a part. My life, as it had been up to the moment the phone rang, had ended—whatever was to come would be something quite different. 'I will make you some tea,' Helga said. Then she sat on the edge of my bed and we had tea and biscuits. At about six in the morning I went to sleep.

I have often since asked myself why I did not go back to the nursing home that night, and I have bitterly reproached myself. Had we gone, as my sister-in-law suggested, we would probably, though by no means certainly, have been present at Diana's death. (There was no change in her condition up to ten minutes before the end and we might have been sent home by the doctor around midnight.) But why did I not go back? I think the true reason is that I could not bear the thought of seeing her die, actually seeing her die. I had been with her those seven weeks, day after day, sharing her suffering, almost merging my soul into hers, going with her, hand in hand to the very gates of the Unknown through which we all must pass alone.

I had taken leave of her when she was still living. I could not go through the same, once again. This would have happened had we been sent home again in the middle of the night. And, as I have said, I could not bear the thought of actually seeing her pass from life to death. Somehow also I had the childish, the magic thought that perhaps some miracle might still happen and we would find her the next day alive and improved.

But when she had died—without my being at her bedside—I was seized by a kind of panic at the thought that she might have regained consciousness, as people do, just before death, and that I was not there to hold her hand and give her peace, love and comfort to the end. But she had died without regaining consciousness; of this the doctors and the nurses assured me, and I have no reason to doubt their word.

We got up early on Saturday. At half-past eight I rang Elizabeth to tell her that Diana had died. She knew already and she said: 'I would like to meet you at the nursing home and be with you when you see her. I also want to say good-bye to her.'

When we arrived at half-past nine, Elizabeth was waiting for us in the entrance hall. It was the first time I saw her not in her nurse's uniform. She wore an orange pink tweed suit with a top-coat to match. She was hatless, her golden hair gathered up over the top of her head and the nape of her neck. There was so much of it; it seemed that no amount of hairpins and combs could hold it up for long. If I remember, she also wore a small black silken scarf pinned on to her hair.

A hush of grief seemed to have descended on the nursing home; everyone, on every floor, knew that Diana had died. People moved in complete silence, and in silence the cleaners and two of the nurses who were in the corridor pressed my hand.

We stood before the familiar door, No. 116. The white card with the name Princess Loewenstein and underneath the name of her doctor was still in its frame as it had been the night before, testifying to the presence of a living person. But what had happened, what mystery of transformation had taken place in these few hours that had elapsed since I kissed her for the last time on her burning forehead? It had still been *her* forehead; she had still been there, her body the expression of her living presence. But now—in a second I would be in the room; would she still be there? No, not *she;* she was no more. She had died. Then whom would I see; *what* would I see?

The dead, I knew, unless death had been violent, look merely asleep—from a certain distance. But even from close by many features must still be exactly as they had been: the structure of the face as a whole, the hair. Especially in her case, the narrow grey streak so touching and so beautiful would still be there as it had been last night; it had for some time lived an independent existence of its own since for so many weeks she had not been able to cover it by a rinse and lately she had not known of it any more.

We stood inside the room. It was as if Paraqlitos, the Angel of the Sorrows of Death, had himself silently opened the door for us.

In the morning of Thursday, the 30th of March, Rosemary had come and had filled the entire room with yellow daffodils. The top shelves of the built-in furniture unit along the walls, the bedside tables right and left, the low round tables by the window, the shelves over the radiators, even the top of the TV set were transformed into banks of yellow daffodils. She lay as in a bed of flowers those two last days of her life. Her pillows were white, her flowing hair like darkest smoky amber, her face like a carving in mellowed ivory; and around her, all around her those yellow-golden daffodils, presided over by the little burning 'Tree of Life'.

This is how we found her that morning, April 1st: surrounded by flowers, the two little Christmas angels in attendance.

Her 'grave little face' was now in the solemn stillness of someone who had gone through a great initiation and keeps her silence; her elegant fingers were holding the crucifix I had found in the rosebushes the summer before.

The yellow daffodils had completed their task.

We all knelt by her bed and prayed.

I kissed her forehead which was now cool; her hair had been

taken back, but there it was, the narrow grey streak dividing her dark hair right in the middle of her forehead, touching, beautiful in death as it had been in life.

I could not grasp that *she,* Diana, my love, my wife, was dead. That never would I hear her voice again, never her silvery laugh; never would I listen again to her quaint stories; never would I see her sweet smile; never hold her in my arms again.

'Let's discuss this, Mr. P.,' she always said; even in the last weeks of her illness. *This, my love, we shall not be able to discuss: not in this life.*

I felt like reproaching her: 'Darling, why did you have to die? How could this happen to *you;* how could you let it happen to *me?* You know you were my reality, the criterion, the yardstick by which I judged everything. Whatever you said, whether it was to do with the weekly laundry, the character of someone we had just met, the name of a flowering shrub or the ultimate things of life and death, I listened to you attentively in the absolute conviction that you *knew.*

'You were the rock on which I based my life; my terra firma. But you were also my companion; my guide, my sense of continuity; you were the burning fire of my altar.

'And now you die, without so much as an explanation. You have let me down; you have proved to be mortal. I never reckoned with that contingency. I knew you could be ill, very ill. But I did not know that you *could,* that you *would* die. You were the centre of my clock: the eternal *Now.* That *Now* has gone with you; my centre is no more. I am like one of those figures by Salvador Dali with a hole right through the middle through which you see a desert . . .

'I am like a gutted house, like a wheel without a hub; and you know from the *Tao-Te-Ching* that a wheel without a hub is no wheel at all. It cannot move; it cannot be.

'Darling, why did you have to die?'

We went back to the nursing home late that evening.

There was no card with a name on the door of No. 116. The

252

room was empty. The flowers had gone. The bed was bare. Her small suitcase stood packed, ready for us to take away.

Wrapped in its tin foil the cherry cake which I had brought less than three weeks ago to enliven her afternoon tea was on a shelf by the wall. We left it there. All her life she had never eaten much.

There was no one about. We went as we had come, unseen.

April, 3rd. Diana's death was announced in the London *Times* and in the *Daily Telegraph:*

> On April 1st 1967, in London. Diana Maria Faith, Princess of Loewenstein-Wertheim, aged 45, adored wife of Leopold; she died as she had lived: *in the Radiance of the Spirit*. Funeral Service and burial Wednesday, April 5th at 3 p.m., St. Mark's Church, Wyke, Normandy, near Guildford, Surrey. Family and close friends. Flowers direct or etc. . . .

When the announcement of Diana's death had made it clear that she had been a Christian, her mother was profoundly shocked. Diana had allowed the unforgivable thing to happen: she had 'been converted'. The very phrasing of this reproach implied that she had yielded to proselytizing pressure. Nothing could have been further from the truth.

Later, in a letter to her elder sister, who like her mother, showed her disapproval by not attending the funeral, I pointed out that what Diana had rejected (like her father before her) was the atavistic concept of the intrinsic 'otherness' of the Jewish people and the whole idea that one particular race or people is endowed with very special virtues which others do not possess. Under whatever labels, I wrote, these notions present themselves, they invariably lead to intolerance, arrogance, injustice and worse. Diana had never rejected her Jewish heritage which was after all part of the common heritage of Western civilization. Nor had she been 'converted'. Like many before her, and from the deepest conviction, she had taken the road that led, as she

253

saw it, from the promise of Judaism to its fulfilment in Christianity. With her it had become a true *Via Crucis*.

I saw her twice more after her death. Each time she seemed a little more remote. The first time her face was like a stone effigy on the tomb of a young nun I had seen in a French Cathedral. The second time she had the ageless face of humanity idealized. But the narrow grey streak that parted her hair in the middle was still there, human and alive.

Wednesday, April 5th. Today, my love, we laid your body to rest; your body to which, from time immemorial, through countless lives, you had given its form. Your body which like everything you did—your painting, your handwriting, your way of arranging flowers, your way of speaking—was your signature in your earthly life—graceful, delicate, beautiful. Your body in which and through which I worshipped you: your incarnate presence.

We laid your body to rest with all the reverence this solemn act demands, with all the compassion we felt for you in memory of your suffering, with all the deep respect we owe to you who tread your via dolorosa with saintly courage and serenity; with all the love we have for you who gave to us all—to every one of us—of your own abundant love; with all the sorrow we felt at parting from you; with all the gratitude we owe to you for your beauty, your kindliness, your gaiety, your childlike purity, your ageless wisdom with which you have enriched our lives; with all the joy we felt at the radiance of your spiritual presence with us, with our faith renewed in life everlasting.

We laid your body to rest, my love, on a sunny spring day— one of those incredible English spring days in which the flowers, the bushes, the trees, the grass, the birds: all nature, all living creatures, only just emerging from the torpor of winter and timidly groping towards the cool new light, are suddenly transported into the golden blaze of a season that is not yet, of a future still to be fulfilled and which seems to say to them: 'Why are you late; I am here waiting for you.'

It was this kind of day, and all of us who came in dark heavy winter coats, shed them, and as we emerged from the church into the caressing warmth of that day, so full of hope and promise, we all looked different people, and to a certain extent we were different people.

It was this sense of your *presence* at the service, so powerful, so real that, in Canon Carpenter's words 'we were all caught up in a common experience', it was this and the wave of love which swept through the church, when Carpenter gave his commendation of you, that transmuted this occasion so irretrievably, irreversibly final, from desolation into exaltation—from death to life.

'*I am the Resurrection and the Life saith the Lord: he that believeth in me, though he were dead, yet shall he live: and whosoever liveth and believeth in me shall never die.*'

Never could the Christian message of Life Everlasting which Gerard Irvine chanted in clear almost triumphant tones as he walked ahead of the procession along the sun-lit path, have rung more true.

I who had never suffered true bereavement before, understood and experienced the full meaing of the words: *Blessed are they that mourn: for they shall be comforted.*

There were flowers everywhere; they covered the lawns around the grave and flanked the paths leading to it. Flowers in incredible profusion of colour and variety. The flowers you have always loved so much, whose language you understood, with whom you conversed, whose essence you could conjure up by a few strokes of your brush; the flowers that kept you faithful company during your weeks of suffering, who were with you when you died—they were here again as your friends. But they were also here to perform their ancient office as mediators between this world and the world beyond.

And with the flowers there were the messages of love. One stood out among all. It read: 'For dear and beautiful Diana—

with love, grief, gratitude and Joy—from her everloving Rosamond.'

It spoke for all of us.

I made these entries into my diary immediately on our return from the funeral. A few days later the undertakers as is customary, sent a list of the names of people who had contributed 'floral tributes'. There was one name against which they had put a query: 'Mr. P.' They even rang me, saying they hoped I knew who that person was.

Part Four

In the deepest sense there is no spiritual dream that is not true, no hope that shall forever go famished, no tears that shall not be gathered into the brooding skies of compassion, to fall again in healing dews.

(From *The Divine Adventure* by FIONA MCLEOD)

The Hole in the Pocket

While you lay desperately ill I took no interest in my surroundings. I lived in other people's houses, and out of suitcases. I took my socks and pants to the flat where Mrs. F. washed them, and I took my shirts to the laundry. I drove through the streets of London as in a dream (my guardian angel must have been keeping close watch over me). I reacted automatically to the changing colours of the traffic lights as though I were myself part of the automatic control system. In the early days at the nursing home you asked me often: 'Are you driving carefully?' Later you did not ask me any more, and later you were not here any more to ask me.

I lived in a limbo, and on your death the clock stood still for me. The rhythm of my days was no more. Winter, spring; cold, hot; Monday, Tuesday; the month, the year, it did not matter to me any more. I read no papers, I watched no television, and if atomic war had broken out I could not have cared less. Nor did I care much about my appearance. All during the weeks of your last illness I had been wearing two suits alternatively, one horrid old winter suit and my dark blue suit with the slight overcheck; we both liked it very much. It is the kind of 'all the year round' suit that fits what I always called our 'national weather', this mixture of all seasons rolled into one (November in May; March in August), and therefore fits almost any mood.

But then in May, for once a real May, I went to the country

again for the first time, and I got out my dark grey summer flannels. They have had a hole in the right pocket ever since I can remember. After many months of dropping money, keys and even handkerchiefs down my leg on to the ground I had become conditioned not to use the right-hand pocket. And many times we said: 'We must repair that hole', and we always postponed it; there never seemed just the right moment for it, and what we really wanted was to buy a new pair.

We actually did go to Harrods once and looked at ready-made 'casuals' in various materials and colours. But they were all cut in the latest fashion with very narrow trouser legs, and as we thought much too revealing. 'I am afraid,' explained the young sales-man, 'they are all like that; we don't go in for the old style any more.' And so we left it.

When I put on the dark flannels on that week-end in May I had forgotten the hole in the pocket, and promptly all my loose silver, pennies and my car keys fell through the hole on to the ground. And here they are with me as before, these old-style trousers with the hole in the pocket, a symbol of an unfinished business, a symbol of the time that had stood still.

But then, the world which had seemed frozen like a film suddenly stopped, slowly began to move again, and I began to notice that it had not really stood still. There were changes, also outwardly, on which, had you been with me, we would have commented as we did on every trivial thing. For example I noticed that new traffic lights based on a new principle had been introduced. (You and I had seen the first preparation, but we did not know what they were for.) New buildings, new shops, new one-way streets, dual carriageways, the mini and the mini-mini skirts. And then, of course, the change from early spring to spring and summer, a glorious, enchanted summer as you remembered from your childhood. You had often said to me: 'When I was a child the summers were real summers, weeks and weeks of sunshine and heat.' Or did you only remember them like that? No, I am sure they were hotter than now;

260

except that summer of 1967 which must have been as good as any of those you used to remember.

And I began to notice changes in myself; above all the desire to give, to give, to give; as though I had received too much and wanted to balance the accounts.

So many things have happened since, which would have interested you, around me and in my own life, my life without you.

The Cherry Tree

As I have said, everything was early in this unusual spring: the almonds, the camellias, magnolias, prunus and cherry, they all flowered three to four weeks before their normal season. The Japanese cherry trees had stood in their full glory on the 1st of April, the day she died.

Three weeks later, when normally they should have been in bloom, they were beginning to shed their petals.

I had left my flat and was staying at my son's house in a quiet street in Kensington, a street of spacious Victorian houses and spacious gardens, recalling a more spacious way of life. This street is protected from heavy traffic by a system of narrow accesses and confusing arrows at both ends; this and the absence of shops helps to preserve its Victorian calm. In the Spring the bushes and trees that line the street on both sides explode in an exuberance of colours: yellows of many hues, pinks, whites, purples and blues. But it is the pink of the cherries which provides the main theme of this colour symphony. Uncontaminated by the diesel and petrol fumes which, in the big cities, blight the flowers, choke and prematurely age the leaves, these well protected trees and shrubs are allowed the full natural span

261

for each phase in their cycle of transformation throughout the year.

For the big cherry trees the cycle of flowering was now nearing its appointed end.

One morning, as I was leaving the house, a sudden gust of wind brought thousands of blossoms down in a pink cloud of whirling petals, each one a perfect masterpiece of Creation, each one to be obliterated for ever. Within two to three days they would all have vanished.

Had her life, in all its beauty, been like the short and glorious flowering of the cherry tree? Had each of those sparkling facets of her character which together had made the uniqueness of her being, been no more than one of those delicate petals now scattered into oblivion? And as the tree, itself oblivious of having shed its flowers would live on and flower again, would she, Diana, the real Diana, live on oblivious of having shed her earthly life?

Or was she but one petal on the *Tree of Life* which cared little for her; perhaps even knew nothing of her?

When a few days later I looked through some of her books I found in *Zen and the Art of Archery* a passage she had underlined and on the margin of which she had written: 'Death'.

She had copied out the passage for the Anthology, and like all other quotations this one too is illustrated by one of her miniature paintings.

It must have been one of her final entries, as is shown by the tremor in her handwriting.

This is the passage: 'It is not for nothing that the Samurai have chosen for their truest symbol the fragile cherry blossom. Like a petal dropping in the morning sunlight and floating serenely to earth, so must the fearless detach himself from life, silently and inwardly unmoved . . .'

Had she known?

Return

The day came when I had to return to the flat (it had suddenly become 'my' flat instead of 'our' flat; it was to take me a long time until I became accustomed to it) and re-establish some kind of relationship to my familiar yet totally estranged surroundings.

It was their very 'unchangedness' which made them so strange and unreal to me. As though nothing at all had happened, every object was in its exact place, concerned, as it were, only with its own particular task that had been allotted to it from the beginning, and ready to continue as before.

Once again I experienced the feeling that inner reality and outward appearances, normal and solid as they presented themselves, had become make-believe, mere 'mock-ups' like the cardboard villages which Potemkin erected along the roads of the Ukraine for the benefit of Catherine the Great.

This especially applied to Diana's studio, that inner sanctum where she used to work and into which I had never entered when she was absent and never without knocking at the door when she was there.

For some weeks after her death I avoided the room. When at last I entered it I found it exactly as it had been on the 10th of February, the day before she had been taken to the nursing home.

It all looked so matter of fact with its paint boxes, brushes, pens, pencils; bottles of India ink, carving tools; the sketchbooks, the little notes pinned to the wall; finished and unfinished pieces of carving, bowls with pebbles and shells, canvasses on shelves and her last unfinished picture on the easel in the middle of the room. It seemed that she had only just gone out for a while and presently would return and resume her work.

But it was not true. She would never return.

As I walked through the deserted flat I remembered that I loved to sleep on the couch of the sitting-room in the afternoon knowing that she was about, busying herself with one thing or other: washing, painting, working on a dress or puttering in the kitchen.

Sometimes she would come into the sitting-room and say: 'Do you mind if I come in; does it disturb you?' 'Do come in as often as you like; it makes me sleep all the more happily.'

Nothing had changed in the flat, but it was all not true any more.

I felt that it was dangerous, psychically dangerous for her as well as for me if I continued to indulge in fantasies of continuity vested in objects and appearances.

To do justice to the new reality, to my living memory of her and to her—whatever her present estate and condition—I must change everything in the flat which suggested a living physical presence that was no more.

Above all I must remove every piece of furniture, together with all the contents from the studio, re-decorate and completely transform the room.

Next I must dispose of all her clothes, personal belongings and objects of daily use; also of all her jewellery including those pieces which had been so dear to her and which she had asked me to take home two weeks before she died. To live on, to live on in their own right, all these pretty things must be given to those who had loved her.

I did not give away her papers, books, sketchbooks, carvings, paintings, nor any of the objects which we had bought together or which she had collected and which though not 'personal' objects like rings, powder compacts, bracelets, handbags, bore the stamp of her unique personality. These to me were symbols of a true continuity which death could not break.

However, the final decision on what to keep and what to give away was a heartrending task. More than once in the hope-denuded hour before daybreak, when one's hold on reason becomes tenuous, irrational thoughts tormented me: 'I must not give away all her clothes (especially her pretty evening dresses); she needs them; how shall I explain it to her when she comes back; I will have to replace everything, begin again from scratch . . .'

Half dream, half fantasy, yet with a logic of their own, these musings kept recurring, pursuing me even into daylight, only to be followed by the comfortless realization that these contingencies would never arise.

Everything I found of hers was a treasure: the small porcelain box containing seven tiny moonstones, two topazes, carnelians, aquamarines; the pretty buttons she collected, the coloured ribbons; her collections of uncut crystals, pink, orange, pale-mauve, golden-black. (I put them on the mantelshelf in the sitting-room.) And the pebbles from Iona and the Cornish coast and the seashells—too many of them, but I dared not throw them away. She had been in communion with them all, even those minute shells no larger than a pinhead. Everything she had left behind she had left in perfect order. There were layers of tissue paper in all her drawers separating the various pieces of lingerie; lavender bags and 'pomanders' giving out a delicate scent of orange and clove. There were many silk scarves (never used) and gossamer-thin handkerchiefs in pastel colours, all folded up with greatest care. And boxes with strings of coloured beads which she had brought back from Italian journeys; coral necklaces, costume jewellery, lengths of materials in silk, velvet and brocade which she had been planning to make into dresses. And many, many miniature paintings (glowing like jewels), flower sketches, line drawings—I never knew until this day that she had done so many.

On Easter Sunday when Canon Carpenter had come to the nursing home to pray at her bedside, he had said to me: 'She was one of the most completely integrated personalities I have ever known.'

Even to one who had not known her, the things she left behind, from her paintings to the seven tiny moonstones in their porcelain box and the perfect order in which she had left everything, would have conveyed this picture of a harmonious, fully integrated personality.

But it was more than that, more than an expression of psychological maturity; it was—in microcosm—an expression of 'the mutual order of all things that maketh the universe like unto God', the vision of universal harmony in accordance with which she had conducted her life.

Chartres

One of the last pictures she was able to see before she became blind was that of the Rose Window over the West Portal of Chartres Cathedral. It was on a postcard from my brother Hubert.

It had been one of her wishes to visit Chartres, one of the many wishes that was not to be fulfilled.

In July 1967, I went on our long delayed holiday to the South of France—alone. It was my first journey since Diana's death; my first holiday alone since before the war.

Julia Ward and I returned to England by car at the end of the month. We took a route which I had always wanted to take with Diana, away from the motorways, and through the provincial towns and picturesque villages which have remained unchanged in centuries and are the glory of France.

From Cannes we went in leisurely stages, via Avignon, Moulins, Bourges, Tours, the châteaux of the Loire valley, to Chartres.

Only twice in twenty years of marriage had Diana and I been able to go by car through France. These journeys had impressed themselves indelibly on her mind. She could recall every detail and mood of those two trips, and though many years had passed, they were to her part of the living present. She never thought in terms of time and the passage of time. Time seemed to surround her like space in which one could move at will in every direction. One direction could be called the past, another the future; yet essentially they were co-existent, like the symbols marking the hours on the face of the clock. Whenever she evoked those trips, it was in the present tense. 'When we drive off the ferry at Calais or Boulogne,' she would say, 'you say to me: 'Now we are in France.' Is this not what you say to me? And then you say: 'Give me a cigarette, darling; light it for me.' And I reply: 'Would you not rather have a banana?' 'I'll have both,' you answer. 'First give me a bite from the banana, and then you light the cigarette. Oh, how I love this moment,' she would add, 'starting our drive through France. I and my man—the man at the wheel, I call him. His arms are bare and he wears his wristwatch. It's all very *sexy,* and he looks serious and determined; he is going to drive the car right through France along the straight tree-lined roads, and he knows all about it. Travel with Mr. P.; he knows France: Louis XIV, Louis XV, the Revolution and Napoleon—the first Empire and the second, or was it the third? Never mind which; he knows them all and tells me about it as we drive along. But I see the pretty houses, the canals, the little châteaux tucked away behind trees. 'Look, Mr. P., here on the right, have you seen it?' He hasn't, he is too busy driving. 'I can't look now.' 'Can't you stop for a moment?' 'No, there is a car just on my tail.' And so we don't stop, and he doesn't see the châteaux. But Diana sees it all and tells Mr. P. And then we arrive at the hotel and Mr. P. speaks French—of course he does; he has been reared by governesses from the cradle on. 'One does not learn French,' he says, 'one knows it.' And so he arranges everything, and they, can all see that Mr. P. knows exactly what he wants: 'Oui, Monsieur, non, Monsieur. On va arranger ça, Monsieur . . .''

And so she would go on, recalling our trips that had been and those that were to come. 'Next time when we go to France' (that was shortly after I had bought the car) 'we must go into the heart of the provinces and take our time over it. No rushing past the little villages, churches and châteaux, no elaborate meals in expensive hotels, but sandwiches—at least for lunch . . .'

My love, it is exactly this kind of trip I have just made, but not with you. I made it in your memory; I made it for you and for me, for us together. And I saw many châteaux—not the little ones; I rushed past those—but the large ones: Chenonceaux, Amboise, Blois, Chambord, Chaumont and others. And at Chenonceaux I saw for the first time *Son et Lumière*. It was a warm and perfect night with a full moon suspended from a velvet blue sky above the castle. There were the vast formal gardens and the river Cher over which the castle strides in graceful arches lit up in rapidly changing colours. And from the microphones placed all over the grounds there came the music of the sixteenth century—which you liked so much—and the brittle laughter of the ladies of the Court, the plaintive voice of Catherine de Medici, as she talked about Diane de Poitiers. 'Who was Diane de Poitiers?' She was the mistress of Henry II; he gave her the castle. But I am not quite so familiar with that period of French history. Anyway, Henry II was succeeded by François II and then came Charles IX and the night of St. Bartholomew. This will do for the moment.

We also heard Henry II repenting of his sins before his Father Confessor when he thought he was dying. And we heard the sound of the carriages and the horses and the baying of the hounds as the royal party went out for *la chasse* in the early morning. The castle was suddenly bathed in pale pink to suggest the sunrise. Then came tragedy. I don't remember exactly of what kind, but we heard thunder and saw the lightning. Then suddenly all was dark. It was all very impressive, but you were not with me, and so my fragmentary knowledge of the history of the castle was wasted. The next day we drove from Chenonceaux via Blois to Chartres through the Beauce, the vast wheat growing plain of France. It was just before the harvest: endless vistas of golden wheat through which we drove on one of those straight tree-lined roads which you so much wanted to see again. Towards the evening there came a moment when all of a sudden, far ahead on the right, the cathedral appeared like a great ship sailing on the horizon of a golden sea shimmering in the light of the descending sun; a sight which must have gladdened the hearts of the pilgrims centuries past and even now, in this disenchanted age gives one the feeling of having reached or, rather, returned to one of the fountainheads of life, *Nôtre Dame de Chartres*. And did you know that this cathedral rose from the ashes of another church at the beginning of the 13th century, and that it took only twenty years to build it. The masterbuilder is unknown; it was all done by the townspeople themselves, and everyone who presented himself on the building site had to give proof that he had been to confession and communion before.

I lack the power of a Péguy or Claudel to describe the majestic grandeur of this cathedral, but it was not in the nature of my visit to study its architecture, sculpture and carvings; nor the details of its stained-glass windows. I came to stand in the jewelled light which fills the vastness of the church with the mystic Radiance of the Spirit.

I came as a pilgrim and with a quest.

It has been said of Chartres that it is *Le Lieu du Monde où tout devient facile*.

Here I found the answer to my quest, and I found acceptance and peace—'the peace which passeth all understanding'.

Epilogue

Si in hoc erro, quod animos hominum
immortales esse credam, libenter erro; nec
mihi hunc errorem, quo delector, dum vivo
extorqueri volo. (Cicero, *De Senectute*)

If I err in this, that I believe the souls of men
to be immortal, I err of my own free will;
nor do I wish this error, in which I find
delight, to be wrested from me as long as I
live.

The idea that one day I would write a book about her, which had first come to me in the early autumn while waiting for her at the pub by the hospital, began to grip me with compelling force during the last weeks of her illness.

I must write a book if only to enable me to come to terms with the calamity that had been visited upon us; to try to discover, if this was possible, some redeeming or transcending principle that would make it more acceptable. If, by faithfully recording my experiences, my thoughts and feelings of that tragic year, I could discover some such principle and could convey its nature and quality, this tale of suffering, anguish, sorrow and death, by raising it from a merely subjective level on to a level of universal validity, could give comfort to others also.

This is what I have tried to do.

To some readers the belief in survival after death implicit in the book may be its most important message. But it is only part of the message, and only if 'survival' is rightly understood, that is, not regarded merely as a continuation or extension in time, of our earthly existence.

In the words of Kahlil Gibran which Diana quoted in her anthology:

If you would indeed behold the spirit of death, open your heart wide unto the body of life. For life and death are one, even as the river and the sea are one.

When Diana spoke to me on that day in February in the nursing home on 'life after death', she spoke with the visionary certainty of one 'whose inner eye is single'. She said: 'I will always be *present*.' Later, I read a passage marked by her, in Arthur Osborne's book on Sri Bhagavan (one of the three books she had taken to the nursing home), a passage which deals with his attitude to death and survival:

Other saints had promised to return to earth for the renewed guidance of their devotees. His promise was different: 'I am not going away. Where could I go? I am here.' Not even, 'I shall be here,' but 'I am here,' for to the Gnani* there is no change, no time, no difference of past, present and future, no going away, only the eternal NOW in which the whole of time is poised, the universal, spaceless HERE. What he affirmed was his continued uninterrupted PRESENCE.

It was the awareness, shared by all, of *her* living presence which made the funeral service into such an extraordinary, exalting experience. Was she present? If by this we mean Diana, as I had known her over all those years, as she had been even a week before, the answer would be *no*. Personality, understood as the totality of the individual's physical, mental, moral and social qualities, whether inborn or acquired, is unlikely to survive the death of the physical body; nor is it likely that it could be 'reconstituted' on any other plane of existence. I think all esoteric teaching is agreed on this.

The late C. S. Lewis in his meditation on the death of his wife† speaks of the irrevocability of death: 'I look up at the night sky. Is anything more certain than that in all those vast times and spaces, if I were allowed to search them, I should nowhere find her face, her voice, her touch? She died. She is dead. Is the word so difficult to learn?'

In this sense then, Diana is no more; she has gone for ever.

* Completely enlightened sage.
† C. S. Lewis, A Grief Observed (1961).

Jung who from many extraordinary experiences with patients as well as from personal experiences had come to believe firmly in continued existence after death, says:

There are two points of view from which we can look at death. The first from the point of view of the ego, the other from the point of view of the psyche. From the first point of view it appears as a catastrophe: as if wicked and pitiless powers had put an end to a human life . . . And so it is. Death is indeed a fearful piece of brutality; there is no sense in pretending otherwise. It is brutal not only as a physical event, but far more psychically. A human being is torn away from us, and what remains is the icy stillness of death. There no longer exists any hope of a relationship, for all bridges have been smashed at one blow. Those who deserve a long life are cut off in the prime of their years, and good-for-nothings live to a ripe old age. This is a cruel reality which we have no right to side-step. The actual experience of the cruelty and wantonness of death can so embitter us that we conclude there is no merciful God, no justice, no tenderness . . . From the other point of view, however, death appears as a joyful event . . . the soul attains, as it were, its missing half; it achieves wholeness.

On the Greek sarcophagi the joyous element was represented by dancing girls, on Etruscan tombs by banquets.‡

I have earlier on, in my reflections on spiritual healing, expressed my conviction that we are infinitely wider, greater, more enduring than we appear in our embodied presence, and that this physical presence is merely the visible focus and operating centre of our own essential being. This does not detract from the importance of life incarnate—the only kind of life we actually *know*. But it does, speaking quite literally, infinitely widen its perspective. This is what all religion is about, and this has been believed by all people at all times.

I had gone through all the feelings of rebellion and bewilderment at the cruelty of death to which Jung refers, and finally

‡ Memories, Dreams, Reflections (London: Collins and Routledge & Kegan Paul, 1963).

resolved to give up any attempt to make the incomprehensible comprehensible; to rely solely on direct experience as it would come to me from moment to moment.

It is therefore not by metaphysical speculation, but through direct experience during the last days and hours of Diana's life that I became convinced that she lives, that she is *present*. When Jung speaks of the joyful event I now know exactly what he means. It is the 'coming into its own' of our essential being—the Self or by whatever name we wish to call our ultimate irreducible entity—enriched by the experience of life. (This does not preclude the idea of 'repeated' earthly existences, but I am not concerned with this here.)

But, whether it be one or many earthly lives, no time process as we understand it is here involved; only different aspects or planes of existence in the eternal NOW.

In this sense she is present.

Was it this I had been searching for; was it this I found? Was this the redeeming principle which would help me to accept the irretrievable loss and the ever continuing memory of her suffering?

No, it was not. What I had been searching for—it came to me in a sudden flash of knowledge as I stood in Chartres Cathedral—had been there all the time and had sustained me throughout: Faith, Hope and Charity, those gifts of Grace which transcend all that is subjective, ego-directed, merely personal in our life. They give direct access to that greater life of the spirit which surrounds and permeates our visible existence. Like a powerful searchlight from the depths of space and time they illuminate our path and point the way beyond. It is through Faith, Hope and Charity that we directly partake of immortality, *here and now*. In them we have our true being. This then is the *motif* which runs through the pages of my book; the message which concerns us all.